THE MONKEY'S PAW

The MONKEY'S PAW

NEW CHRONICLES FROM PERU

ROBIN KIRK

UNIVERSITY OF
MASSACHUSETTS PRESS

AMHERST

Frontispiece: Peasants from Iquicha, on the Huanta heights
© Orin Starn

LC 97-16068
ISBN 1-55849-108-2 (cloth); 109-0 (pbk.)

Designed by Dennis Anderson
Set in Dante

Library of Congress Cataloging-in-Publication Data

Kirk, Robin.
    The monkey's paw : new chronicles from Peru / Robin Kirk.
        p.   cm.
    Includes bibliographical references (p.   ).
    ISBN 1-55849-108-2 (cloth : alk. paper).
— ISBN 1-55849-109-0 (pbk. : alk. paper)
        1. Peru—Politics and government—1980–
2. Sendero Luminoso (Guerrilla group).
3. Peru—Social conditions—1968–   . I. Title.
F3448.2.K55   1997
985.06'33—dc21   97-16068
                                                        CIP

British Library Cataloguing in Publication data are available.

This book is published with the support and cooperation of
the University of Massachusetts, Boston

TO ORIN

There is a side of war which is human, which is lived like a love affair or an intense hatred and which can be recounted like a novel. So that if someone goes about saying that strategy is a science, he understands nothing about war, because war is not "strategic" . . . even if one supposes that war is scientific, still it would be necessary to describe it . . . from illusions, from beliefs that are only rectified bit by bit.

Remembrance of Things Past,
Marcel Proust

CONTENTS

Acknowledgments

MANY PEOPLE HELPED me write these pages. Among them, I give special thanks to Richard Almonte, Enrique Bossio, Lotta Burenius, Cromwell Castillo, Elsa Chanduví, Lucien Chauvin, Pilar Coll, Isabel Coral, Alejandro and Edilberto Coronado, José Coronel, Mario Cueto, Carlos Iván Degregori, Garry Emmons, Israel Galván, Kevin Goonan, Gustavo Gorriti, Virgilio Grajeda, Virginia Hamilton, Claudia Koonz, Anne Manuel, Francisco Mattos, Mónica Newton, Angel Páez, Carmen Rosa Páez, Ponciano del Pino, George Ann Potter, Francisco Reyes, Rick Roth, Irene Silverblatt, Francisco Soberón, Rosemary Underhay, Carlos Valer, Mónica Vecco, Cesar Villanueva, Sabina Villarreal, Coletta Youngers, and the social workers at the Episcopal Conference for Social Action (CEAS); to Vera Lentz, tireless travel companion and teacher; to Víctor Córdoba, Francisca Paz, Profelinda, Jesús María, Jorge, and my dear *ahijado* Edwin; and to Betty, who for the space of a day was brave enough to take the full measure of her life.

Florence Ladd and Renny Harrigan at the Mary Ingraham Bunting Institute at Radcliffe College gave me the necessary push to complete this manuscript. Among the editors who helped and encouraged me are Mark Abel, Merrill Collett, Paul Derouisseux, Richard Lingeman, and Tom Uhler. Paul Wright at the University of Massachusetts Press saw the book in a manuscript I was still struggling to complete. I especially thank Sandy Close of Pacific News Service, whose dedication to the difficult questions and the uncharted paths has formed, educated, and inspired a generation of journalists and writers.

My parents and parents-in-law were uniformly supportive and knew when not to ask the questions I couldn't fully answer. Finally, Orin and Frances Dorothy Starn not only put up with my early morning work habits, but were generous with both the encouragements and the distractions I needed to complete this manuscript.

GLOSSARY

Arrepentidos. Literally repented ones; former guerrillas or their supporters who surrendered to the authorities and informed on their former colleagues in exchange for a reduced prison sentence.

Bola. A rumor presented as inside knowledge or fact.

Ccarhuac (har-WAK). An Ayacucho village.

Ccochacc (HO-chack). An Ayacucho village.

Ceibo. A thick-waisted tree common to the Andean foothills of Peru.

Chaveta. A long-blade knife.

Chivato. A goat-bodied demon with coal-red eyes.

Cholo. Often a derogatory term for mixed-race Peruvians and Peruvians of Indian descent from the mountains.

Chutos. A derogatory term for highland Peruvians of Indian descent; dirty, savage, pagan, from the puna.

Creole. A term used in the past to describe Peruvians born in the New World, but of European heritage. The Spanish term *criollo* is still used to describe Peruvians from the white middle and upper class who live on the coast.

Cunya (COON-ya). An Ayacucho village.

Delincuentes subversivos. Literally, subversive delinquents; the phrase used by the authorities and some journalists to describe guerrillas.

Huaychao (why-CHOW). An Andean village.

Huayno. A type of highland music played with guitar, flute, and Peruvian mandolin *(charango)*.

Iglu. The igloo-shaped temporary structure built to house families attempting to take over land.

Maquinita. A slang term for money-printing machine.

Marccaraccay (Mar-har-ah-HI). An Ayacucho village.

Misti. A Quechua term for whites, particularly Peruvians of the middle and upper classes.

Mitimaqs. The Incas would move conquered groups, like the Chaukas, to unpopulated areas as mitimaqs, forced colonists.

Moreno. A person with some African features, like brown skin or curly hair.

Nakaq. An Andean vampire. Instead of sucking blood, the nakaq, or pishtaco, sucks fat. While in colonial times, nakaqs were often described as Spaniards, today, the nakaq has taken on the shape of foreign tourists and aid workers.

Palomillera. A gossip and general live wire.

Pampa. An open space, often a yard in front of a dwelling or building.

Paquetazo. Economic measures usually presented together, often including dramatic price, wage, and tariff changes.

Pueblo joven. Literally young town; the Peruvian term for shantytown.

Puna. High-altitude desert.

Purus (PU-ruse). An Ayacucho village.

Razuhuillca (rah-zoo-WILL-ka). The peak that dominates the heights above Huanta in Ayacucho.

Ronda campesina. Literally peasant patrol; a neighborhood watch group.

Senderista. A member of the Shining Path *(Sendero Luminoso)*.

Serrano. Literally, from the mountains, or *sierra*.

Sinchi. Specialized anti-terrorism police.

Tiracha. A homemade gun of wood and pipe used by highland civil defense committees.

Toccto Lake (TOCK-toe). A lake above the city of Huanta, Ayacucho.

Uchuraccay (Oo-chew-rah-HI) An Ayacucho village.

UNSCH. National University San Cristóbal of Huamanga, a public university based in Huamanga, Ayacucho.

Vara. Clout, influence.

Yanauma. Literally blackheads in Quecha, an insult used by the Shining Path against members of civil defense patrols, who often wear black balaclavas.

THE MONKEY'S PAW

1

HEROES

ON MY FIRST trip to Peru in 1983, I slipped a note into my pocket to give to the guerrillas in case they stopped the bus and searched the passengers. The note introduced me as a journalist who wanted to interview Abimael Guzmán, the leader of the Communist Party of Peru—Shining Path, an insurgency that had by then taken hold in the southern highlands. At the gas station where the bus would fill its tank for the journey, the driver first turned to the passengers to take a vote about whether to proceed. Our destination, Ayacucho, was where the guerrillas were strongest. Often, they had lists of names and culled like damaged fruit the passengers who were police officers or had committed a perceived crime, like skimming money from a potable water project or wheedling a peasant community out of land. These passengers were shot, kneeling, at the side of the road.

Among the Peruvians, there was anxious consultation. I felt only excitement. If only the guerrillas would stop the bus! At that instant, I was sure I could talk my way into the interview. I saw myself in the brilliant high beams, negotiating interview terms with some masked *comandante.* He would be wary, but intrigued. My audacity, I thought, and calm control of myself despite the havoc around me would win my exclusive. When the passengers voted to continue our journey (there being no off-duty police officers among them and all conniving landowners long since using the twice-weekly airplane route), and the driver filled the bus's tanks, I felt sharp anticipation, like a hunger about to be satisfied.

In retrospect, my plan perfectly described my ignorance. Ferociously anti-American, the Shining Path was more likely than not to kill a Yankee foolish enough to travel cross-country in the midst of war. Their revolutionary plan was not to reform Peru, but to destroy and by destroying extirpate every last vestige of capitalism from Peruvian soil, including the tourists who had filled their pockets with capitalist dollars. Although I had thought ahead far enough to write the note and fold it into my pocket, I had forgotten the bus would spend most of the fourteen-hour trip at above twelve thousand feet, at night. My partner, Orin, and I, having rolled our sweaters into the backpacks lashed to the roof, spent the night covering each other with our bodies, too frozen to complain. Around us, our fellow passengers drowsed under layers of wool and alpaca ponchos.

The bus churned over the *puna*, the high-altitude moors that the Shining Path had made its own. I don't remember seeing a single other vehicle. All the towns and villages we passed, shuttered and locked and as dark as the puna itself, seemed to crouch low to the ground and willfully turn their backs to our passage. I had the notion our driver could have taken us straight over any one of the cliffs that periodically yawed out beneath my frost-encrusted window and we would just vanish, a spent breath, the road suddenly quiet and whatever birds and rodents that populated the thickets free again to use it as their causeway. The windshield and the print of the headlights on the rough road silhouetted the driver's helper, the boy who had lashed our backpacks to the roof. He talked to the driver, fiddled with the cassette player, and watched each curve as if to pluck from the darkness a suspicious shape in time to stop the bus, turn, and flee. I saw a hare and what looked like a dog curled into a ball. I think I dozed, though what I most remember is the cold.

When we reached Ayacucho city, it was Orin who was singled out, not by a guerrilla but by a soldier at a checkpoint. As the other soldiers looked at IDs and poked at baggage, he placed the muzzle of his semi-automatic rifle in Orin's ear. At the time, gringos—the catchall term for white foreigners—were believed to be the Shining Path's patrons.

"We should just shoot these people," the soldier grumbled.

But there were too many witnesses and traffic had backed up and besides, such things are best accomplished at night, on the puna, without words. He shouldered his gun and moved on. As we descended to the city, the bus no longer seemed an icy prison to me. It was shelter. I had no wish to leave it.

There is much that I have since forgotten about Peru, learned, and sought to know again. But that moment of leaving the bus—my plan vanished, my marrow chilled, my heart still racing from the soldier's casual hatred—has never lost its peculiar thrill. A piece of the world had peeled away before my eyes. And still I stood, blinking in the fantastic sun that wheels so close to the skin of the world that marks Peru.

IT TAKES STUBBORNNESS, perhaps arrogance, and a certain faith in the face of long odds to write about someone else's country. Nothing binds me to Peru, no family or history. Yet that is not the same as saying that writing is impossible. Perhaps it takes an outsider to discover in details invisible to natives a window onto a national soul. In this type of writing, there is a tension between ignorance and vision, between history and lived experience, that can either inspire or doom a manuscript.

I have not aspired to be a Peru expert. In my mind, the fact that I have lived for a time there and seen certain things, talked to some people and traveled a fair amount qualifies me only as adventurous. Peru is a place I've been, but not always. It has occupied my thoughts, but not without respite. The stories I heard, some told in these pages, conclude with no prescriptions for Peru's many ills. In a decade, what will Peru be? Besides still poor, I can't say.

As a writer, though, I confess an aim in writing about Peru. Through the writing of this book, I came to the realization that place mattered less to me than an idea, that details can be a kind of pitch, a way to an idea but not by themselves a meaning. Which is to say that I could have written a novel or about the Sudan or placed a kind of neo-noir mystery in the house next door to me now, where a gay couple lives an apparently quiet life behind shades that never roll up or flutter with interior breezes. My idea would have been the same: how is it that people craft moral lives in times of trouble, against temptation, when choices are few and hard, and what message do those lives hold for me?

By moral, I don't necessarily mean good or admirable. I mean when people embrace an idea of what it means to do right in the world, then take that idea to its terminal consequence. Perhaps they knelt with the poor. Perhaps they made the poor kneel. And everyone else, with me among them, watched and listened and walked away changed. On some nights, I slept as peacefully as the child I had once been, secure in the solidity of the walls and doors and ceiling above. Other nights, I did not sleep. I knew my bed for the flimsy shelter it was.

Peru is my lens, a country where the challenge to lead a moral life is perhaps greater or more present than in my own. It is not a country founded on morality, but rather the exploitation of natural wealth: gold, jewels, people, cotton, guano, rubber, coca. Yet it is also a place where morality has been taken to a lethal extreme, most recently in the war between the government and the Shining Path. Inspired by that same Abimael Guzmán I was so eager to meet, young Peruvians set out to destroy the world they knew in order to build something that was barely a waking dream, where all that was unjust and cruel would be replaced by the perfect sphere of equality. To stop them, the government also destroyed, so that what was left in the battle zone was emptiness and ruin and death.

To say I have no physical connection to Peru does not mean I lack an emotional or intellectual one. I found Peru's struggle absorbing. At times it inspired me and at times it left me wrung as a rag. I engaged and took strong positions, which both sharpened my vision and left me blind to certain kinds of stories, particularly those from the wealthy or the soldiers who saw in their fight a right and rational response to pure evil. As a result, I have both friends and enemies there. I have been called a paid agent for the government, a facade for guerrillas, a rat, a useful idiot, woolly, and a "pseudojournalist and human rights trafficker, totally reactionary, bourgeois, imperialist, old and rotten." Which is to say I left more than marks on a page. I have a history, albeit brief, in the scheme of things, and a place to stand.

I AM NOT THE first to see in Peru a moral challenge. Although I did not know it at the time, the bus route that was my introduction to the war approximated one frequented in the 1600s by another writer, an Ayacucho muleteer named Felipe Guamán Poma de Ayala. "Falcon Puma" is the Quechua translation of his name, in the Inca language that once dominated Peru. Guamán Poma was, he claimed, the descendant of native royalty that predated the Inca. But he had a mestizo half brother, and his father had adopted a Spanish last name after saving the life of a Spanish captain named Ayala in a battle against the Inca. In 1613 a fourteen-hundred-page manuscript written by Guamán was delivered to a Spanish ship for transport to Spain and King Philip III. Included

Woman selling telephone tokens, 1985.
© Robin Kirk

were dozens of line drawings of customs, personalities of the time, and cities, and reports about the conduct of the various characters of the Conquest and the later consolidation of Spanish rule: cruel land owners, lascivious priests, corrupt officials, grasping mestizos.

Guamán's *Nueva corónica* [sic] *y buen gobierno* (New chronicle and good government) is among the most astonishing manuscripts to have come out of Latin America. Probably begun around 1567 and finished when Guamán was near death, it begins with a description of the Inca empire and the Conquest (he was too young to have witnessed either one first hand) and the consolidation of Spanish rule (which he lived and knew intimately). While Guamán doesn't minimize the brutality of the Conquest, neither does he entirely blame the great suffering he saw around him on the 150 men who had, in the space of months, defeated the Inca. Although they were not blameless, Guamán described them as profligate with violence, spending almost as much time killing each other as they did killing Indians. As a devout Catholic, he embraced the salvation they had brought with them, proving himself a man astonishingly able to see in a half-empty cup the promise of deep rivers of cool and refreshing water.

For Guamán, the true culprits of despair were the bureaucrats—the middle managers, as it were—of empire. Not the viceroy, but the *corregidores* and *encomenderos*, administrators and estate owners, not the archbishop, but the local priests. And not the Incas, who were, he believed, just and wise, but the local chiefs and mixed-race Peruvians who colluded with brutal, gluttonous, thieving, lascivious, petty, and needlessly cruel Spanish officialdom.

Historian John Hemming has described *Nueva corónica y buen gobierno* as wild and often incoherent, which is accurate. Yet, as Hemming notes, it is also passionate, visionary, and deeply moral. Guamán wrote it as an appeal to a king he presumed capable of reform. If only the king knew the truth, Guamán believed, he would promote justice in the New World. For Guamán, Peru could be a utopia of collaboration between Spaniard and Indian. Despite the genocide of the Conquest—out of an estimated population of 9 million at Pizarro's arrival, native Peruvians numbered only 600,000 a hundred years later—Guamán imagined something better, not a reversion to Inca rule, but a new and amalgamated Peru, better than before. Although his book is full of evil deeds, it is grounded on the belief that evil was not the inevitable way of things.

But Guamán's quest went awry. His manuscript was delivered to the ship that was to carry it to Spain, but what happened next remains unclear. It may have been wedged under a cotton bale or lost behind yet another bulging sack of golden idols in the ship's hold. So many marvels packed the caravels headed for Seville—jungle Indians, llamas, huge gold effigies, dried mummies, emeralds, cloth fashioned from the pelts of vampire bats—that a simple book was easily mislaid. While the book eventually reached Madrid, it ended up in the hands of the Danish ambassador, an expensive curio perhaps. He took it home in his luggage. Probably, King Philip III never read it. It was not found again until 1908, when a German scholar took it from a shelf in a Copenhagen archive.

Rediscovered, Guamán's words no longer resonated with possibility and high purpose, but tragedy. A relic, *Nueva corónica y buen gobierno* never brought justice to those for whom it was intended; but it does show that some not only saw and recognized the vast waste of the Conquest, but were at work to harness that roiling energy of contact to make something better. Of course, even if King Philip III had received and read Guamán's book, he would very likely have simply admired the drawings and wondered at the mash of Spanish and Quechua that Guamán used to express himself, then put the manuscript aside. He was, by most accounts, an inept king. But maybe not. Maybe not.

Guamán was the victim of a spectacular fumble. Yet in Peru, as I came to learn, although frustrated, such quests are often still portrayed as heroic and used to teach virtues considered uniquely Peruvian: unwavering loyalty even to known scoundrels, gallantry when all is lost and lost beyond any hope of victory, risky adventures based on assumptions that even to contemporaries must have seemed flawed (like Guamán's conviction that if King Philip III only knew of the abuse, he would scrap the system that had brought such fabulous wealth to Spain). Certainly, the United States has its failed inventors, the dreamers whose life's work is burned to cinders in a single night. But they are secondary in our national drama, used to highlight the brilliance of our true heroes, who overcome odds, embrace independence, and win.

In defense of the port of Arica against Chilean invaders in 1880, Col. Francisco Bolognesi uttered words now recorded in every Peruvian history textbook: "Tengo deberes sagrados que cumplir, y los cumpliré hasta quemar el último cartucho" [I have a sacred duty, and I will carry it out until the last bullet is fired]. He was outgunned and outnumbered and was killed for a country that existed in little more than name. In the same battle, Alfonso Ugarte rode his horse off a cliff to keep the Peruvian flag from falling to the Chileans. The grade school depiction I have shows Ugarte and his horse not as they leapt defiantly into the air, but in the act of falling, underscoring not the nobility of the gesture, but the sickening twist of free fall to the rocks below. Admiral Miguel Grau, Peru's most venerated war hero, died in the battle that turned the course of the war against Peru and led to the three-year occupation by the Chileans.

Not only war heroes die gallant, pointless deaths. The hero of Peruvian medicine is Daniel Carrión, who at twenty-six attempted to find a cure for a fever killing the men building the rail line from Lima to Huancayo in the 1880s. As a research subject, he used himself, injecting his arm with blood taken from an infected fourteen-year-old. "What importance is there to the sacrifice of one's life if I am serving humanity?" he is said to have told the friends who attempted to dissuade him. Immediately, Carrión felt a change, which he noted in his journal. "I feel an itching followed by fleeting pain." Soon too ill to take further notes, he died thirty-eight days later.

On an anniversary of Carrión's death, the Peruvian Congress spent a day debating a bill that would elevate him from "martyr" to "hero." Some deputies protested it wasn't really a promotion. They eventually approved the bill, and Carrión's remains were moved to the official Heroes Crypt.

One grade school text I have collects heroes on a single page, and in chronological order they are cast from a battlement, beheaded, beheaded, drawn and quartered, run through with a saber, shot, shot at the stake, shot at the stake, propelled from a cliff (Ugarte, hand raised in triumph), shot, blown up, assassinated, and killed by friendly fire. In each case, defeat in whatever cause they have embraced is inevitable. The gesture is what counts.

"Somos un país de desgraciados" [We are a country of scoundrels]. In a War Ministry office, the army public relations chief, a general, offered me a crystal tumbler of ice and Johnny Walker Red. He played me a *vals* (waltz), coastal music prized by native Limans. "Don't touch my Peru," he sang, "Like Cáceres and Grau, that Bolognesi and Quiñonez, I will give my life for you, but before I will fight with a couple of good . . . reasons."

On the last word, the general looked at me, eyes twinkling. The word "reasons" *(razones)* suggested *huevones* (balls). The lyric was part of an ad campaign meant to improve the army's image, then unfortunately dominated by an overabundance of balls and the kind of discipline that allowed soldiers to rape and pillage with the apparent consent of the War Ministry.

Later, the general was forced into retirement, brought down in an internal army scandal over the division of cocaine booty. His vals continued to be played on the radio, though, especially before soccer games or after some particularly effective guerrilla attack. He meant it to be rakish and defiant. But, on those who heard it, it seemed to have a different effect. It produced a kind of melancholy. It was almost as if the very fact that these heroes had embarked on lost causes—lost spectacularly, with panache—gave solace, and reassured them that defeat was the very marrow of nationhood, the bond that neither history nor race nor common language could deliver.

I SHARE WITH Guamán both a compass and a challenge, to bring to life a world that may seem different and harsh, but is, inescapably, part of our own. Guamán hoped to bring the king to his senses, to open for him like an oyster the rich history and potential of Peru and thereby prove not only its worth, but its worth to the king, to his treasury, to the place history would assign him. My readers are not potentates; but I insist that, although we do not see or feel it every day, the choices we make as individuals and a people are important and have consequences far beyond our homes and communities.

There are heroes described here, usually uncelebrated, and scoundrels. Despite all, and in Peru facing stifling odds, I met people for whom moral questions were not simply to be considered, but forces that shaped their lives, their axis and molten center. They believed and acted on those beliefs. In part, my aim in writing this book is to recognize them and put them in a context, to explore what a hard and astonishing thing it is to carve this path out of that wilderness. And I measure myself there, and wonder: where do I stand?

It is one of the basic questions, to ask what, if circumstances were different, would become of me. What is my essential self and what, if my comforts vanished, would I become? What if my child died? What if my electricity stopped and my faucets ran dry? What if my money lost its value in the space of an hour? What if my labia were clipped to a car battery? What if I were taken into the glare of the headlights on the rocky road, with the fleeing hares and the prick of the puna wind, and made to kneel? What if I forced the kneeling?

Perhaps it is the conceit of a writer to believe that the questions I find absorbing are more poignant now than they ever were. But I also wonder whether what all the modern world has given me—my soft chair, my tight roof, my full belly, my peacefully sleeping daughter, my

Man making freeze-dried potatoes (chuño)
on the puna. © Orin Starn

cash machine and my safety belt and my hope and my vacation time and my birth control pills and my assumption that I will never be completely without a choice—makes me and those like me almost a different species from most of the rest of humanity and certainly most Peruvians, whose lives revolve around finding a meal, a night's sleep, a bit of money, a place to rest. To Peru, the centuries have brought not progress but a place on a precipice. Any of the winds that periodically blow can crack away a tenuous purchase, won at high cost and never, ever sure.

Can I bridge the gap? Is my quest doomed? Is there, in all of this, a place to stand?

And then?

2

JUSTICE

IN 1986 I WENT to live in Peru. I had no single purpose. Orin was living in a village that would become the subject of his dissertation for an anthropology degree. I was lonely and curious and joined him. It seemed romantic and adventurous, to find some exotic place and bond with peasants, who out of friendship might give me handicrafts and tell me wise, strange things by candlelight that I could later publish to acclaim.

I got my first look at the village while leading a donkey loaded with the wrought-iron bars Orin said were necessary to keep animals and children out of the adobe house he had built. Like San Francisco, where we had been living, Tunnel Six is built on hills. There, the comparison ended. Somehow, I had imagined it tucked into a fresh, green mountain valley, not stifling hot foothills covered in scrub. The houses were like dusty beads broken from their chain and scattered down the slopes. A gritty wind bit at my eyes. I began to regret all the books that weighed down my suitcase, then felt a wild joy that they were there. Huge, misshapen *ceibo* trees provided no shade and the only color was the faint green of the fungus on their bark.

The first native to greet me was a naked and filthy boy. He had the long, matted, fragile hair typical of malnourished children in Peru who have yet to be baptized. Only when his parents had chosen godparents for him would it be cut, in a ceremony known, unromantically, as "the hair-cutting." The boy had been hitting a pig with a stick, a lean, muscular piebald raised wild on shit and garbage.

I was hot. Trash hung from the thorny bushes. The boy whacked the razorback on the snout. "Piggy!" he shouted. "Greedy piggy piggy!"

We reached the house in a swirl of dust that left me blinded. There was no water to wash. The house had two small rooms and a dirt floor. Children climbed in the unbarred window. I sat on the bed of cut bamboo that Orin had struggled to find for my comfort and wept until my eyes were clear enough to see my new surroundings.

TUNNEL SIX IS in the state of Piura, which borders Ecuador. The village name comes from the tunnel built for the irrigation canal that divides the village in two. Although the Quiroz River winds through the floor of this valley, its water supplies only the farms on its banks. Tunnel Six came with the canal, as mountain families realized they could siphon out water and turn the scrub below it into plots that were tillable year-round. The brown monochrome—what I saw as I crested that hill—was after the twice-yearly planting transformed by an explosion of green below the canal that reached all the way to the river.

Technically, only those who paid for the water—corporations, mostly, that ran huge rice and sugar operations on the coast—were supposed to draw it. But the authorities didn't have the time or money to monitor the hundred-mile length of the canal. In Tunnel Six, the men had dropped narrow iron tubes into the canal, then had run them underground to an irrigation ditch that linked their plots of corn, rice, yucca, beans, and banana. After a couple of long sucks, the water flowed.

Canal overflow also fed the creek where we bathed and drew water to drink and cook with and wash. The water had the look of hand-me-down clothes, used and reused and used again. After an hour in the red plastic bucket, a syruplike sediment would collect at the bottom. Since boiling took too much time and kerosene, we mixed in a capful of bleach or iodine before drinking it.

About a hundred families lived in Tunnel Six. Víctor Córdoba, his wife, Francisca Paz, and their six children lived at the summit of the hill that defined the northern half of the village, near the school and the two stores and overlooking the canal and road. Orin had built our house next door.

For me, the days quickly took on a predictable shape. Our neighbors woke before dawn, to feed the animals, take the goats to pasture, and start off for the fields, sometimes an hour or more distant by foot. Throughout the morning, children sang and played in the schoolyard.

There was a long sag at midday, when the sun was full on the bare hills and the wind twisted dirt devils into the air. By late afternoon, there was movement again—back from the fields, back from the washing rocks in the stream. On weekends, parties held in the school lunchroom filled the air with the thump of Colombian cumbia tapes played on an old boombox fed off a car battery. There was nothing fancy in the two stores—tuna, matches, noodles, and hard, neon-colored candy. But compared to the village's southern half, tucked up a canyon, Víctor and Francisca, known as Pancha, and Orin and I lived a hustle-bustle life.

Considering that I had appeared in their midst with little warning, my neighbors were surprisingly friendly. Of course, I was news. Never before had whites, let alone foreigners, set up housekeeping among them. Otto, a German with business dealings locally, had married a local woman and bought a house in Paimas, a truck stop a half hour away on foot. Some of the engineers who built the canal in the 1950s had been foreigners. But Otto had died long ago, and the engineers had left. Now Orin, the *doctor*—a term of respect used for educated strangers from the city, not for medical doctors—had brought his *doctora* partner.

Plans to marry Orin to a local woman, as Otto had done, were kept quiet. Visitors began to arrive with small gifts—some mangos, an egg, a sack of corn. In exchange, we would give powdered milk in bags or canned mackerel or colored markers for the children. Dollar for dollar, our visitors got the better deal. But seen in terms of what their gifts cost them, their value in relation to the gift-giver's net worth, we accumulated riches. In Tunnel Six, poverty was like nothing I had seen before or could imagine in the United States, where even the poorest among us can find a meal, see a doctor, or buy a trinket.

Although I realized it only later, we had come to Peru's countryside at the perigee of a decades- or even centuries-long decline. As chroniclers like Guamán told it, the Inca empire had known no famine, and fed, clothed, and housed all its loyal subjects. But by 1986 no country in the hemisphere save Haiti was poorer than Peru. Most Peruvians, which is to say urban dwellers, perhaps from the farm but long ago transplanted to town, saw farm life not as dignified or healthy, but abject, disease-ridden, and starved. Peasants grew food but ate little, raised hogs, goats, chicken, and cattle but could not afford to eat them. Besides Christmas, the few times meat was plentiful in Tunnel Six was when there was a *peste,* a livestock epidemic. An animal would sicken, and suddenly there was meat for sale. Orin learned of this only after buying some pork for his dinner and watching amazed as the bean-sized worm cysts typical of trichinosis popped and deflated in the heat of the frying pan.

Poverty frightened me and made me pity my neighbors. Suffering! I thought. Misery! That lasted awhile. Then men started to ask for large loans and say accusatory things about Orin and drink away the rice harvest. Women schemed to get rid of me and get the house Orin had built, the kerosene stove, Orin himself—and cast spells. My pity was far too fragile for that harsh climate.

One of the first things I learned was that until Orin had appeared with me on the crest of the hill, several villagers had believed him gone for good, captured by soldiers and taken to the highest ceibo they could find, up a rocky canyon that no one quite remembered how to find (since no one had gone to rescue him). So, it was said, the soldiers placed the noose around his neck, looped the rope around one of those piss-green branches and pushed him to oblivion. But he was a damned gringo, too tall to hang properly. And, as the story went, he struggled there still, heels scuffing the bare ground.

When Pancha told Orin this story, she laughed, covering her mouth with her hand. "Don Raimundo," she said, using the name he had adopted to avoid being called "Orines," the Spanish for urine and an endless source of amusement for young or tipsy peasants. "Isn't your neck still a bit sore?" I'm not sure what about the story most amused her—the fact that her neighbors had so insisted on it despite what Don Raimundo had told them about going to the coast to meet his señora or the thought of those poor little soldiers still scrambling in the brush in search of a ceibo high enough to hang their huge gringo.

LIKE MOST OF the women my age in Tunnel Six, Pancha's belly was permanently distended from her six pregnancies, like a jar waiting to be filled. Her oval eyes gave her a distant, thoughtful expression, and she was quite beautiful despite the mottled mask of pregnancy that lingered on her cheeks. Pancha could not read or write, but knew how to sign her name, her fist gripped around the pen.

I had first met Pancha through Orin's letters, written as he lay on his cot in the dust and flies of the broiling afternoons. The letters were an amalgam of discovery and despair, seen through the lens of a tenacious case of diarrhea aggravated by Pancha's cooking. Coming from the Bay Area, where food rivals art in importance, it was easy to parody her dishes, meant to blunt hunger: Pancha's Slimy Noodles, Four-Starch Pork, Petrified Fish Bake, and Grease-Poached Eggs over Half-Husked Rice. But Pancha was a sweet and attentive hostess. Once we began to cook for ourselves in our house, we were liberated of the dismay that had accompanied each heaping plate. In the afternoons, I would join Pancha as she rested in front of her house with Marco, her sixth and youngest child, in her lap.

Pancha and Víctor's house had four rooms: a bedroom with two narrow beds, the storeroom for harvested corn and rice, the kitchen with the cooking fire built on a low mud platform, and the front room, which showcased their largest piece of furniture, a long, thick wood table. The roof was of corrugated tin, red tile, and plastic fertilizer sacks. Pancha's kitchen tools included a knife, a mismatched set of metal plates and cups, metal spoons, a small meat hook, one pot, a tea kettle, and a frying pan. Children's drawings provided the only decoration. But because of the adobe, within days they would be stained the dun color of the bricks. Wool saddlebags and blankets were thrown over the central roof beam, a thick trunk stripped of its bark and aged dark and smooth from smoke. At night, it was the chicken roost. When the eldest child, Profelinda, studied or when men gathered to talk, Víctor would hang from it a hurricane lamp.

The house of Pancha's mother, Margarita, shared one wall. Across the dirt yard, where goats, turkeys, pigs, and chickens milled at feeding times, lived Víctor's elderly parents and his younger sister. In Tunnel Six only a few families had latrines—"pig-powered" versions, with the hole open to their ravenous snouts. Although we lived in the most densely populated part of Tunnel Six, not once during my six-month stay did I see an adult shitting. In this (as in little else) they were fastidious, and looked upon our habit of going to a latrine with a hole dug deep into the ground as not only wasteful (since the pigs couldn't get to it), but also brazen, since everyone within a mile radius could see us and imagine our purpose.

There was no electricity, mail, or telephone. The Quechua still spoken throughout southern Peru was in the north whittled to solitary words—*huishqu* for buzzard, *pampa* for dirt yard, *chacra* for field, *choza* for shack. Every couple of days, Pancha, Profelinda, and Margarita trekked into the hills for wood, which they lashed into bundles and balanced on their heads to carry home for the kitchen fire.

All the objects in Pancha's house, and the house itself, would barely net a hundred dollars if anyone were buying. In Tunnel Six, the only thing worth real money was land, and the only land worth having was beneath the canal. Until 1968, it had been part of an estate called Pillo belonging to the Leigh family. Peru's estates can be traced back to the conquistadors, who received from the Spanish crown grants of Indians to entice them to remain as part of the occupation army. In exchange for the Spaniards' "protection" and instruction in the Christian faith, the Indians had to deliver tribute in crops, animals, precious metals, or goods, like cloth. These encomiendas, as they were called, also had a strategic function. The Spaniards did not live with the Indians, but in town, where together they could easily fend off attack.

The system was similar to the one that had existed under the Inca, who also demanded tribute. But many encomenderos were extremely abusive. Although the crown expressly prohibited the enslavement of the Indians (though not of imported Africans), in practice the encomenderos branded them and bought and sold them freely. The system soon faltered as the number of Indians plummeted due to overwork, disease, and starvation. By the century's end, four out of every five natives were dead.

Encomiendas were replaced by huge estates owned by a handful of wealthy, mainly white, men, born in the New World and known in Peru as creoles. Although the Indians no longer "belonged" to anyone, they owed for the right to farm and live on estate land. By then, to be *indio* meant to be backward, primitive, responsible for whatever was bad or faulty about Peru. One turn-of-the-century president believed the country would be better off if all the indios, *los indiecitos, la indiada,* were replaced by Germans. H. H. Leigh, an Irishman, bought the estate known as Pillo on the eve of the U.S. Civil War, and made his fortune when the demand for cotton shifted to Peru. Meanwhile, the peasants who lived at Pillo and tended successive Leigh generations during their visits to the estate house, and carried the cheeses and meats and blankets and corn and rice to their Piura mansion, slipped deeper into poverty.

Margarita Paz weaving a saddle blanket.
© Robin Kirk

Both Agripino, Víctor's father, and Margarita had worked for H. H. Leigh's great-grandson, Antonio Leigh. As children, Víctor and Pancha tilled the Leigh's fields and herded their stock. One afternoon as I sat with Pancha, Marco asleep beside her, Margarita told me that she had woven wool saddle blankets and saddlebags for Mrs. Leigh. The subject came up after I had admired the saddle blanket she was weaving on her back strap loom.

As a girl, Margarita said, she remembered feeling angry and afraid of that white woman, Señora Leigh, who praised the color and quality of Margarita's blankets but never paid for the wool or the labor. Mrs. Leigh considered them her due.

"That wasn't fair," I commented, to silence. I was uncomfortable with the train of thought that had led from Señora Leigh to me.

Margarita shrugged. I reddened, aware of the inanity of my words. The idea of fairness seemed shallow and weak against the enormity of the injustice woven into the blankets Margarita had made. For Margarita, it wasn't the blanket itself that counted or even the money it was worth, but the fact that this woman who did not know the machete or hoe or man-pulled plow could order her around just because she was white and named Leigh.

"The planters forced us to bring them the best of the corn harvest," added her son-in-law, Víctor. A small man, Víctor had bowed shoulders, ropy muscles and leathery skin. Most of his teeth were gone and he had never bothered to visit the local denture-maker for a new set. "When a family didn't pay, they would send men to throw them out. When I was ten, they did this to a Mr. Jiménez, who didn't want to pay. His neighbors told him that all his family—the babies, the women, the grandparents—should sit on the roof so they wouldn't tear down the house. They thought that the presence of women meant they wouldn't be mistreated. But the men came and they knocked down the walls with everyone on top. And they let the boss's cows roam in the fields, eating the harvest."

In Tunnel Six, everything changed in 1968. At the time, the president was Fernando Belaunde, an architect. Belaunde had the white skin, elegant manners, and foreign education of a successful creole. "The Architect," as Peruvians respectfully called him, believed that technology, implemented and administered by an educated elite, was Peru's salvation. His political party, Popular Action, drew together estate owners, merchants, and professionals, who built roads and dams along with an extensive graft and patronage network.

In contrast, Gen. Juan Velasco, who deposed him and installed a military junta, was brown and born poor in a Piura slum. Velasco had worked his way up through the ranks of the army from soldier to general, one of the only avenues open to *cholos* for advancement. Cholo—which means mixed-blood, from the mountains, brown, uncivilized—became for Velasco a badge of honor. For Velasco, "the Architect" personified misrule. Velasco blamed Peru's poverty on the estates and multinationals he believed whites such as Belaunde had allowed to run the country like a lucrative franchise. To kill Belaunde, however, risked transforming the pink and portly president into a martyr. Instead, Velasco ordered him hustled out of the presidential palace clad only in pajamas before a bank of willing news photographers. While elites railed against this unheard-of insult, the millions who slept in the same clothes they labored in and had only seen pajamas on Mexican television soap operas roared their approval.

What Velasco called "the Revolutionary Government of the Armed Forces" was different from its Latin counterparts, which generally defended the status quo against what they perceived as the Communist threat. General Velasco nationalized foreign holdings, devoted state resources to organizing workers, and announced a land reform. All holdings over 125 acres on the coast and 75 acres in the mountains were redistributed, along with livestock, farming machinery, and tools. Land was either handed over to the people who worked it or consolidated in peasant-run cooperatives. Agripino and Margarita, who had gone from harvest to harvest barely able to pay for the privilege, suddenly found themselves the owners of coveted land beneath the canal and owing nothing to the Leighs.

Before the reform became law, Antonio Leigh sold the cattle that should have been handed over to the peasants and bought a Piura hotel. Some of the government bonds he received in exchange came due in 1987. When Orin visited him that year, the bonds were still in his desk. Leigh said he was too embarrassed to cash them. At the current rate, the value would have barely covered the cost of a Lima newspaper.

I listened to the tape of Orin's interview in Tunnel Six. By then, we had installed the window bars and calico curtains over them. Yellow paint over walls finished in concrete made the house cozy and agreeably cool. Nights, especially after the dust and heat of the afternoon, were like a refreshing drink.

On the tape, Leigh's voice was bitter, that of a man who nurtured grudges. The reform had instilled in him a great hatred for General Velasco and the people he had once considered his.

"Because of the land reform, land was given to people who knew nothing about it," he told Orin. "They are completely ignorant. Everyone wants land now, but that does a lot of damage to the nation. Do you know why? Because peasants only produce for themselves and their house, it doesn't interest them to sell. So the nation goes further down the tubes every day. Every man has four or five women, children everywhere, they have no control over birth."

When Orin asked why this was so, Leigh, who had ten siblings, pointed to his head. "Very small," he replied.

General Velasco was also a devout Catholic, and he imposed strict laws regulating marriage and prohibiting adultery. When Víctor was twenty, he was jailed for eloping with a minor. At the time, he was working on a citrus farm on the coast. Víctor's job was to spray the tree branches from a tank of the insecticide parathion strapped to his back. He says he was always careful to dodge the lethal residue. Other, less-experienced men would often be found dead in the rows, suffocated by fumes.

He had met the sixteen-year-old girl in town. Though many peasants never legally marry, Víctor says he offered it to pacify the girl's parents. But they refused to settle. After his arrest, the judge offered to free Víctor for a bribe that was for him a fortune. The foreman of his work crew offered to pay it. But on the day the money was due, the foreman got drunk instead. Víctor spent the next four years in the Piura jail.

It was in jail that Víctor learned to read and write. He said he also discovered that while some of the men who shared the patio were thieves and con artists, others were men like him, who lacked the money to buy their way out of trouble. Disagreements with landlords, foremen, or the policemen in their pay was enough to put a poor man in jail for years. The experience changed Víctor. In his mind began to percolate ideas about peasants and the idea of being a peasant that could only have come in the wake of prison and Velasco, who had further disgusted the former estate owners by declaring an entire day, June 24, Peasant Day.

"My youth was squandered in jail," Víctor told me once, "and because of this, I can talk about injustice and give counsel to young people now."

After serving his sentence, Víctor returned to Tunnel Six, where he and Pancha set up house. She was also sixteen, but Margarita did not object to the pairing. In 1980 Víctor and Pancha finished building their house.

By then, General Velasco was dead. Ousted by his own generals in 1975, he ended his life as bitter as Antonio Leigh. Illness cost him a leg. From his easy chair, he obsessed on the conspiracies and intrigues he claimed felled his dream for a more egalitarian Peru. He lived just long enough to see his land reform dismantled in some areas, reversed in others. In the end, less than a quarter of Peru's peasants benefited. Much of Peru's south remained untouched. Though one of General Velasco's dreams was to free Peru from what he called "imperialist domination," by the time he was forced out, the amount Peru owed to foreign creditors had ballooned. The countryside, even his beloved Piura, ended up poorer because of his reforms. Bureaucrats took control of many coastal cooperatives, which fell prey to mismanagement and corruption. The state-owned rice- and corn-buying companies only paid the people of Tunnel Six for their harvests long after inflation had erased the value of the checks.

But in Peru, such spectacular failure more than qualified General Velasco as a hero to the people he had tried to help. He is remembered in Piura as a man of the people, the cholo who did not forget his roots. Perhaps he made them poorer, but he gave them dignity. In one Paimas bar, a stained and dusty poster of General Velasco is hung on the wall, garlanded by plastic pink flowers. He is in his uniform, chubby-cheeked, with a look of firm purpose in his eyes. Many believed, totally without basis, that General Velasco was assassinated by the sons of the estate owners for standing up for the cholos—for them.

For Víctor, General Velasco was the ideal against which all current and future Peruvian presidents will be compared. Víctor had come to believe his prison time was a gift, when the hand of General Velasco mysteriously reached out and bestowed on him pride. People called Víctor "Brother Cholo," a nickname that would have been an insult before Velasco's time. Many times, I saw Víctor at the family table long after the meal was finished, absorbed in a first-grade textbook. When there were important documents to digest, he preferred to have Profelinda, the best student in her sixth-grade class, read them aloud. The text books he read for pleasure. He especially liked the rhymes. He mouthed them carefully and they slipped out as little bursts of breath between his lips, inaudible in the storm of children and animals around him.

TUNNEL SIX NEVER had a *varayocc*, a traditional chief, or even a mayor. Nor did the natives have especially interesting or exotic customs. Men still wore wool ponchos, dyed a deep purple and woven by their mothers and wives. But beneath, like an aquarium fish, lurked brightly patterned polyester shirts bought in the city. Women wore polyester dresses over bell-bottomed polyester pants, with black plastic combs stuck in their hair. The home-woven straw hats that had once pro-

Profelinda (*top*) and Santos painting a sign.
© Orin Starn

tected them from the sun had been replaced by "John Deere" and "Caterpillar" tractor caps, stand-ins for the machines no peasant could dream of buying.

It was their *ronda campesina*—literally, peasant patrol, though it came to mean much more—that drew Orin, and me after him, to Tunnel Six. In 1987 Tunnel Six was the headquarters of the twenty-two ronda committees in the Quiroz River Valley, and Víctor was their president. It was on his pampa that I heard the story of the ronda's beginning told and retold, usually after the youngest children were asleep.

The story always began with the land reform. Though the two- to four-acre plots families were given barely supported them, they represented a victory, a breathing space, unthinkable twenty years earlier. For the first time, families began to accumulate possessions others coveted or that could be sold and were therefore worth stealing. No longer would the estate foreman, known as the *mayordomo,* punish thieves with his whip and stocks. Perhaps a bucket would disappear from its nail hook or a precious pair of sneakers. The theft of a cow, the peasant savings bond, could shatter a fragile margin of survival. Families began to sleep in their fields at night to keep from losing whole sections of ripening crop to midnight threshers.

When El Niño, the warm ocean current, hit the Pacific coast in 1983, torrential rains ruined the harvest. Theft became a life-or-death issue. In the night, a cow or a pig or a chicken would disappear, rustled by a neighbor and slaughtered in the hills or delivered on the sly to the truck drivers who bought animals on the Paimas road. As Víctor tells it now, the road was a kind of mobile bazaar. The drivers would bribe their way past the two police checkpoints to arrive at the Sullana market by morning, *negocio redondo* (a good deal). They even stole the dogs, he said.

"At three or four in the morning, you would hear a truck on the highway, and its lights would be off," a man who came to Víctor and Pancha's pampa one night said. Blacked out under the new moon, the man was almost invisible to me, a shape against a sky brilliant with starlight. "It would stop at a certain point. Someone would creep up with his neighbor's cow and would sell it to the thief for a certain amount. The thief would then load the cow and drive off to Sullana."

Five hours away by truck, Sullana is a clutch of low adobe buildings surrounded by a vast warren of tar paper and wood market stalls where produce and animals from the countryside are shipped in, sold, and reloaded on trucks bound for Lima. It is not a place for the meek. In his novel *The Green House*, Mario Vargas Llosa described the Sullana wind thus: "As it crosses the dune region, the wind that comes down off the Andes heats up and stiffens: reinforced with sand, it follows the course of the river, and when it gets to the city it can be seen floating between the earth and sky like a dazzling layer of armor." People in Tunnel Six feared Sullana's cunning merchants and gangs of thieves. The more cholo they looked—stained clothing, tire-soled sandals, a straw hat—the more likely they were to be cheated and robbed. When Víctor went to Sullana, his disguise was an old pair of army boots and a polyester shirt. Nothing could hide his dried-apple face, though, his goofy, one-tooth smile. He would quickly sell his sacks of limes and rice, then plant his skinny rear on the pile of purchases he had loaded on the next truck pointed toward Paimas.

But while the residents of Tunnel Six were considered bumpkins in Sullana, in their fields General Velasco had made them masters. In the fields, there were no police and no laws save the ones they imposed by force. The security they needed had to come from themselves. In the cities, wealthy Peruvians built fences, installed alarm systems, and hired private security guards. In Tunnel Six they began to *rondar* (patrol). Inspired by radio reports of rondas in the nearby department of Cajamarca, several of the village men began patrolling at night armed with flashlights and thick leather whips. Called *chicotes*, the whips were braided leather the length of an arm. At the tip was a flowering of thin strips bound to the whip by a hard leather knuckle.

The patrollers made convincing examples of well-known thieves, to prove their resolve. One man was hung *periquito*, little-bird style—by the arms tied behind his back, then hoisted up a ceibo—until he confessed. Obstreperous drunks were subjected to an on-the-spot "re-education" in front of their drinking buddies. One well-known thief accused four patrollers of dangling him upside down from a rope above the brown torrent in the canal. The closest most peasants get to deep water is the stagnant pool collected in pits left after dirt has been dug out to make adobe bricks, so this was an especially terrifying torture. The patrollers denied it. But there was about the accusation a convincing fury, the authenticity of the patrollers' rage. Peru has seen worse

24

punishments. After the Inca general Rumiñavi captured a noble accused of collaborating with the Spaniards, historian Gonzalo Fernández de Oviedo wrote, "[Rumiñavi] extracted all the bones through a certain part leaving the skin intact, and made him into a drum. The shoulders formed one end of the drum and the abdomen the other, so that, with the head, feet, and hands embalmed, he was preserved intact like an executed criminal—but transformed into a kettledrum."

The four patrollers were held in a provincial jail for a week, then released.

If a thief was caught red-handed, a whipping was measured in what they called bushels. A bushel was equivalent to twelve whipstrokes. A bushel received kneeling in a muddy field, by a fist of angry men, was a lesson few had to learn twice.

As trucks labored through the ruts on the Paimas road, suddenly men with whips would loom from the brush. They searched the trucks for stolen cattle, just-harvested corn, muzzled pigs. Such uppityness was unprecedented. With their tonguelike bellies, their beer cologne, hair shiny with sweat pomade, truck drivers personified city corruption and its hidden loyalties—to the police they drank with, the store owners they gave special rates to, the thieves in their confidence. Before, families from Tunnel Six treated them with great care, for the drivers could make or break a family by refusing to load a harvest or by charging an exorbitant fee. Once the ronda was afoot, though, the drivers were the ones with debts.

Víctor liked to point to the week the four patrollers spent in jail as the spark that ignited the ronda in Tunnel Six.

"The police, the politicians, and the judges are corrupt," he told me. "You have to pay them for justice and we have nothing to pay with. We have the ronda because we know best about our own problems and how to solve them."

Not only outsiders felt the lash of the ronda whip. Though on Víctor's pampa the men talked a lot about truck drivers and corrupt judges, the wraithlike figure of the erring peasant, pushed to the limit by poverty or flood or chronic drunkenness, was ubiquitous. Along with theft, the ronda outlawed the knives, called *chavetas*, men used to carry in leather sheaths and pull out when they were drunk and belligerent or felt insulted. Punishment for flouting the new rules varied from place to place: cold-climate villages preferred frigid water baths to the whip, while others levied fines in adobe bricks or days of labor. In some villages, if ronderos were chronically absent from their weekly patrol, the women's committee would give them a dress to wear. But whipping was preferred in Tunnel Six.

"If you get drunk, you want to keep on drinking," explained Víctor. "People would steal their neighbor's goat, or take them to eat, and afterward toss the skin in the canal."

Serafím Gómez, the Tunnel Six denture-maker, was more direct.

"Since the ronda was formed, people have forgotten their bad habits. Young men used to get drunk and bother women, and sometimes beat them if they wouldn't sleep with them. With the ronda, it's like a new world here. And we've done it by ourselves, because the judges, the police, and the government authorities are even more corrupt than the thieves."

The local judges and policemen who once depended on the steady flow of cash, goats, and turkeys to "settle" disputes suddenly saw their incomes deflated. They fought back with the law. Between 1986 and 1987 twenty-one arrest warrants were issued for Víctor, for kidnaping, abuse of authority, and assault, among other charges. But nothing stuck. For Víctor, the ronda was about *levantando cabeza*—lifting their heads—above centuries of servitude.

He seemed to take it all in stride. The phrase I heard Víctor say most often was this: "Me duele toditito el cuerpo" [Every single inch of my body hurts]. Then what he did was recline on a pile of Margarita's blankets on the pampa, in the night darkness, and debate and explain and resolve until morning the disputes that once were taken to outsiders. Bouts with the bubonic plague, worms, measles, and various torn and twisted muscles had aged his body, but his words were always vigorous. He had a profound patience with the intricacies of village leadership—land disputes, a husband beating his wife, the theft of a lamb—and was a tireless promoter of peasant unity and strength. And he never seemed to tire of talking.

If he had been born in the city rather than a farming village, Víctor would not have been a lawyer or judge or mayor. He had no thirst for neat conclusions or the corruption that permeates official life. Strict adherence to a penal code or party doctrine would be too binding. Víctor had a cleric's zeal. He believed. The occasional days he had to work the fields with Pancha were flavored for him with resignation, a

Victor Córdoba with *chavetas* seized
by the patrols. © Orin Starn

schoolboy compelled to get the grammar out of the way before writing the poem. Víctor had seen the light and it was ronda justice.

THEFT PROVED EASY to stop. But this idea of moralization, of shared community values, was thornier. People in Tunnel Six began to bring to the ronda the land disputes, charges of incest and filial negligence that had once ended in bloody chaveta duels. Shadowy figures would collect on the pampa, and as I read or washed up after dinner, I would hear the slow murmur that meant a case was being discussed. Víctor would ask questions. Talk often wandered into stories about past disputes and how things used to be, before the ronda. Pancha, silent, would listen from the doorway, where she could hear Marco cry. From birth, he had been a sickly, troublesome baby, and Pancha nursed him often since he could rarely keep down more than a mouthful of her milk. After everyone had left and Pancha and Víctor were settled in bed with their children, Orin and I would often hear their low voices in the stillness, mulling over details, noting possible discrepancies and outright lies, and predicting the response of the implicated party, who, in all probability, would show up within a day with a very different tale for the ronda's eventual consideration.

Víctor alone never decided cases. In keeping with the notion of group responsibility for individual transgressions, important cases were brought before a community assembly. On the chosen night, Víctor would hang his hurricane lamp on the bars of the school lunchroom window. The lunchroom was a musty cavern of a place and smelled strongly of beer from the dance parties held there. Save for the pampa, though, it was the only place where a crowd could gather. Gradually, shapes would be drawn by the lamp's glow. That and the lure of scandal. Few willingly missed the chance to listen in on the latest village doings.

The first case I heard had to do with a charge of excessive gossiping. The case pitted Chavela against Hermelinda, her cousin, who accused Chavela of spreading gossip out of jealousy over Hermelinda's love affair with a young bachelor named Hércules. Everyone agreed that Hércules had once favored Chavela, who at twenty-two, unmarried and with two children, was considered by many villagers to be a *mujer de mal vivir*, a loose woman. At fourteen, Hermelinda was plump and childless. She was considered ready for a steady man.

People gathered early, anticipating a juicy fight. In the lunchroom, they formed a deep semicircle around the head table, where Víctor and the elected officers of the ronda sat on wooden chairs. The only other seats were crumbling adobe bricks. A patroller elected "delegate of discipline" was in charge of decorum and making sure those who spoke were not shouted down. As I later learned, the same man was always chosen. I assumed it was because of his astonishing ugliness, his face a puzzle of conflicting planes. One ear was still ragged from a bout with a chaveta. People called him "Gacha-Gacha" for the sting of his whip, and he had the most crushing handshake in the valley.

Anyone visibly drunk was ejected. Whisperers were glared at. With the butt of his whip, Gacha-Gacha poked dozers awake. To him, excuses were irrelevant.

"If you want to sleep, go to your own house," Gacha-Gacha would growl. "You're here to listen."

The men commandeered the bricks used as seats. The few women present settled on wool blankets and tucked their children inside their shawls. Although the ronda preached equality, disputes were still largely settled by men. Women weren't prohibited from joining the assembly or even speaking. But they had to guard against appearing too forward, too strong-willed. The punishment for such behavior was to be tagged a "gossip," "egotistical," or even a *machona*—a woman who acts like a man.

I had first heard the word used to describe a female donkey who refused to let the male brought to mount her approach. As children watched with glee, the female, firmly tied, would again and again smash her delicate, sharp hooves into the male's nose, causing his long, engorged penis to flop in the dust.

"What a machona," one of the boys commented.

For this case, Víctor had decided to try something new. Throughout the previous week, he had been talking to the men about forming a women's committee within the ronda. Peasants in Cajamarca, he explained, who thought up the idea of the ronda, had women's committees. Women were invaluable spies, he pointed out. They always knew the gossip and on trips into the hills for wood or while herding their goats or washing clothes beside the stream were always alert to suspicious movement.

And, Víctor added, sometimes other rondas put women in charge

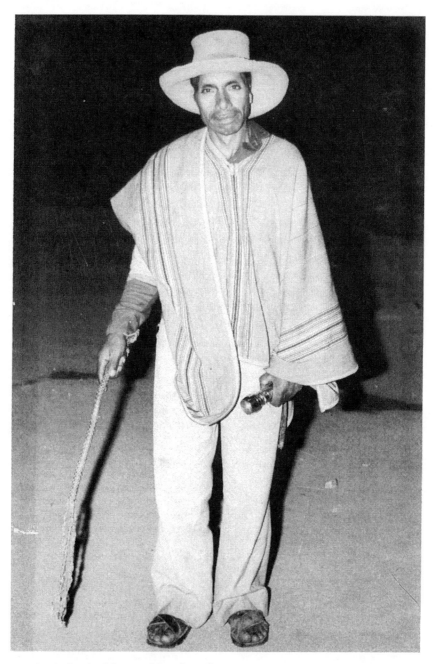

Gacha-Gacha, the delegate of discipline of
the Tunnel Six patrol. © Orin Starn

of whipping the guilty, to inflict maximum shame, especially on drunkards.

"What's a little beer, once in a while?" one of the drunkards had countered. "Are they going to whip us every time we have fun?"

"If women are allowed to whip men," replied another, "then men will be even worse off than women."

Víctor had finally won them over by arguing that as long as women were excluded from the ronda, all ronda decisions would be taken apart by gossip and even witchcraft the next day, a kind of supernatural Monday morning quarter backing. A women's committee was formed, in time to help settle the dispute between Chavela and Hermelinda. The title of women's committee president was first offered to Angélica, known as "La Sargenta," the Sergeant. At forty, La Sargenta was built like a stalk of cane: skinny and straight, elastic but able to straighten with a vicious snap. Her braid hung heavy as a whip down her back. Her nickname, like Brother Cholo for Víctor, demanded respect. But it also drew a surreptitious snigger. Although her wisdom and fairness were acknowledged even by her enemies, her audacity, her presumption, were criticized by friend and foe alike. Behind her back, people called her a machona and said her husband was *saco largo* (pussy-whipped).

But La Sargenta had declined the post because she could not read or write. Instead, Víctor had made the wife of the village catechist, Bárbara, president of the women's committee. Pancha became its vice-president. That night, although neither Bárbara nor Pancha sat at the head table, they stood near the front of the lunchroom, within the circle of yellow light left by the hurricane lamp.

With her tight town permanent and boxer's swagger, Chavela looked the part of a home-wrecker. Her thin body gave unexpected angles and planes to her worn blouse and skirt, which had clearly been the day's uniform for field work, cooking, and baby care. Chavela was notorious for having left her husband while he was away on the coast selling corn. She was the kind of woman women dislike, and she knew it. Yet she launched her defense with spirit, though her nervousness was apparent in the way she addressed the one empty corner of the lunchroom. She accused Hermelinda of being vain, lazy, a snooper into other people's business, and a general pain in the ass.

In contrast, Hermelinda's round body filled out a spotless cherry-red shorts jumper. During her turn to speak, she waved her arms,

An assembly in Tunnel Six, with a local man
defending his case. © Orin Starn

rattling the plastic jewelry around her wrists. Her hair was long and
heavy, country hair. She was cute and peppy and in love with Hércules,
which she thought proved her innocence. As Hermelinda spoke, her
mother, Gucha, commented about Chavela: *muy metida* (very nosy),
and *no dice la verdad* (she's not telling the truth).

Hércules sulked in the corner, a little ashamed at the attention and a
little proud of being the prize.

Gacha-Gacha meted out more than one poke that night. Eduardo,
the store owner, sold individual cigarettes by marking down debts on
his forearm with an ink pen. All who made sweeping moral judg-
ments—like admonitions to chastity, marriage, and responsibility for
children—risked having their own past transgressions immediately and
salaciously introduced. Finally, Bárbara and La Sargenta conferred.

Bárbara approached the head table. "One stroke for the three of
them, Chavela, Hermelinda, and Gucha," she pronounced. "I hope it
will teach them not to gossip."

Hermelinda was told to sit on a metal kerosene drum placed in the
middle of the lunchroom. She sat firmly, but was unsure of how to

position herself. In the hush, a patroller arranged her shoulders gently, so that the whip would land squarely over her shoulder and lay the length of her back without coming near her face or her bare upper arm. The cherry-red jumper was folded back neatly, exposing a swath of smooth, brown skin.

Her brother, who held the whip, faced her. He had the nervous authority of a boy called upon to do a man's work. He hooked his heavy poncho over his shoulder so as not to hamper his arm. He shouted, his voice as shrill as a girl's: "I don't want you gossiping, you are an embarrassment to your family. Learn to stay at home. Learn to stop shoving your nose in where it doesn't belong!" Then the whip curled tight as an arm over the length of Hermelinda's back.

Chavela received her stroke from her father, a brawny, tall man who settled himself before her purposefully, intending to do a quick, credible job.

"Don't gossip," he told his daughter sternly. "Behave better. I want you in the house." The stroke made a singing sound. Chavela shrugged, a ginger shrug, her parting shot at her cousin. Gucha also took her stroke with a shrug.

At the time, I was struck by the brutality of the scene, bare flesh in the smoky light and the sound of the whip. Later, though, after I had seen other cases, many of which ended with no physical punishment, I couldn't help comparing this face-to-face administration of justice with what I knew and had grown up with, the professional justice of the American courts.

Certainly, the cases heard by the ronda were rarely heinous. Although no one was murdered during my stay, I knew that Víctor would not accept such a case. The armed robbers had been outsiders quickly chased away by the threat of the silent men with whips.

Yet the impact of animal theft in Tunnel Six did compare with car theft or burglary in the United States. And the other charges frequently brought—slander, breach of contract, spouse abuse, nonpayment of debt—are the bread and butter of civil litigation. I assume most outsiders would cringe as I did at the prospect of a public whipping, barbaric as it appears in the light of modern theories of punishment. But was the American way so superior, I wondered? My question wasn't confined to the whip itself, but took in the people gathered in the lunchroom, who not only witnessed the punishment and meted it out but determined its scope and argued out its effects in public and before the litigants' families.

In contrast, Americans delegate justice to experts. Even juries are admonished into silence during proceedings and told daily to reserve judgment and pay attention only to words approved and shaped by legal experts. In U.S. courts, guilt is assigned and punished, victors and vanquished, winners and losers. Blind justice lets her balance tip to conclusion. And once punishment begins, it is within a separate space, out of sight and forgotten by all but the guilty, the victims, and their families.

The U.S. system is certainly more fair; but is it more just? In Tunnel Six patience rather than vengeance ruled debate, truth by consensus rather than discovery, and a collective desire to resolve disagreements rather than simply punish. Assemblies were called *arreglos,* arrangements, and the word was apt. While guilt was important, the goal was not just to assign it but to position it, to reweave a relationship between the two opposing parties, with the community around them. All had the power of the word—not just good words, legal words, but all words, words of friendship, jealousy, hidden agendas, religious conviction, exhaustion, indifference. Words could be used, but they could also be countered and questioned and stripped of their disguises. In Tunnel Six decisions were never neat. Division, closed chapters, finished stories were unknown. No justice was without its history, its circumstance. It was Víctor and his neighbors' ability to strike again the balance of daily life that was considered justice. The face above the whip was perhaps the dearest in the world to the face beneath it. "Behave better"—no one was ever completely condemned, yet no one was ever completely innocent.

"We have no use for cells," Víctor often said. "What good would it do us to throw a poor man in jail for stealing a chicken to feed his family?"

For Víctor, the physical punishment was secondary. Public humiliation and community intervention were what he considered the ronda's most effective tool.

"We only give a sanction when it's a second or third offense. All of us make mistakes, and we have the opportunity to mend our ways. But if we don't listen to what the community says, then we deserve a reminder."

Before the arreglo ended, Hermelinda, Chavela, and Gucha signed

Natividad working in his rice paddy.
© Robin Kirk

the minutes kept by Natividad, the ronda secretary and the most highly educated person in Tunnel Six, which meant he had finished high school. As long as records were kept, the patrollers believed the authorities, including the police, couldn't toss them in jail and throw away the key. In part, their belief was based on a victim's knowledge of the Peruvian legal process. For generations, peasants had been the losers, since they had no papers to defend themselves. But now, the ronda had paper, the thick *libro de actas* (official record book) that contained the minutes of every arreglo, their shield against attack. If someone tried later to dispute an arreglo, Natividad would draw out his book, which showed the signature of the parties involved, their agreement to submit their dispute to the assembly. Whippings were never explicitly mentioned. Instead, they were called "punishment in accordance with the customs of the ronda." The ronda leaders also had a perverse and canny faith in the vendettas, petty gripes, and toadying endemic to the bureaucrats who occasionally pursued them. When Víctor was thrown into jail for his ronda activity, the papers were often just the tinder a bureaucrat needed to set his sticky-fingered boss alight and skim for himself the fat of the land.

Like any organization, the ronda had its critics. Within the village, men murmured that Víctor was egotistical and stepping in where he didn't belong, specifically between their family and a coveted object or piece of land they wanted to acquire without undue fuss. One of Víctor's most virulent enemies was Eusebio, the warlock. Víctor's Tuesday night patrol once surprised Eusebio in a field as he was bent over a candle laying a curse on Víctor. Occasionally, a disgruntled villager whispered that the ronda was a cover for a gang of bandits. Others, more dangerous, stopped in at the local police station to report on recent events.

But allegiances shifted with each case. Brothers-in-law were pitted against nieces, grandmothers against greedy grandsons. Support gathered and dissipated, depending on the harvest, interest in the case, the probability of punishment. When dissension in the village was high, Víctor would consider buying a charm—the plaster figure of a saint or a simple wire cross to hang over the door—and would add, when he complained that his whole body hurt, that the cause was probably "evil eye." When he took sick, Pancha would blame a village witch or warlock bent on winning a case.

But when consensus was high, when the ronda had achieved some goal—celebrating an anniversary, facing down the local police sergeant, resolving a divisive case—Víctor would rest on folded-up blankets in front of his house, his children clambering over his bony frame, and spin stories of defiance and strength until even his voice grew dim and drowsy across the broad pampa.

IT WAS WHILE Víctor was away on the case of a stolen mule that his youngest, Marco, fell ill. He had been born two weeks early, and when Orin saw him at fifteen days old he was wrinkled and blue and looked ready to die. At the time, Víctor had brought a goat to the house to kill for Marco's funeral. He and Pancha seemed resigned. Their second child, José, had died at age three, struck by a sudden seizure and dead before dawn.

Orin consulted one of the books he had and guessed that Marco was probably suffering from septicemia, a blood infection common to newborns. He walked with Pancha to the clinic in Paimas to buy her a bottle of ampicillin, a wide-spectrum antibiotic often used for children.

Earlier, the same health worker had sent Pancha away with Ex-Lax, for Marco's constipation. But with the ampicillin, Marco improved. Although Marco was never a healthy baby—he always seemed to have a rash or a runny nose or strange bumps on his head—when I would hold him, he wriggled and kicked and made cooing sounds. He even gained weight, and Pancha would take him with her to the fields and set him under a bush as she worked with her machete.

But after Víctor left, Marco caught a cold, the same one that every child in Tunnel Six seemed to have. But with him, it was worse. The acnelike pustules on his scalp migrated to his neck where they clustered in an angry ring. Throughout the day, Pancha tried to get him to eat. Although he had a high fever and the temperature outside was near one hundred degrees, she had him wrapped tightly in soiled scraps of clothes. She didn't believe my explanations that it was better to bathe him or at least unbind him, but I hardly believed them myself. Marco was too sick for our book anymore. What he needed was a hospital. But it was too late to get on one of the trucks that would take us to the nearest one four hours away. Besides, Pancha said, people only went there to die.

The Paimas health worker gave Marco an injection, to no effect. By nightfall, his breathing was ragged and hard. He sounded like an old smoker. Pancha took a chicken feather, dipped it in the ampicillin, and dabbed it on his raw throat.

"He is going to die," she said tonelessly.

Of course I said no. In my world, babies didn't die this way.

At 2 A.M., Profelinda stood beneath our barred window. "Pancha says to come because the cholito is dead."

Pancha was sitting on a bed, Marco in her lap. Beside her were her mother and sister-in-law. When I touched Marco's forehead, it was hot as an iron. He had burned straight up, like a twist of paper. Pancha had started to moan, a low and throaty sound. Tiny bubbles would appear at Marco's lips, and his sisters would dab at them, dry-eyed. People began to come and go. They would lift his limp head and touch his cheek. With Margarita's help, Orin and I slipped the baby from Pancha's grasp. By then, Marco had begun to cool, and his wrinkled face, so haggard and sad, softened.

Pancha's sister-in-law considered herself an expert on pustule death.

Pancha with Marco before his death.
© Orin Starn

Periodically, she would thrust her hand into that sad little pile and announce: "He's still warm!" And he was, for a baby two, then three, then four hours dead.

Among Pancha's children, Marco's death seemed to hit Profelinda hardest. Although she was still just skin and bones, a twelve-year-old with a sharp and playful intelligence, people already talked about her as soon to find a man, move out, have children of her own. Some nights, after finishing the day's washing, pasturing the goats, going to school, shelling beans, tending Marco, and completing her homework, Profelinda would visit us. She would squat under the kitchen table, bright-eyed and curious, and tell me about absolutely everything: who was beating whom, an aborted fetus she had touched, where to find wild herbs, multiplication, jokes, the ghosts of drunkards who had fallen into the canal. For her, Marco's death was a kind of coming of age, the moment when she looked at something not as a child does but as an adult. If she were to stay in Tunnel Six, this would be her life: children, a farm, the ronda, early death. I wanted to think that she would reject it, like some of her aunts, escape to the city for something,

38

anything else. She was as tender with Pancha as she had been with Marco and managed to get her mother to sleep at dawn with her two-year-old, who had slept through his brother's death, in her arms.

It was custom in Tunnel Six to celebrate the death of an infant with a dance party, with music to accompany the journey of this newest angel to heaven. In the morning, Orin helped Pancha's brother catch and slaughter one of Margarita's pigs. A sister-in-law bathed Marco and dressed him in shorts and a T-shirt with a faded picture of a clown. An altar, consisting of two sacks of corn and a sheet of metal covered with a white cloth, was where she laid him. Marco's sisters gathered flowers for the arch over his head. Margarita, who had lost six of her thirteen children, cut a crown out of gilt-paper supplied by his godparents. I used typing paper to cut initials to paste on the crown, since Margarita could not read or write.

All day, we waited anxiously for Víctor's return. Pancha crouched before the altar and moaned. She worried that Víctor would not return in time to hire the casket-maker, and they would have to bury Marco in a cardboard box.

But he came. Somehow, Víctor had learned of his son's death. "My cholito is dead," he said as he walked into the house and stood before the altar. He looked completely defeated. No one touched him and he did not touch Pancha.

That night, musicians played on the pampa. The first to dance were Marco's godparents, who took out their handkerchiefs in the traditional style and whipped them over their heads as they stamped the dirt to a *huayno*, a kind of Peruvian bluegrass. I remember the full moon. Men started to drink and the party became raucous and loud. The theme of the ronda was never far, though, and the mourning had a decidedly political tone, as Víctor's supporters grumbled about how much his work had taken him away from his family and his rivals grumbled about how he couldn't even manage his family, so why trust him with the ronda. To one side, under the brilliance of the hurricane lamp, Víctor and the casket-maker labored over the casket, which they painted robin's-egg blue.

Marco was buried the next day, in a part of the graveyard reserved for infants. It was brutally hot, and the graveyard was barren, a hill marked only with rough sticks marking the newest graves. After the funeral, Orin told me that while he and Pancha's brother had been digging Marco's grave, they had broken into the casket of another child, which they had hastily covered up before Marco's procession arrived.

Afterward, there was more food. The goat bought months ago was finally slaughtered. Pancha moved silently, without seeming to touch the earth, as she handed out plates of rice, yucca, and goat stew. When the band arrived and the dancing began, Pancha's weeping punctuated its rhythm. Far from dampening spirits, her grief seemed to lift them, to push people into a wild and fierce motion, as if the stamp of their feet and the swing of their arms and the handkerchiefs blooming like night flowers from their fists would smooth the way and lift her infant boy as he made his way beyond the moon that shed its light so freely on the pampa.

AFTER MARCO'S DEATH, the next case to face the ronda involved land and women, in that order of importance. Segundo Neyra was accused of raping his sixteen-year-old daughter, Saturdina, the day after his wife's death. It was not the first time. But Segundo was caught by his mother, who came to the house to prepare her daughter-in-law's body for burial. The house was closed and her other granddaughters cried outside. Saturdina's muffled screams were audible from behind the barred door. Saturdina was well known in the village as a hard worker, tilling her family's four acres alone with a crowbar and a shovel.

Caution convinced Víctor to pass the case to the local police. Chicken-stealing is one thing; incest and rape quite another. Segundo was rumored to have friends among local bureaucrats. Like any successful leader, Víctor liked to pick his battles, the battles he thought he could win.

But he later regretted not taking action. Segundo apparently paid a healthy bribe to police in exchange for his freedom. The night he returned to his house, Saturdina left Tunnel Six to work as a maid on the coast. Segundo sold the house and farm for $3,400 to a man who sold it again, to Serafim, the village denture-maker. Segundo left Tunnel Six, abandoning his remaining daughters, who moved in with relatives.

Segundo entered popular legend not as the respected patroller he had once been, but as a demon. At night, people began to say, he became a *chivato*. Pancha explained to me that a chivato is a huge goat with coal-red eyes who walks upright. Since Marco's death, she had been at loose ends and would wander down to our house to chat. Her face was often swollen from crying. She told me she couldn't sleep. Both she and Víctor were taking doses of a perfume called Water of Chances, which had been prescribed for heartache.

She had seen Segundo one night across the pampa, she said, coming toward her. Only the sudden appearance of one of the children saved her. Before she packed her one bag for the coast, Saturdina told Pancha that Segundo had murdered her mother, blocking the windows and doors against her invalid screams.

There the case rested until the morning weeks later that Saturdina returned to Tunnel Six. Husky and narrow-eyed, she had the sleek, unmarked complexion of a childless girl. At Víctor's house, she announced her claim to the family farm, even though it now belonged to Serafim. For her interview with Víctor, she wore a bouncy miniskirt and a "Kiss Me!" T-shirt, neither of which masked the power in her arms. She was determined to work the land herself. She had already been to visit the local police sergeant, who told her to wait until she had paired up with a man who would help her. From the station, she had gone to Víctor's pampa to ask for justice.

The question of land rested heavily with Víctor. Land is scarce in this valley and fought over fiercely. The best land—beneath the canal and already sculpted into paddies—had been divided and subdivided within families, and rarely went on the market. Only five years earlier, the father of Natividad, the ronda secretary, had been killed during the attempted takeover of a nearby cooperative. Although he was stumbling drunk at the time, he was considered a hero. Since Velasco's reform, the sale of land had been strictly regulated. To own land, peasants had to reside nearby and work it themselves. In practice, though, the wealthy still trafficked in land, holding it through shadow "relatives." To Víctor, the man who had bought the land from Segundo and resold it for a nice profit to Serafim was like a pimp, buying and selling a sacred thing.

"There are some of us who live as *peoncitos* (little peons) and some of us who are like *patroncitos* (little bosses)," Víctor said to Saturdina. "If there is a sale, the land goes to the one with more money. But the ones who have no land need it, not the ones with money. Otherwise, we'll have what we had before. The rich with land and the rest of us without a mouthful of bread."

Any land sale was of vital interest to the community, and therefore to the ronda. Land was life. Sales were public, not private, matters. According to General Velasco's reform laws, families had an inalienable right to land even after it was sold. If a son claims land a parent sold, he had a good chance of reclaiming it. But in Saturdina's case, the test was to see if a daughter could defend the same right.

The dispute split the village in half. The houses on the hill, Víctor's neighbors and relatives, supported him and through him Saturdina. But up the stream canyon, where Serafim lived, sentiment was clearly in his favor. Alliances showed themselves in unusual ways. During one cockfight, Víctor's faction bet on the white rooster while Serafim's bet on the black. Although the black rooster broke the white rooster's back early in the round, leaving it agonizing in the dirt, it did not die, prompting Víctor to declare the match a tie. Since Pancha's brother held the money, Víctor prevailed, over much drunken shouting.

Some patrollers reasoned that Saturdina was plump and pretty and anyway, the rape was understandable since Segundo's wife had been chronically ill and was unable to fulfill her wifely duties. Víctor complained that Segundo wasn't even very drunk when he did it and was a fool to stick around long enough for the ronda to catch him. Later, Víctor added in a story about another villager named Bartolo, who didn't have the sense to leave the village after raping his daughter. He ended up killing her and burying her on his land, and was only caught after people started asking about the livid scratch on his cheek. "Threshing rice," he told them, though he had none planted. A story circulated about Segundo's desire to flee with his daughter and begin a new life in another village, as husband and wife. Serafim and his wife, who had waited years to buy land, planted corn and yucca on the disputed field, bolstering their claim. Meanwhile, villagers crept in to steal it, sure that the ronda would not punish them.

Some of Saturdina's aunts stood by her while others blamed her for blabbing and losing them the occasional jobs Segundo used to pass their way. Saturdina's most loyal supporter was her Aunt Leonila. Tenacious and bulldog stubborn, Leonila often derided Saturdina for being a "useless girl" because Saturdina would cry or not pay attention or inadvertently blurt out that she would rather be off chasing boys than stuck in another ronda meeting. But Leonila had grasped at once the essential issue—women's power to own land—and dedicated herself to Saturdina's cause.

Leonila cleaning raw wool. © Robin Kirk

Leonila and Pancha and La Sargenta spent many an afternoon swapping gossip about the case. La Sargenta's house was built up the stream canyon, under the spread of a tall, thick-waisted ceibo. La Sargenta raised the best turkeys in Tunnel Six, and her ducks loved being so near running water. But what she raised best were boys. At her house, there were boys in the trees, boys sleeping in the sun, boys tormenting the dog. Boys sucked wedges of fresh sugar cane and lounged against the turkey roost. Boys carried her messages across town, bought kerosene and noodles at the general store, and boys followed her in a single file when she returned home from tilling her fields, kicking the stones in their path.

Until Saturdina, Pancha and La Sargenta had been unfriendly, even though they were *comadres,* La Sargenta being godmother to one of Pancha's boys. But Saturdina's cause brought them together. One broiling afternoon, the three of us sat at La Sargenta's house commenting on the peccadilloes of various neighbors, in absentia or as they passed by on their way to and from the fields. The two women spoke rapidly, of the case as well as past events well known to both, and I didn't understand much of what they said. I looked out over the valley as the conversation wound on, at the distant mountains that mark the climb into the Andes. To me, Saturdina's case seemed to combine everything that was wrong about Tunnel Six—the powerlessness of women, poverty, seemingly casual violence—with the things that were so admirable and right, including the ability of Víctor, Pancha, La Sargenta, and Leonila to organize to solve a problem with profound moral and social implications, like the fair distribution of land. Most people in Tunnel Six seemed to recognize and agree that simply leaving the matter up to the marketplace was wrong. And for me, it was heartening to see how women had embraced the issue and were beginning to recognize their power to establish new rights.

As I best remember this was the conversation when Pancha placed her small, rough hand on my arm.

"He beat her," she insisted. "She would come out black and blue."

"Who?" I asked. "Today?"

"Six years ago," interjected La Sargenta. She held her arms turned out, flat, to show where the bruises had been.

"You?" I said, unsure of how the conversation had arrived at La Sargenta.

They nodded. La Sargenta explained that her husband had once had an affair with a married woman. The woman's husband "found them" behind the house, where the pigs were fed. When La Sargenta's husband returned home, he beat her. Only later did she learn what had happened in the pig pen. For the next several months, whenever he returned home drunk or they had an argument, he beat her. Occasionally, La Sargenta still considered bringing the case before the ronda.

"Husbands shouldn't beat wives," I volunteered, tying the incident to the misdeeds of men, Segundo among them.

La Sargenta shook her head.

"I want the woman whipped," she said, "so she won't go around trying to steal my husband."

EIGHT ARREGLOS TOOK place on Saturdina's claim. Víctor traveled frequently to the city and was arrested twice. The first time was after Serafim complained to the police that the ronda had threatened him with a whipping if he did not hand over the land to Saturdina. The police sergeant satisfied himself by keeping Víctor for a couple of hours in his airless office and calling him a "peasant dog." The second time was more serious. Víctor was on his way to get yet another official order mandating the transfer of the land to Saturdina. He made the mistake of boarding the truck that was to take him to the city in front of the police station, where Serafim had alerted the sergeant to be on the lookout. This time, the sergeant threw Víctor into the cell where they kept drunks. The cell was shiny with urine and stank of vomit. Without a bed or blanket, Víctor slept on the floor.

One morning, Orin and I brought him a papaya and a soda. Others came and went, and Víctor conferred with them through the bars. There was no lock on the cell door, but the handle was so rusted that it must have taken special effort to open and close it.

Only a steady stream of supporters—and the implacable presence of Pancha, Bárbara, La Sargenta, and Leonila outside the station—kept him from being masacrado as people said later, beaten and hooked to the grimy car battery the sergeant kept in a closet. For those three days, Pancha had Profelinda consult what she called "her oracle," a worn copy of Napoleon's Book of Dreams to answer the question, "When will my friend come?" She also considered leading a prison escape, but her brother, calmer, argued that given Víctor's well-known aches and

pains it was unlikely that he would survive long as a bandit. Andrea, a
witch who supported Serafim's claim, brought me eggs and palm-size
cheeses in the hopes of gleaning new gossip. After Víctor's release, I
didn't tell her that Pancha and Profelinda had been put in charge of
ferrying Víctor's overnight bag to Paimas, so that no one would know
when he was to travel. Meetings were held, confidences whispered,
spies crisscrossed the village, hungry for news.

Despite Víctor's efforts, Saturdina still did not get the land. After
many months, Víctor quietly let the case drop. The impasse clearly
proved what he had always told us, directly and through his stories: no
decision was possible without broad community support. Though
much had been made in Peru about the ronda's whips, about vigilante
justice, the truth was that Víctor and ronda presidents like him could
force no decision. Their role was to persuade, to teach by example.
And lessons often lasted years in the countryside. No ronda could set
Saturdina in her straw hut and maintain her there, like some extraterrestrial mandated by a higher order.

In many ways, the case was profoundly disturbing. Which landless
peasant should win, Saturdina or Serafim? Was the store owner, showing initiative and ambition, wrong to sink his life savings into a disputed plot? Had Saturdina bitten off more than she could chew, since
she steadfastly refused to simply claim the land physically by squatting
there, a tried and true technique? How far did women still have to go
to defend land claims?

Víctor made no pretense of objectivity. He thought Saturdina had
the better case. For him, the issue was not just her right to the land but
community autonomy and the power to regulate its internal affairs.

Yet his heart lay elsewhere, not in acrimony but in accord, in agreement. Only occasionally did the tension of the case seem to affect him.
The evident fragility of the ronda—of any justice system based not on
force but consent—didn't seem to worry him, but individual events
did. The day after his release from jail was the first time I ever heard
him openly attack Serafim. That afternoon, Víctor seemed fully capable of turning Serafim into a kettledrum to pound out the village news
down through the ages. Much talk was devoted to witchcraft, which
could make worms crawl out of your eyes or your skin break out in
shivering sweats or a *mal viento* (bad wind) grip your shadow and cause

your children to die or your cow to abort or the tin roof of your home to peel off with the next mountain storm.

But the next day, the humiliation and anger would be behind him, saved perhaps, but silent. Communities create their leaders, and Tunnel Six had made Víctor, to lead them, surely, but also to listen closely to how they should be led. The ronda was not the answer to all their problems or even most of them. It certainly hadn't saved Marco. But, as Víctor constantly repeated, it had given them dignity, and that was something they could never have before claimed.

On the nights he was not traveling on ronda business, Víctor took to his favorite spot on Margarita's saddle blanket with one of his children, a dark lump against the smoky interior light. One night, not long before I left Tunnel Six, we sat with Víctor and Pancha and Margarita and all the children to watch a storm roll slowly toward us across the valley. Lightning illuminated the mountains furthest away, then the farms and the river itself, flashing silver with each bolt. One of the girls wept in Margarita's arms, terrified by the noise. I said to Pancha, sitting beside me, that I wished my mother were there to hold me close. She laughed, not bothering to hide her smile behind her hand.

As the storm passed overhead, everyone whispered, as if to speak aloud would increase its strength. Once the storm passed, the conversation resumed. We had been talking, as always, about the ronda.

"We still remember Juan Retete, who walked the mountains in a poncho with only a sack of corn to eat," Víctor was saying. "They say that he died when he was 130. He would call meetings in the most distant villages, trying to organize people like we are organized now in the ronda. He said, 'Don't be afraid, my sons, the estate is going to be a village. The boss-man's going to leave the estate and go far away.' Because we were so young, we didn't know anything so we said, 'This old fart's screwing us around.' But what the old man said was true."

3

BLACKOUT

AFTER LEAVING TUNNEL SIX, I did some things in the States and thought about going back. The news from Peru wasn't good. After the election of Alan García in 1985 and some high hopes, Peru seemed headed for disaster. It surprised no one. After the boom, the bust was a familiar coda in Peruvian history. But the coming bust looked especially grim. García had won the election handily, and many Peruvians seemed to support his defiance of the international lenders, who he said would get no more than 10 percent of the country's export earnings as payment on the $14 billion foreign debt. He was handsome, charismatic, and had a penchant for bold, dramatic gestures. He liked to appear seemingly spontaneously at the balcony of the government palace (there was always a crowd assembled to cheer him) in what came to be known as *balconazos* and wave his winglike arms and say eloquent and funny things about the glorious future of Peru. García was a tall man, and when he spread his arms he looked as if he could swoop over the heads of his audience, provoking exclamations of delight if not any particular surprise.

Foreign correspondents compared García, Latin America's youngest leader, to John F. Kennedy. "Austerity without misery" became his catchphrase. He subsidized food, suppressed inflation by imposing price controls, purged the police, and hired thousands of the unemployed to sweep streets. He threatened U.S. oil companies with expropriation, which elicited raves from many voters. People tended to dismiss his political party, the American Popular Revolutionary Alliance (Apra) as a bunch of corrupt, violence-prone thugs, *búfalos* according to the political terminology of the day. But "Alan," as people chanted from beneath the balcony, seemed different, above and greater than the Apra. Alan had huevones (balls). "The Apra didn't win in 1985," one Peruvian told me, "Alan did."

His debt plan was bluster and bravado, but it also made a kind of sense. It was the first time a Latin leader had explicitly linked debt payments to a fixed percentage of the country's earnings, unpopular among lenders, to be sure, but an arrangement that took the immediate burden off the people, who had never asked for the debt in the first place and who had never reaped many benefits. Paying on the debt by pushing the population deeper into poverty wasn't going to make Peru healthy. Alan's rationale even won over the *New York Times,* which praised the "dashing Mr. García" and mused in an editorial, "How much austerity are these nations to endure?"

But García's plans failed on his scale—spectacularly, hugely, with voracious panache. The lenders cut him off, and subsidies, bloated state enterprises, and corruption drained the state's reserves as surely as the Tunnel Six canal drained the reservoir above it. In Lima slang, *cutra* means graft. "Alan," a friend's mother said to me, "is king of the cutra." García's Argentine economic adviser, who had helped preside over his own country's disastrous bout with hyperinflation, fled Lima after being excoriated in the editorial pages. The Shining Path intensified its urban campaign. For the first time that decade, a curfew was imposed in Lima. After the security forces quelled a Shining Path–led prison riot in 1986 by slaughtering prisoners who were captured or had surrendered, García no longer looked like a young reformer, but a demagogue willing to say or do anything to remain in power.

On Peru's Independence Day in 1987, García announced his plan to nationalize the banks, insurance companies, and all financial institutions. Although he explained it as a way to force the rich to invest in Peru and democratize credit, many saw it as cutra, a way to get his mitts on the last ready cash still lingering in Peru. They were probably right. Even then, it was clear that corruption in the ministries, teeming with new employees with nothing much to do, was rampant. García desperately needed money to prop up his flagging presidency, and had few scruples about where he got it.

Yet among Peruvians, I noted a certain satisfaction at the spectacle of the sleek and cosmopolitan bankers going apoplectic at the thought that they would no longer have their way. Of course, they person-

Woman voting for Alan, 1985. © Robin Kirk

ally wouldn't have been ruined, since most could quickly move their money out of Peru. But, like Velasco, García had suddenly stepped up and grabbed something they believed was a divine right. Much later, Mario Vargas Llosa, who led the opposition to the bank nationalization, wrote wearily that, "Alan García had found the ideal scapegoat to explain to the Peruvian people why his program did not produce the fruits that he had promised: it was all the fault of the financial oligarchies that made use of the banks to take their dollars out of Peru. . . . Is anyone in the world," he added, "fond of bankers?"

Vargas Llosa opposed the nationalization as part of his defense of what he called modern democracy, which he believed should play a much-reduced role in business. Instead of nationalizing enterprises, as Velasco had done and García attempted to do, Vargas Llosa proposed selling off what the state owned and abolishing intrusive and graft-producing red tape. But to poor Peruvians, Vargas Llosa's plan sounded like a return to the days of monopoly, when the very few operated in a world without rules and kept for themselves the country's lucrative natural resources—gold, guano, cotton, coca, sugar, rubber, oil. Only through bold, unexpected grabs, some believed, would Peru's plutocracy ever flinch.

In an echo of the Velasco years, when soldiers stormed the newspapers, an army personnel carrier battered at the huge metal doors of the Banco de Crédito. Bankers slept in their offices and workers refused to work until García gave up and the nationalization law was annulled. To cover the country's ballooning deficit, García turned to creating money. Money changers on Ocoña Street, Lima's informal Wall Street, swore they heard the gears of the *maquinita* grinding late into the night, spitting out yellow, orange, and brown bills.

The bust seemed complete when, in December 1987, the crash of a navy plane killed the entire Alianza Lima soccer team. Alianza is the favorite of Lima's poorest, especially in the African-Peruvian neighborhood of La Victoria. Games against Universitario, the white, *pituco* (snob) team were each season's highlight. At the time, investigators blamed the landing gear, which stuck in the housing until the plane ran out of gas as it circled Lima and crashed into the Atlantic. It was a grim omen: men in their prime trapped in a machine that couldn't land and dove nose-first into the sea. It was like the country, trapped in the grip of the Cutra King and headed straight for the sea.

WITH PROMISES FROM some newspapers and magazines that they would buy my stories, I returned to Peru in 1990. A friend picked me up at the airport. We spent the day, a Sunday, hanging around her house and watching the variety programs that dominated the day's television schedule. What I remember is that most of the advertisements were for candidates for Congress and the presidency. All told, they numbered close to three thousand. Most of the ads were for candidates from the Apra and FREDEMO, the right-wing coalition behind Vargas Llosa. An Apra ad showed a huge and ghostly head devouring the screen, a stand-in for the economic "shock" they said Vargas Llosa would impose on Peru to halt inflation. The makers of the ad had plagiarized the head from the Pink Floyd video for *The Wall* album.

Other ads were more prosaic: one man offered to give poor Peruvians free vacations; another danced with black women whose ample buttocks shook at the television screen. Another, referring to Peru's deepening poverty, chirped enthusiastically, "Necessity is a sport! Something happy!" It was their way of appealing to what was called *Perú popular.*

There were those, however, who considered an appeal to Perú popular beneath them. When I asked Jorge Salmón, Vargas Llosa's advertising director, about the wisdom of devoting so much time and money to television when so few voters owned a set, he dismissed my question. "Many do," he said, "at least a black and white. But that's not the problem. Most Peruvians don't have the sufficient cultural level to interpret our message."

Offscreen, there were armed strikes (imposed by the Shining Path), work strikes (imposed by the failing unions), postal and garbage strikes (imposed by the bloated, yet poorly paid government work force), and shortages of all types: noodles, flour, eggs, fish, electricity, medicine, chicken, even potatoes, a Peruvian staple. While shopping, I never knew what to hoard, so always lacked something essential, like milk or aspirin. One taxi driver told me he couldn't find a new brake piece, so had to lash the cable to his shin.

By then, inflation ran between 30 and 40 percent per month. Far from pulling Peru from its crisis, García had dug it much, much deeper. About the only thing better off about Peru at the end of his five-year term was the Apra party itself and some of its leaders, who had moved to mansions in La Molina and Chacarilla del Estanque, the ritzy neighborhood where García himself had moved.

That year, economic damage inflicted by guerrillas was estimated at $2.65 billion, including lost work time in factories darkened by power outages. In eight years, the Shining Path had blown up about fifteen hundred electrical towers, sometimes twenty at a time. Most were along the Mantaro Interconnected System, three separate trunks that deliver power from the Mantaro River dam in the central Andes to the 10 million Peruvians who live in Lima and along the central coast, half the country's population. Guerrillas liked blackouts because they were spectacular and shut down industry. The fact that hospitals, schools, and homes also went dark was, for them, a side issue. According to their logic, they had to destroy to rebuild, to devastate in order to lay a solid foundation for their new society.

Pundits even spoke of an eventual stand-off between the government and the Shining Path, which up to that point had been considered mainly a threat to the southern highlands. Half the country, including Lima, had been put under emergency legislation, in effect suspending key civil rights. In the Upper Huallaga Valley, where most of the coca leaves made into the cocaine shipped to the United States is grown, the Colombian cartels had negotiated a pact with the Shining Path. The guerrillas set the price of raw cocaine, called *pasta básica,* and charged a landing fee to each Colombian plane. In exchange, the Colombians could depend on a steady supply of product. The Shining Path had no need to look elsewhere for support. The crumbling of the Berlin Wall meant nothing to them, since they had always considered the Soviets traitors to the true Marxism epitomized by Mao Zedong. From a distance, it seemed absurd, the world's ultimate capitalists in league with radical Maoists. But in the Peru of the day, it made a peculiar kind of sense.

ALTHOUGH THE PRESIDENTIAL elections were at their highest pitch, at first I didn't pay much attention. It took all my energy to find and equip an apartment, which meant not only some place with a toilet, a shower, a telephone, and electricity, but also a place where all those things worked. It was during that time that I first became acquainted with Don Miguel—his voice, at least, which had come to be the voice of Peru's blackouts. When the lights went out in Lima, people would switch their battery-powered radios to Don Miguel. His full name is Miguel Humberto Aguirre, and he was the general manager of Radioprogramas, Peru's most popular radio station. When he was on the air, though, callers addressed him as "Don Miguel," Sir Michael, which rather than formal came off as an affectionate, friendly tribute to the man who tried to talk Peruvians through their worst moments of darkness.

For maximum effect, the Shining Path timed blackouts for week-nights at about eight o'clock, when the streets were crowded with people headed home from work. Young people hoping to get into university or land an office job were in front of their night school computers. At home, with the televisions tuned to a soap opera, Lima's middle-class families were sitting down to the rolls and margarine and freeze-dried coffee that were the dinner staples.

Then the lights would flicker. The light never winked out immediately, but would lurch like a drunken dancer, still agile but heading for a fall. Strong, weak, less strong, more weak. Watching a lamp, I could almost feel the towers staggering. The government protected about 30 percent of the towers with electrified fences, mines, and even thick, dynamite-proof "pants." But there wasn't enough money to do them all. In 1990 it was a safe bet that Lima would go dark at least once a month.

When it did, the gas-fueled generators that powered the Radioprogramas seventh-floor studio rumbled awake. Aguirre was in the studio when the first blackout occurred in 1980. A Chilean, he was once the deputy director of the government newspaper, *La Nación*, under Salvador Allende. After the military coup, which caught him in Europe, he never went back. Radioprogramas offered him a job editing the 8 P.M. sports roundup.

"All of a sudden, guak! No light!" he told me about his first blackout. I had gone to his studio to interview him for a story on blackouts. Aguirre had thick silver hair and a wide belly tucked into a blue alpaca pullover. Young reporters whizzed around him in the studio, dropping off urgent messages. Even with the lights on and morning mist spattering the windows, Aguirre exuded the calm that was his blackout trademark. "The city was in total disorder," he said. "The announcer on air sounded as upset as the people looked on the streets below. I was getting desperate on the other side of the glass, telling her, 'You lack sensitivity, you lack love!' "

The only announcing he had done was a commercial for a stomach antacid. But it proved the perfect training. The Radioprogramas owner, hurrying in from the street, pointed Aguirre to the microphone. Since then, he had managed to be at the microphone for almost every blackout. Don Miguel never liked to focus too much on news. "A young boy once called and told me he was all alone," Don Miguel told me, "and he began to cry. I told him that of course he wasn't alone! I was there, so were the reporters in the Mobile Units driving around the city to report on the blackout. One by one, we all talked to him. For me, it's a way of saying you are not alone. And soon, the light will be back on."

IN THE MORNINGS, I would awake to the faint but penetrating smell of burning garbage. There would be a hint of autumn in it, from eucalyptus leaves and dry grass. Yet there was always an unmistakable undertone of paper cartons, rags, bits of food, and shit. Because of the humidity, the smell was never sharp enough to sting my eyes or color the air. When I ran, I would often come across the source in El Olivar Park—a tamped-down heap, smoldering under the eye of a municipal worker, himself dressed in what looked to be burnable rags. The piles never seemed to completely disappear, but were lit according to some schedule I was never able to learn. As I typed at my computer or shopped or spoke on the telephone, I would notice it in the air, persistent, like a melody from a nearby apartment, picked out over the daily rhythm of the street below.

Dawes, a moneychanger I knew, was my first dinner guest. I was working with an English television crew, and Dawes was to be their link to ready cash. Inflation and the sinking value of the currency known as the inti meant that dollars had to be exchanged in increments, every couple of days. Dawes had taken some dollars and returned with the first installment of intis in neat blocks suspended in his underwear.

I don't remember what we ate, but given the shortages and the blackouts and the lack of water and the sorry collection of pots and plastic plates and spoons I had inherited from the previous renter, it couldn't have been elaborate. What I do remember is hurrying to get the hot food on the table, since I feared a blackout would knock out my electric stove. It was around the time of the anniversary of the start of the Shining Path insurrection, May 18, which the Shining Path celebrated with bombings and blackouts.

"Don't worry," Dawes commented from my single chair. "It won't be tonight." His theory was that the bombs would come several days later, when everyone had relaxed.

Dawes ate ravenously, hunched over the table and with the single-minded attention of someone who never took meals for granted. His body was wiry, and his fingers were long and elegant. I remember them because after he finished eating, he pretended to flip through a stack of dollar bills and said all he had to do to get a cocaine high was lick his fingers afterward.

Dawes was what people in Peru called a *vivo*, someone who is cunning and lives by his wits. He had the face of the Inca noble featured on tourist postcards—high cheekbones, a royal nose, lips that revealed strong, white teeth—and the mind of a venture capitalist. Everywhere, he saw opportunity. His only problem was consistency— he couldn't stick with any one project for more than a couple of days. Sometimes, he appeared with clothes to sell, other times with investment schemes or proposals that involved the sudden sale or purchase of dollars. Once, Dawes introduced me to Black Cat, a scissors dancer he hoped to promote in the central highlands. The scissors dance dates from the Taki Onqoy, a seventeenth-century protest against the Conquest. Natives said they caught the "dancing sickness" from indigenous spirits banned by the Catholic priests, and would dance to rid the country of the Spanish invaders. Modern scissors dancers use elaborate mirror and rhinestone costumes, but keep in their hands the pair of scissors natives once considered an instrument of the Devil. Mountain towns hire dancers, young and very athletic men, two at a time for their local saint days, and the men compete by dancing until one collapses with exhaustion, after several days. Black Cat was in special demand. When in a dancing trance, Black Cat would mutilate himself with the scissors and thereby add drama to the contest.

Dawes never had enough money to really get in trouble, though a knife scar creased his eyebrow. Every so often, Dawes told me, he would fly to the jungle to collect bales of dollars in black Hefty bags and deliver them to Ocoña, the downtown Lima street where dollars were bought and sold like fruit. At the time, these dollars were an indispensable part of Peru's economy. Even the national bank and state-owned businesses bought dollars on Ocoña, one of the few sources of fresh cash.

Didn't he get scared, I wondered. Dawes had polished off the chocolate squares I provided for dessert and was licking his long fingers.

"Are you kidding?" Dawes replied. He narrowed his Inca eyes and his noble nose flared. "I'm dead with fright!"

I WAS USING TAXIS to get to interviews and the airport since buses were too crowded and slow and full of thieves. A curious thing began to happen. The drivers would tell me secrets. By then, most Lima taxi drivers were amateurs, people who were moonlighting or had lost their jobs, so *hicieron taxi*—worked a taxi—for a living. A taxi could be a rattletrap Volkswagen or a smoked-window Saab. Vendors sold TAXI signs on street corners, and fares were negotiated at the beginning of every trip.

In retrospect, the secrets I heard in taxis were often more interesting or provocative than the interviews I was hurrying to make. Once, I traveled with a colonel in the antidrug police, who told me about a top secret investigation. Another driver was an air force pilot, one of the few trained to fly Peru's French-made Mirage jets. On one ride, I heard the story of how the driver, a former army officer, had survived a Shining Path "popular trial," their euphemism for a public execution. According to him, while his fellow soldiers killed for pleasure, the guerrillas only did so for cause. Far from unusual, his admiration for them was something I came to hear often from war veterans, usually to the detriment of their fellow soldiers and the officers who commanded them. During our trip, the former soldier controlled the speed of the Volkswagen by pulling on the emergency brake, since his left leg was so full of shrapnel he could barely lift it.

I asked one driver about the picture of the saint taped to his dashboard and heard the story of Sarita Colonia, the informal saint of the informals. A peasant girl, Sarita Colonia died in Lima in 1940. Because her family was poor, she was interred in a mass grave. Nothing was remarkable about her life or death. But in the 1970s rumors began to circulate about her miracles. When I visited the shrine, I had to wait in line to go inside. It looked like a city bus, a low concrete rectangle with one door to board (marked 1914, the year Sarita was born) and another to exit (marked 1940). Inside was a mountain of flowers, mainly gladiolus, which I will always associate with cemeteries and the faint stench that emanated from the aboveground niches that surrounded us.

A Shining Path drawing of one of their early
public executions (*juicio popular*)

A vendor at Sarita Colonia's shrine, holding
her image. © Robin Kirk

The woman selling trinkets outside the shrine—necklaces, amulets, good luck charms, wallet cards, all with Sarita's pleasant face—was herself a devotee. I bought a wallet card and took her picture. No one claimed great works for Sarita, no miracle healing or disasters averted. But by the time I visited, her family had taken note of 891 miracles attributed to Sarita Colonia, 753 of which involved finding a job. That number includes the miracles Sarita regularly performed for her family, which produced and sold Sarita's image at a shrine built in a city cemetery, and the one performed for me, since I sold the story of my visit to Sarita's shrine to the *San Francisco Chronicle*.

Before long, evaluating and taking risks became routine for me. There were the big risks, usually involving travel over or through guerrilla-controlled areas. But the little ones sometimes caught me up short and made me wonder how my mind had come to work in this new way.

For instance, one afternoon, I went to a mall to see a movie. It was a new mall, full of glass and chrome and stocked with items few Peruvians could afford to buy. So the shop girls—sullen-faced and paid some miserable starvation wage—spent their time knitting things to pass to friends who had market stalls, or reading movie magazines, or forming tight little groups to complain. In the mall, I noticed an un-usual number of security guards and bomb-sniffing dogs and con-cluded there was either a threat of a car bomb or the imminent capture of some guerrilla chieftain at hand.

A bomb seemed more likely. As I stood in line to buy a ticket, I weighed my options, forgo the movie (I can't recall what it was) or risk a bomb. I bought my ticket, and this was my reasoning: even a big bomb wasn't likely to destroy the whole building. The theater—on the sixth floor and well away from the street, where a car bomb would detonate—would likely be untouched.

A month later, a car bomb did detonate outside the mall, punching out each and every one of its black smoked-glass eyes. But my reason-ing proved solid. Despite the bomb's power, the movie theater was unscathed.

"Don Miguel!" cried a housewife, his first caller during a blackout. Her children made a clatter with pots in the background. "Here in San Borja, we have no light!"

"Tranquility!" Don Miguel crooned. It was his favorite word during blackouts. When I stuck my head out my window, the darkness was eerie and shape-filled, fractured by car headlights. For thirty minutes, guerrillas set off dynamite charges at banks and public buildings, and the sound of distant explosions gave an almost electric charge to the air. But seeping from the houses up and down my block was also Don Miguel's voice. It's the voice that did it—honey-smooth, tuneful, rum-bling in a low register, and never hurried or the least bit upset.

He asked the woman for her name, where she lived, what she was cooking when the blackout began. Other callers gave Don Miguel information about what was happening around them ("Uyyy!" Don Miguel said when one caller reported explosions nearby, and "Uyyy!" again when a man, calling from a pay phone, said he witnessed an armed robbery).

Blackouts used to cause panic. After so many years and Don Miguel, though, people took them pretty much in stride. The rich had their gen-erators; the middle class and poor, their candles and kerosene lamps. And everyone had Don Miguel, his soothing, antacid voice. Within an hour or so, the power company usually came up with some light. Don Miguel tracked it as it leapfrogged the coast—Jesus María, Callao, Chorrillos, Chincha, La Victoria. Some people believed Don Miguel had a say in when the power came back on, and when they called they asked him, politely, to put in a good word for their neighborhood.

Lima has been called proof that there are no knowable limits to what people will put up with. But listening to Don Miguel, I could just as easily have said that when limits were passed, there were moments of eerie calm. The night I listened so carefully to Don Miguel's blackout broadcast, the light in my neighborhood had still not returned when he signed off and the station resumed its regular programming. By then, though, I was too sleepy to notice. At 3:15 A.M., I woke to find the bedroom brilliant with light. When I was turning off lamps, I looked out the window. In the house across the street, I saw my neighbor wrapped in a robe, hair tousled with sleep. He was turning out his lights, too. The streets were quiet and I didn't hear a single radio. The grayness of the fog had turned to night and the weird, pulsing glow of the reawakened city. I returned to bed feeling my way, and was asleep again in an instant.

4

RECORDED IN STONE

Wild weed, pure of scent!
I beg you to follow my path.
You will be my balm and my tragedy,
my scent and my glory.
You will be the friend that flourishes on my tomb.
There, let the mountain shelter me,
let the heavens answer me.
In stone, all will be recorded.

Edith Lagos

"BETTY" WAS SEVENTEEN when she ran away from home. Her mother had abandoned her as an infant and her father was dead. She was raised by an aunt, a drunk who beat her. Unlike most runaways, though, who don't know for sure where they will land, Betty had a plan.

For months, friends had told her about the guerrillas in the hills. They said they fought to end poverty and set up a government of the people. Betty had never gone hungry or lacked a bed. With her white skin and education, she knew she was better off than the peasants the guerrillas moved among. Yet her aunt's raised hand had taught her something about suffering, she thought. Betty decided to join, to do something about injustice.

At twenty-seven, Betty still looked to me much as she probably had at seventeen—young, but cautious with her words, a thinker. Her black cap of hair just brushed the collar of her polo shirt. Her slanted eyes and high cheekbones gave her a fragile, almost Asian beauty. Yet she was like so many other young women in Peru. By then, if I had passed Betty on the street, I don't think I would have taken particular notice of her.

I met Betty in 1991, introduced by a mutual friend who had gone to elementary school with her. I interviewed her in the car I had hired to drive from Huamanga, the city where the Shining Path was born, to the parking spot where we spoke. The backseat, with the windows rolled up, insulated from prying ears, was the only place Betty felt comfortable talking about her life as a *senderista*—a member of the Shining Path.

To tell her story, Betty adopted the kind of fixed, relentless rhythm of someone describing images flashing past on a movie screen. On the appointed day, she told me she rolled up a pair of sneakers in pants and a T-shirt, and packed them in the bottom of her school book bag. With her best friend, she walked the three miles to their rendezvous, like truants out for a picnic.

"We agreed that we would not be afraid," Betty said. "We were leaving home to fight for a cause."

That young Latin Americans joined guerrilla groups wasn't news; for much of this century, it's been a rite of passage, like being a campus radical before joining a prestigious law firm. But that was the only thing usual about Betty's militancy in the Shining Path. In no other modern guerrilla movement have women played such a prominent role. According to Peru's penal authorities, a third of the people held on terrorism charges related to the Shining Path are women. In 1990 police intelligence documents listed eight women among the nineteen members of the Party's Central Committee and two of the five members of the Political Bureau. At the insurgency's peak, more often than not it was a woman who gave the coup de grace to the police and military officers the Shining Path hunted down in specially trained assassination squads. Guerrillas claim 40 percent of their militants are female.

Betty left her aunt a letter saying she would never return. "My family is the people," she told me she wrote. "I no longer belong to this family. When people ask, tell them I left one day without looking back."

It made her happy, as happy as she had ever been. She and her friend swung their bags with their rolled-up secrets. In the distance, peasants chipped at their rocky plots. Betty felt like shouting to them that help would soon arrive. There was hope.

"It was the beginning," Betty said, "of what I thought would be my new life."

WHEN CHE GUEVARA and his boys-only band marched into the Bolivian jungle in 1967, they were symbols not only of an ideology but a *style*. It was young, daredevil, intellectual. It was combat-ready, but sensitive, even poetic. And it was male. No women packed in, slogged the muddy trails. Women were expected to fight the enemy (in this case, capitalist imperialism) the way most societies have always expected them to fight: defending their homes, perhaps, or deploying their bodies to steal enemy secrets. But a woman train in the art of the kill? Even revolutionaries have taboos.

In many cultures, a woman with a gun means something very other than a man; it is armed emotion, violence pushed beyond the rules of formal combat. In the place of the mother is something terrible, in the sense of full of terror. The few women who have led modern guerrilla insurgencies are remembered for their savagery and fatal beauty: for example, Fusako "Mistress of Mayhem" Shigenobu of the Japanese Red Army, and Ulrike Meinhof, cofounder of the West German Red Army Faction (better known as the Baader-Meinhof gang), who ended her guerrilla career hung by a towel from a Stammheim cell. When the Sandinistas sent Nora Astorga into a hotel room with a Somoza general, it was not her skill with an automatic they prized, but her astonishing beauty, which clouded the general's senses long enough for the gunmen in the curtains to adjust their sights. Although women made up an estimated 30 percent of the Sandinista army before their victory, afterward women were the first demobilized. Future president Violeta Chamorro was the only woman ever named to the five-member junta. She lasted nine months.

Even revolutions that claim they defend equality between the sexes rarely do. Although Mao Zedong once said the success of revolution depends on women, only thirty women made the Long March, most of them, like Jiang Qing, wives of Red Army leaders. Overall, the ratio of women to men never surpassed one to eighteen. Some historians believe the Central Committee allowed Mao and Jiang Qing to marry only after she agreed to confine herself to domestic life for twenty years. The end of that ban coincided with her appointment as the first female member of the Politburo.

After Mao's death and her fall, some critics said her ruthlessness during the Cultural Revolution was born of repressed ambition and living so many years in Mao's shadow. But Jiang Qing rejected any hint of "feminine" hysteria. "Liberty: there is no word sweeter in resonance," she once wrote. "But for women it is as incompatible as snow with fire. To be a woman and free is to be dead . . . and I want to live."

I also had my notions. As I listened to Betty, this was the thought I couldn't shake: how could she be fooled? Aren't women too smart, too *canny*, for war? I buy into the idea of women as peace-makers, nurturers. Certainly political figures like Margaret Thatcher can play the war game. But to mold oneself to what the Shining Path calls its "killing machine"? When I mentioned my curiosity about Shining Path women to some feminist friends, they looked at me in disbelief. For them, it was an obvious lie that women supported this group, a ploy guerrillas use to appear more powerful than they were. Women? they said to me. Only the crazy ones.

In the newspaper photos, though, they didn't look crazy. They had the stout, powerful bodies of market vendors, of maids, of thieves. They wore jeans and pullovers and sneakers for running fast. Their hair was cropped short, no frills. They looked like Betty.

After I began to ask around, I discovered that the idea that only crazy women join was widely shared. For the dailies, there were only two kinds of female senderista: a sexless automaton, cold as gunmetal; or alluring bitch-goddess, a bloodthirsty nymphomaniac. Talk dwelt on their cruelty, their beauty, their sexual appetite. Like the stories about "La Chata" (Shorty), who led fifty guerrillas on a raid of the ranch of a prominent Lima political figure in November of 1990. Witnesses said La Chata forced the owner to kneel in the dirt for a "popular trial." Although the workers insisted he had treated them fairly, La Chata was stone. "Bad weeds," goes the Shining Path saying, "must be torn up by the roots."

She shot the man twice in the chest. According to one newspaper, she knelt to fire the coup de grace into *la nuca,* the base of his neck. Hours later, police shot her down on the highway. Two men, her lovers the male reporter suggested, died with her.

These "personality traits" were taken from a 1990 police training manual on "subversive women": "They are more determined and dangerous than men, they behave in an absolutist fashion, and think them-

Page from an army comic book showing a
Shining Path female commander

selves capable of carrying out any mission, they combine the dichotomy of weakness with hardness, they are indulgent, very severe . . . they exploit and manipulate the nearest to them, they are impulsive and take risks."

The police liked to show off "suspected subversives" in press conferences, to demonstrate that they could capture the *delincuentes subver-sivos,* the *terroristas,* display them, command them, control them. But they hadn't realized there would be so many women. "What are these *muchachas,* these girls, doing there?" I heard people say when the images appeared on the nightly news. At first, they shook their heads. They wondered at this ominous sign, like a comet or freak rain in rainless Lima. Although U.S. viewers were shocked at the image of a disheveled American woman, the New Yorker Lori Berenson, as she was brought before the television cameras and accused of subversion in 1995, for Peruvians, her gender was by then the least unusual thing about her. For once, a friend commented, Peru's smaller insurgency, the Túpac Amaru Revolutionary Movement (MRTA), had grabbed the spotlight with a *camarada,* a comrade.

What was the world coming to? people asked. It was as if Nature had delivered a totally new creature: a two-headed calf, an infant-fish, complete with flippers instead of feet and hands. It frightened, and gave guerrillas an aura of unnatural, witchy power. There was something wrong out there, it said. There was something beyond your ken.

It was beyond mine. During our afternoon of conversation, it was hard to look Betty in the eye. In the oven-hot car, as I listened to her, this was the image I couldn't shake: the fact of Betty in the clearing as the accused man was dragged out and pushed to his knees for a "popular trial." She was not the passive observer or even just one of the gang, but had her finger on the trigger when she bent, like a penitent, to pin another star on the red banner of the People's War.

FOR THREE DAYS, Betty and her friend waited in a peasant house. A man and a woman came to ask them if they were serious. "I became even more determined," Betty remembers. "I was doing something that I knew others would find too difficult. It made me feel strong and grown up."

The comrades were thrilled. Betty and her friend were the youngest ever to join their unit. At first, camping out was like a game. Betty had visited farms before, but she was a town girl at heart, used to the nearness of the square and its belled church. Some days, they would march twelve hours up and down the steep gorges. It was exhausting. She fantasized about collapsing beside the streams that cut the trail, sucking in her fill of thin, cold air. But she didn't. Her legs grew strong, her lungs, too. At night, the star-shine was so intense it threw its own shadow.

She studied harder than she ever had in school. They carried no texts, instead noting down passages from Marx and Lenin and Mao and especially President Gonzalo, the Shining Path's leader, memorized and recited by the more experienced comrades. Betty used her algebra notebook from high school, but wrote in red ink only. Soon, her script was as neat and ordered as a typewritten page.

At first, she rarely opened her mouth, in awe of the other comrades. There were so many things to learn! They were a unit in the People's Guerrilla Army, which the comrades shortened to EGP. The year 1980 marked the ILA—Inicio de la Lucha Armada, beginning of the armed struggle. The Party—that all-powerful entity people talked about reverently—was based on MLM-PG: Marxism, Leninism, Maoism and *pensamiento Gonzalo,* Gonzalo Thought. Sometimes, the lessons seemed as complex as the algebra she thumbed through to get to the red pages. What is the enemy of revolutionary thought? Revisionism! In what stage is Peru? Semifeudal, bureaucratic capitalism, imperialist domination, principally Yankee! She learned the stages of guerrilla war, why they must destroy to rebuild.

Criticism sessions were held almost every night. Once, she was criticized for not speaking up. How could she become a true revolutionary if she never opened her mouth? She vowed publicly and in grateful tears to reform. Comrades clapped her on the back. To Betty, it felt like love.

The goal, she was told, was to forge true revolutionaries. The Iron Legions! She was to hide nothing—nothing!—from the Party.

Betty learned how to hold a gun and clean it, how to storm a police station, and set an ambush. More important than skill was the Thought—Gonzalo Thought. She would even dream it, their glorious President Gonzalo before her, his shape huge and imposing against a brilliant red dawn. Soon, Betty shouted like the most experienced cadres, her fist clenched and her face filled with love. Love for the Party, love for the people, the comrades, love for battle. President Gonzalo said it could take fifty years. She was ready! It made no difference that she was a woman. They were revolutionaries—warriors—equal in the quest for justice.

She kept the notebook tucked inside her jacket. Sometimes, the peasants would give them gifts, like a wool poncho or hat. But Betty lived by the golden rule: never take even so small a thing as a needle from the house of a peasant. She ate from the common pot: potatoes, potatoes, and more potatoes. Occasionally, there was soup with *quinua*, a high-altitude grain, or a wedge of freshly made cheese, moist and salty. Only on holidays—the anniversary of the Russian Revolution, the ILA—would a peasant slaughter a pig. Breakfast would be a steaming plate of its entrails, tossed in oil and onion over a wood fire. Later, there was barbecue and stew, a day-long feast, washed down with the sour beer called *chicha*.

"People welcomed us, and we would teach them about *la lucha*, the struggle. I would think of my other life, and wonder what had taken me so long."

Betty's language skills made her indispensable. As a child, she had learned Quechua, the Inca language still spoken throughout the southern Andes. In contrast, the older comrades had never learned more than they needed to understand their servants or swear on the playground. Betty became their interpreter. At night, the comrades would call villagers to meetings. They would tell them about the People's War, about rising up. The People's Army had to kill the wealthy, kill the corrupt, kill the adulterers, kill the thieves. They would fall on the cities, dens of corruption, and destroy with the cleansing fire of revolution. Betty made her sentences ring so that even the ones crouched beyond the veil of light from the lantern could hear.

She had a new life. She chose a new name: Rita. No longer Betty: abused Betty, poor Betty, silent Betty. She was Comrade Rita, interpreter and cadre. She was changing the world.

Only later, thinking back on those evenings and the clutch of faces turned up to hers, did Betty realize she was the only one among the comrades with her face uncovered.

"How could I speak to them of these things in Quechua with my face hidden?" she asked. "They wouldn't have believed me. Now, though, how many people look at me and think, There she is—there goes Comrade Rita, who is responsible for all this suffering?"

ON THE WAY TO my meeting with Betty, César, my driver, told me his theory about Shining Path women. César had a potbelly and cheeks swollen by occasional bouts of marathon drinking. He had lived all his life in Huamanga, the capital of the department of Ayacucho. Although he was sly, given to name-dropping and promising more than he delivered, I liked him. César drove his rusted red Toyota anywhere and was boundlessly patient.

César began by saying he once dated Teresa "Techi" Durand, a fugitive member of the Shining Path's Central Committee. As a youth, he played drums in the Happy Boys band. She loved to dance. César told me she had straight brown hair and a slim, compact body. He called her a *palomillera*, a gossip and general live wire.

Her family lived just outside town. People thought Techi and her older brother, Maximiliano, were going places. For Teresa, that meant a husband and children and perhaps a part-time job. They thought Maximiliano would be a lawyer or engineer. Success meant moving to a house in Lima with a gardener and maid brought from Huamanga, and shopping junkets to Miami and New York.

In a way, both fulfilled those expectations. Maximiliano Durand became an internationally known specialist in alternative energy development. When he was arrested in 1981, the Argentine writer Julio Cortázar signed a plea for his release. Afterward, Durand went to France where he became the Shining Path's European ambassador. Another brother, Jorge, ran the Shining Path newspaper, *El Diario,* until his arrest in 1992. Techi married Osmán Morote, the Shining Path second-in-command. They had two children, Elena and Osmán Jr.

There, the path of expectation and revolution diverged. Techi left the children with peasants and slipped into the shadow world inhabited by the highest Shining Path cadres. Later, the children were delivered to Techi's mother. Like Techi, Elena studied social sciences in college. In April 1991 Elena was arrested outside a Lima shopping mall for attempting a bombing aimed at Peru's vice-president, Máximo San Roman. At nineteen, she was sent to the prison where her father was serving a twenty-year sentence. Her brother followed several months later. There, walking the concrete breezeway to the Shining Path cell blocks, they may have glimpsed their father peering from his cell window for the first time since they were toddlers.

"Their house was one point on the Bermuda Triangle, I call it," César said about the Durand home. The Bermuda Triangle, it turned out, was formed by houses belonging to the Durand family, the Cáceres family, and the Morote family. Many of the children joined the

Shining Path. "That's where they got lost," César said, grinning. "That was like a black hole."

He didn't understand why Techi married Osmán Morote, "that sourpuss," he said, "that monk!" Discussing Morote's sexual deficiencies took us above the shallow Huamanga valley, where the mountain slopes turned steep and rocky. There were no people, no animals, no roadside stands. The land seemed empty. Recently, this area had been the scene of clashes between Shining Path units, the army, and the civil defense patrols set up by the army to fight guerrillas.

A journalist friend in the backseat was pallid from what turned out to be a case of typhoid. He sat up long enough to name the grassy spot next to the bridge that marks one of the route's few hairpin turns: Ayahuarcuna, Quechua for the place where the dead are hanged. Here, soldiers took suspected guerrillas, executed them, and left them for the vultures, the *huishqus*, to eat.

Techi made a mistake in marrying Morote, César repeated. What he meant was she probably still pined for the former Happy Boy. "Girls are led in by these types," César insisted, shaking his head. "Hood-winked, maybe."

He finally got around to his theory. He believed Techi's story was emblematic. Women from the mountains were strong-willed, warlike. They called the shots. Like his wife, who recently left him. She too was from Huamanga, a *huamanguina*. Like Techi, she had her own ideas about life. They included living in Lima, not a backwater like Huamanga. She wanted movies, restaurants, a night life. She had it up to here with the killing, he said. And his drinking. She wanted to set up a fancy dress boutique and live a little, for a change.

Twice César tried to raise the fee he charged me for his services, to pay off her Lima debts, he said. He added that someone—an aunt, a cousin—has Techi's high school graduation picture. For a price.

"It may look like the man is the chief of the family," he finished, sweeping his arm across the dashboard to take in the valley below and all the invisible women he imagined there, lying in wait. "But if you scratch the surface! The woman is really in charge."

A lot of people told me about tough *ayacuchanas*: like María Parado de Bellido, who faced a firing squad rather than give information to the Spanish during the Independence Wars, and the lady butchers who protested the introduction of paper money at the turn of the century

Ayacucho woman with child.
© Robin Kirk

by marching on Huamanga's central square with their freshly sharpened cleavers. Women on the Huanta heights were supposed to be "as
fierce as their men, urging them on with shouts and applause" according to one soldier who fought Indians protesting the salt tax in 1896.

Historian María Rostworowski recounted one version of the Inca
creation myth that had Mama Huaco leading her siblings to the cap-

ture of the Cuzco valley, which later became their capital. When the Incas attacked the *guallas*, who occupied the valley, Mama Huaco grabbed a gualla soldier, tore out his lungs with her bare hands and blew them into pulsing red balloons, scaring off the enemy. Some chroniclers say the Incas defeated the *chancas* by calling on the *pururauca*, magical stones that transformed into male and female warriors. Contemporary feminist scholars suggest that before the Conquest, Andean women could be leaders and warriors as well as wives and mothers.

After the Conquest, however, Spain and the militant bearers of Catholic morality decreed a new social order. It fell especially hard on women, considered less human than their men. The equation couldn't have been more direct. Spanish law held that the testimony in court of one Spaniard was equal to two male Indians, itself worth the testimony of three female Indians. Since women often supervised the worship of pre-Columbian idols, which the Spanish sought to destroy, they were considered sorcerers and consorts of the Devil.

Far from docile, Peru's indigenous population mounted many challenges to Spanish rule. The most celebrated was that of José Gabriel Condorcanqui, who called himself Túpac Amaru II, after the last Inca murdered by the Spanish. Although it lasted less than two years, between 1780 and 1781, the uprising extended across half the Peruvian Andes. Condorcanqui may have been a visionary, but it was his wife, Micaela Bastidas, who gained fame for military skill. Once, she publicly upbraided her husband for failing to attack Cuzco in time to rout the Spanish.

After Túpac Amaru's defeat, the Spanish killed Bastidas in front of him. First, they cut out her tongue. But the iron vise they used as a garrotte was too large. Instead, the executioners looped ropes around her neck, and kicked at her stomach and breasts as they pulled in opposite directions.

Even creole women were considered tough. While French traveler Flora Tristán awaited the ship that would return her to Europe in 1834, she noted in her journal that Limeñas were taller and "more vigorous" than their men. "There is no place on earth," she wrote, "where women are more free or exercise more dominion than in Lima."

Yet Tristán's own experience in Peru, published later in Paris as *Peregrinations of a Pariah,* revealed a radically different picture. Daughter of a wealthy Peruvian expatriate and his French lover, Tristán was raised in Paris and received the upbringing typical of the bohemian middle class: piano and dance lessons, poetry, painting, and a taste for polite rebellion, encouraged by the young Simón Bolívar, who once escorted her through the family garden. But when her father died, never having formalized his marriage, she and her mother joined the poor.

An unhappy marriage and the desire for independence convinced Tristán to ask her Peruvian relatives for a share of her father's inheritance. Although her uncle Pío, owner of a huge hacienda in Arequipa, paid for her voyage to Peru, he granted her only a small pension. He severed it after reading her salty observations on upper-class, provincial Peru. Her book was later publicly burned in Arequipa's central square.

Even wealthy women had to wait until 1956 for full voting rights, late for Latin America (in neighboring Ecuador, women began voting in 1929). Literacy laws kept uneducated women from voting until 1980. On the left, women have yet to break out of the secretary-mistress mold (*machismo-Leninismo*, it's called). Too often, I heard the saying "Más me pegas, más te quiero" [the more you hit me, the more I'll love you] tossed about at leftist cocktail parties like charming folk wisdom. "Women," wrote the founder of Peru's Socialist Party, José Carlos Mariátegui, "lack a sense of justice. Woman's flaw is to be too indulgent or too severe. And they, like cats, have a mischievous inclination for cruelty."

One friend called Peru *el país de las nalgas*, not some forgotten Amazonian tribe but asses, women's asses. In Peru, asses are massive, otherworldly, suns to the minor planets of breasts and legs. The respected news weekly *Caretas* ends every issue with "La Calata"—a naked woman whose exposed dorsals float like egg yolks in a pan of black newsprint. Yet in this very macho culture—where a man who, for neglecting to beat his wife, can be called saco largo (pussy-whipped)—the ass is a wicked, double-sided image. After all, what other corporeal feature is so pleasingly androgynous, so apt for all tastes, than the breastless, penisless, vaginaless ass?

At the intersection of Mama Huaco and La Calata, I wondered, where lay the Shining Path?

IN AYACUCHO, TALK inevitably circled back to a man: Abimael Guzmán, who once taught philosophy at the university there. Although he lived in clandestinity from 1979 until his arrest in 1992, when I visited the city in 1990, his presence lingered like scandal. Straight from the airport, César took me on his "Stars of the Shining Path" tour: where Guzmán was known to drink, Techi's house, the spot where their first bomb went off. "Have you seen the Kremlin?" he asked, before swinging by the walled-in bungalow where Guzmán once lived.

Guzmán was no handsome Che. The photos taken of him when he taught at the National University San Cristóbal of Huamanga (UNSCH) in the 1960s show a barrel-chested, jowly man with a head round as a billiard ball. He had changed little at the time of his arrest, adding only a full beard, trimmed sharp as a sickle around his chin.

Guzmán called his doctoral dissertation "On the Kantian Theory of Space." Like the philosopher, he was a practical man. He also got a law degree. People remembered him as bookish, intense, a skilled political infighter who yet charmed close friends during the boisterous *jaranas* (dance parties) that often lasted until the icy mountain dawn. He danced and drank. He talked literature and music, though he approved of only "serious" artists, like Beethoven. Vivaldi, for example, was "drivel for palace suck-ups." Even his enemies admitted he was charismatic, even brilliant. The name he chose for his group—the Shining Path, from a phrase written by Mariátegui about the "shining path to revolution," had a mysterious, mystical air, something that might suddenly shimmer open to lead the way to a Communist Camelot.

Guzmán once said he never intended to spend more than a year in Huamanga. But there, he said, he "discovered the peasantry."

"One proposes and the classes decide, the masses and the people who make many things of one," Guzmán was quoted as telling the editor of El Diario, the pro–Shining Path newspaper. "Ayacucho has been of transcendental importance for me."

It was his laboratory for revolution. The state is a moonscape of puna cut by the gorges that reach into the Amazon's tropical headwaters. It is among Peru's poorest states. For centuries, white estate owners treated the indios as animals, good only for manual labor. But after the Second World War, industrialization and land reform forced change. Country people began to migrate to the cities in search of jobs and a better life. Fired by the idea of progress, Peru's leaders began to build new city universities. Between 1961 and 1985, forty new universities opened. These state-funded institutions were meant to train a new generation of doctors, lawyers, agronomists, and social scientists. No longer just the children of elites, or *mistis*, many new students were cholos, *serranos*, from the mountains known in Peru as the *sierra*. When the University of Huamanga reopened in 1959 (it had been closed in 1876 after Peru's disastrous defeat to the Chileans), enrollment increased by more than fifteen times in as many years.

Carlos Iván Degregori was a colleague of Guzmán's. Like him, Degregori is a misti, son of a prosperous provincial family. On the shelf behind his cluttered desk at Lima's Institute of Peruvian Studies, where we spoke, were pre-Columbian pots mixed with contemporary ceramics on sale in the Indian Market for about fifty cents apiece. Although centuries separated them, the ceramics shared the same ocher patina, a hand-fashioned roundness.

When I admired the ceramics, Degregori smiled absently, anxious to get on with the interview. As one of Peru's leading "senderologists," students of the Shining Path, he was a busy man. He waved off any intention to make a grand statement on cultural continuity with his pots. But he agreed that in Peru, the concepts of past and present are slippery. While history and exoticism are the everyday fare of tourist brochures, such forces are by no means easily understood or particularly benign when translated into current events.

An anthropologist, Degregori blinked often, as if surprised by the turn and play of the things he talked about. It can be easier, he told me, to go back five hundred years to explain what is happening than use polls or even scan the day's headlines. For example, to explain why peasant children flooded universities in the 1960s and 1970s, Degregori told me a tale—myth or fact, it wasn't important—from colonial times. "A conquistador decided to send some melons to a friend in Lima," Degregori said,

> so he gave the Indian bearers a letter explaining the gift. He warned them not to eat any melons lest the letter give them away. Halfway to Lima, tempted by hunger and the fragrance of the ripe fruit, the Indians carefully hid the letter and ate some melons. The tale ends with their stupor before the power of the printed word, when the recipient takes this piece of paper and tells them exactly how many melons they ate.
>
> From the very beginning, knowledge of the Spanish language, reading and writing, was a tool of domination. To educate oneself meant to stop being tricked, a process which gives education an explosive power.

Poor families were more likely to scrimp to send a boy to college. But girls also began to enroll. These were the brightest, most ambitious ones, willing to defy tradition. In 1968, of the 1,451 students enrolled at the UNSCH, 403 were women. Over half were from Ayacucho. They gravitated toward the departments of Social Work, Obstetrics, and Education, where they outnumbered men.

Degregori gave me the name of a colleague from his UNSCH days, whom I arranged to meet several weeks later. Like Degregori, "Sylvia" also taught at the UNSCH. Although she was raised in Lima, she did her doctoral thesis in the jungle, on a theme that interested Guzmán: why Communist revolution had so far failed to take hold in Peru. The fact that Sylvia was also beautiful and spirited must have added a special intensity to Guzmán's attentions. A former colleague and frequent drinking partner had told me that the dour Dr. Guzmán had an eye for feminine beauty.

Over mineral water in a Lima deli, Sylvia described Guzmán the suitor: in his gray suit and white shirt with its firmly buttoned collar, offering books, tea, conversation. By then, Sylvia had heard the gossip about Guzmán's male followers, who would invite freshmen females to parties to *enamorar* (seduce) them, thus winning them to the cause. Affairs between Shining Path professors and the colleagues they wanted to recruit were commonplace. (Chinese writer Ding Ling, referring to Mao's stay in Yenan, called this "undisciplined guerrilla warfare.") But Sylvia wasn't interested, physically or politically. "I had read Mao," she said, "we were all Maoists then, it was part of the times we were living. I knew his line, and disagreed with it."

Nevertheless, their relations were friendly. One evening, she said, she stopped by the Kremlin for tea. Grouped around the kitchen table were the men and women who were already Shining Path leaders. As he held forth on revolutionary theory, Guzmán was imposing, insistent, even witty, but with a sharpness and ferocity that Sylvia said left a chill on her arms. Despite the presence of others, Sylvia felt he was talking directly to her, wooing her even as he expounded on Maoist doctrine.

"It was as if he was trying to capture me, seduce me with these words," Sylvia told me. "He continued trying to recruit me until one day when he came by my house unexpectedly to drop off some books. He saw two of his political rivals leaving my house, and he realized I belonged to their side. From then on, he looked at me with hatred, as if I had betrayed him. He never spoke to me again. Later, when I was walking down the street, Katia Morote [Osmán's sister] crossed the street just to spit on me. She was married then to Julio Casanova, an important cadre. The wives were like that: loyal to their husbands, and therefore the Party."

Guzmán's early interest in her work was why she preferred not to use her real name for our interview. Friends had been questioned and arrested by the security forces. And then there was Guzmán. From potential disciple, Sylvia became the object of some of Guzmán's most lurid tirades. He was fascinated by filth (his best grades in high school were in hygiene and conduct), and that fixation translated into the redolent style that became a Shining Path hallmark: enemies are reptiles, cretins, sewer-drenched monsters who will be crushed, pulverized, annihilated, blown into oblivion.

Sylvia left Huamanga and went abroad. When she returned to Peru a decade later, friends showed her paintings Shining Path prisoners had done of Guzmán, now known by his war name of "Gonzalo." She no longer recognized her ideological suitor. His cheekbones, once nestled in baby fat and a five o'clock shadow, jutted like mountain cliffs. A tender potbelly was a torso hard as rock. Socialist realism, she thought, meets the fitness craze.

She saved her nostalgia for her students, the shy, respectful, obedient Catholic schoolgirls who had once addressed her as Madam Professor. "There was a certain feeling among them that we have to excel more, be more dedicated, more heroic than the men, something I see in my own background as a daughter of the middle class."

For Sylvia, Guzmán's genius lay in harnessing that ambition to his political project. These new graduates discovered that race, not their degrees, still determined success in official Peru. Even a poorly paid secretarial job required *buena presencia* (white skin), not good grades. They had their degrees, but no prospects. Ambition, and no jobs. Progress—that tricky notion—had left them stranded.

And as women, their future was especially grim. Female poverty was on the rise in Peru, visible in the statistics of child and mother mortality, malnutrition, and infectious disease. Although poor women were frequently praised for forming local "survival" organizations like soup kitchens and mothers' clubs, these groups, as hard and well as they worked, had only blunted its effects. In four months in 1990, more children died of diarrhea and preventable disease, like tetanus, than in a decade of political violence. Although rape was one of Peru's most common crimes, according to official estimates, less than 1 percent of the rapes committed annually resulted in conviction. A leading cause of maternal death was botched abortions, many practiced on rape victims. Often, procedures were performed clandestinely by midwives, who provoked abortions by introducing foreign objects into the womb or pumping in liquids like soapy water or kerosene. Key battles—for instance, to make so-called sentimental abortion, abortion in the case of rape, legal—had been lost.

In medieval times, European women could detour around the physical hardship of being female by joining a religious order. By joining the Shining Path, women also accepted a mystical contract that exempted them from a female fate. The Shining Path remains the only Peruvian political group ever to actively recruit women, then place them in positions of power. By joining, these women became better than whites, the rich, other women—anyone not inside the Party. They went from the bottom of Peru's social pyramid to the top of the Shining Path's.

They also won equality with *men*. For the Shining Path, class, not gender, was what mattered. For them, biological femininity is the equivalent of, say, being freckled or a good dancer. It was interesting, but not relevant to the struggle at hand. Unlike other Communists of the time, who insisted that gender equality was a "secondary contradiction" to be dealt with after the revolution, the Shining Path magazine *Rima Ryña Warmi* (Women speak out) asserted that both economic and gender equality would automatically result from a Maoist victory.

By 1965 Guzmán had formed the Popular Women's Movement as part of the Maoist faction of the Peruvian Communist Party. As director of student teaching, Guzmán spent much of his time organizing the Education Department, where women were the majority. By 1981 half of Ayacucho's teachers had received their degrees from the Shining Path–controlled UNSCH Education Department.

After her return to Peru, Sylvia visited a prison where Shining Path women were held. As she stepped inside the gate, the women shouted:

"Querida profesora!" (Dear professor!) "They were my students, all of them, even the shyest ones, the fattest ones! And the ones I did not see were dead, they told me, or *en las filas*" (in the ranks).

WHEN GUERRILLAS DECLARED their war in 1980, the most famous Shining Path member after Guzmán was Edith Lagos. In a high school photo, Edith is startlingly beautiful, with mist-gray eyes and full, rounded lips. Like Betty, Edith was not a peasant but a misti, third daughter of a wealthy store owner. Her parents named her after a popular singer of criollo valses—city music, the music of whites and the coast-bound descendants of African slaves. They wanted her to study law, so sent her to Lima. During her brief stay, Edith often skipped classes to catch Indian movies downtown, *peliculas hindú*. Edith watched them, her sister told one journalist long after her death, because she liked to cry. The rest of her time was spent with union organizers, talking revolution.

In a mug shot taken after her capture in 1981, Edith had visibly changed. Her nose and cheeks were swollen from a beating. Her black hair was shaggy, her clothes travel-stained. What struck me most, though, were her eyes. Gone was the curiosity, the sense of promise so evident in her high school photo. Here I am, they seemed to say, with my mind made up. She was eighteen.

That year, guerrillas controlled the northern third of the state. These were the students who had studied under Guzmán and were now the vanguard of his protoarmy. They recruited their friends and friends of friends. And they did more than talk about change. One of their most popular moves was to hold public trials for adulterers and men who abandoned their families and cheated on their wives. They told wife-beaters to reform or face the ultimate punishment. Peasant families welcomed them by clearing their storerooms and putting in extra beds. Unlike the government, they backed their promises with *obras*, works. *Los mejores hijos del pueblo* (our best and brightest), Guzmán liked to say.

Edith helped orchestrate the Ayacucho prison break that liberated 78 guerrillas and 169 common prisoners in 1982. One guard and one senderista were killed. Later that night, 3 guerrillas were murdered in their hospital beds by enraged police. Within six months, Edith herself was dead, shot down by police on a mountain road. Legend has it that she and her lover had stolen a pickup truck so she could learn to drive.

When it stalled, they tried to commandeer another one. Unfortunately, they chose one filled with police officers dressed as peasants.

When her coffin was carried out of Huamanga's stone cathedral, a crowd of more than ten thousand received her. Carlos was there to record it. At the time of Edith's funeral, he worked in the university audiovisual department. He was learning how to use the newly do-nated Panasonic 3800 video camera by recording university events and the recent rash of bombings and attacks people said were the work of Guzmán and his faction. At the time, these were novelties, strange and exhilarating. But they gave Carlos a sense of purpose. Huamanga was a small city, ingrown around the university, yet still resistant to the out-siders, like Carlos, who ran the school and staffed its offices. Although by the time I spoke with him, Carlos had lived in Ayacucho for twenty-four years, he still rented a single room and ate his meals in a restaurant where he paid a monthly fee, every day except Sundays and holidays, when he was on his own. At the beginning, several years passed before he was invited to a private home for a meal, even when the Shining Path shut down the city with armed strikes and bread was scarce as rubies. *Mamitas*, the market ladies, would hide stale *chaplas*, like pita bread, in their blouses and offer them to him like cocaine, at exorbitant prices.

With the Panasonic 3800, though, and through its lens, Carlos found his own solitary way into Huamanga society. He collected its images, much as some collect old photographs of people they do not know. Years of editing video in dark rooms left Carlos with pale, almost translucent skin, remarkable in this land of open slopes and harsh sun. He still worked in audiovisuals, although the Panasonic had long been replaced by lighter handycams.

Carlos had viewed the Lagos funeral tape hundreds of times. But when he showed it to me, it was clear that it still moved him. For that reason, he didn't like to show it to strangers. I had to plead. He worried that I would see only the sensational content, the cinematic crescendo to tragedy. For him, it was personal. He believed he had captured the precise moment at which everything changed.

"When we heard about the funeral, me and the guys who worked around here grabbed the camera. It wasn't far—we set up a spot on a second-floor balcony overlooking the square, which gave us a great shot of the cathedral door. But we had no idea what we were about to

The grave of Edith Lagos in Huamanga.
© Robin Kirk

film. It didn't take us long to realize it, though. Even as the camera was rolling, we knew we had something extraordinary."

The video opened in the softening light of afternoon. A crowd pressed to the cathedral gate. Inside, a bishop was giving Edith's funeral mass. On the tiny screen, I made out the hats and dark skirts of peasant women. There were schoolchildren, office workers. Men and women. When the coffin was borne out, over the heads of the crowd, people moved forward, drawn to it. Clapping began: "Commander Edith is present! The people will never forget your spilled blood!"

Hands pulled a red hammer-and-sickle banner over the coffin. One young man seemed to be leading the chant, "a commander," Carlos explained, "who I think was killed soon afterward."

The crowd grew, spilling into side streets. The coffin and its inner circle of family members circled the central square once, twice, three times. Each time, the crowd grew larger. At one point, the screen seemed to shake. "We had been told that the entire military command of the Shining Path was on its way," Carlos said, his fingers stroking the screen. "We didn't know what would happen if we filmed, say, Guzmán. I was terrified." The last scene was of the road to the cemetery, a solid carpet of people.

Since that day, Edith's grave has been blown up three times, probably by an army paramilitary group. Each time, her father, Manuel, has rebuilt it. He rebuilt it even though, after the first blast, there was probably nothing much left to put inside. On the anniversary of Edith's death, her mother puts a bouquet there, yellow for the broom flowers that, for the Shining Path, mean resistance. Each time a new concrete slab has been poured to cover the grave, the Lagos' have ordered that Edith's poem, which she wrote to be her epitaph, be reinscribed.

The Lagos family still lives in Huamanga, where they prosper. People whispered to me that they made a fortune in cocaine. Although known for its mountains, Ayacucho reaches into the jungle where coca bushes thrive. Every day, Mrs. Lagos, round as a barrel, attended customers in their general store. Too many have come nosing around for a shred of girl guerrilla glamour for her to suffer them gladly, and she would not speak to me about her daughter. But Commander Edith was also a public, shared myth. There are Edith sculptures, poems, and banners. César made her grave a regular stop on the "Stars of the Shining Path" tour. César asked me to take his picture there, as the boys who tended the cemetery trees watched.

Edith became the Shining Path's rallying cry, their martyr. They needed one. Three months after her death, then-President Belaunde declared nine provinces in the southern Andes in a state of emergency, including Huamanga. Control was ceded to the military. For them, it seemed a simple problem. If the guerrillas were fish in the sea, then the soldiers would drain that sea. The minister of defense had been trained in Argentina and was known as El Gaucho. Like his teachers, El Gaucho believed that Communism was a disease to be torn out of the body politic. Then, the surrounding tissue needed to be sterilized. No one needed to tell him that Peru wasn't Argentina. In Peru, he once told journalists, you couldn't be as thorough or scientific.

Before a single soldier had been sent to the emergency zone, El Gaucho told reporters, "In war, there are no human rights."

"So mass graves will be daily occurrences?" a reporter pressed.

"If it is necessary, yes. A war is won or lost. To win it, there are two methods: either the adversary surrenders or is destroyed."

There are many ways to measure this period in Ayacucho's history, none precise. Politicians kept death statistics even though they based them on reports by the security forces that routinely listed anyone killed as a "suspected subversive." By the time I watched the video of Edith's funeral with Carlos, there were more *huamanguinos* in Lima than Huamanga, forced there as internal refugees. Any glance at a market on a busy day revealed that half the women wore widow's black.

César measured distance by telling me about the things he began to find on the road. For instance, a partially flayed man. One dip in the road marked the starting place of a footpath that led to a mass grave. Once, the Shining Path stopped him and took one of his passengers, a teacher. They said she was an army collaborator. They waved César on. In his rearview mirror, he says he saw her fall to her knees.

Often, soldiers simply blew the bodies up. Years later, if you were in the right place, César told me, you could collect tiny finger and foot bones, picked clean. Amnesty International refused to be pinned down to a number for the dead, saying the scale of killing "could be estimated in part by the high number of clandestine graves or cemeteries, and of places where numerous cadavers are thrown to the side of the road."

Although blunt and inexact, El Gaucho's science drove the Shining Path from its strongholds. Many villages were destroyed by the army as punishment. Guerrillas countered with patient work among the survivors, especially young people who had seen their siblings or parents killed. People who opposed the Shining Path were no longer tolerated, and "public trials" became commonplace.

Edith's memory came to mean not only justice, but vengeance. Not just an end to poverty, but the beginning of a new science, Guzmán's

A Shining Path drawing depicting
Guzmán greeting graduates of the first
military school

science, that would blast their enemies, "blood-crazed hyenas," to use his phrase, from the earth.

"The trumpets have begun to blare, the rumbling of the masses grows and will grow more, it will deafen us and will draw us toward a powerful vortex," Guzmán pronounced in his most famous speech, to close the Shining Path's first military school in 1980. A painting made later to commemorate the event shows a beaming Guzmán welcoming cadres. The first two in line are women. "We will convert the black fire into red and the red into light. This is us, this is the new awakening. Comrades, we have been made anew!"

FOR THREE MONTHS, Betty couldn't have been happier. "They made us repeat the morals we were supposed to learn, especially that we were a family dedicated to the same cause," Betty told me. "Men respected women. We had the same rights."

But trouble came in the form of a conversation with a man from another unit. In time, they talked every time they met. Betty shrugged as she told the story, to show that it meant nothing to her—just a man, a distraction, as she studied more important things. Yet it came to be everything, including her ruin. One night, the man—she never named him—told her he was in love with her.

"This wasn't in my mind," Betty insisted. "It hadn't occurred to me."

He wanted to marry. She refused. She wanted nothing more than the Party, the *lucha*, the struggle, she said. He cried. She said no and no and no again. By then, she was his lover. Yet she didn't mention his proposal to her superiors, afraid they would blame her for his passion. He even promised to marry her according to Shining Path rules. By then, the guerrillas had their own ceremony, officiated by the political commissar of the area, who united couples under the vow to "better serve the revolution."

"One night, he threatened to kill himself with the revolver he had if I refused to go with him to Huancayo, where his parents lived," Betty said. "He told me they were ill and ready to die. I thought, if it's only for a couple of days. If I come right back. I had no intention of marrying him. But I told no one."

It seemed, at first, so simple. In the morning, they caught a truck hauling *tuna*, the fruit of the prickly pear cactus, to Huancayo. She hadn't expected to feel excitement. But the pitch and roll of the truck filled her with joy. She had never left Ayacucho. The road followed the valley's edge, then climbed to the frozen puna. Against the brilliant sky, she saw a condor. Once, a small red fox leapt across the road. A black-and-white *chinalinda*, a kite, swooped across the road, hunting mice and hares. After hours skirting immense gray boulders, the truck nosed down, into the Mantaro River watershed.

It was only then, with the mountains of Ayacucho blue and distant, that her lover said, "Perhaps we can make contact with them in Huancayo." Make contact with the Party, she wondered. Why bother, if they were returning immediately to their units? He shrugged off her questions. Just a thought, he said.

"Of course, when we got to Huancayo, his parents were fine," Betty said. "It was all a trick, to trick me into coming. And it was so terrible in that house, just like my aunt's. His father was a drunk. They would throw us out of the house screaming for all the world that we were just dirty terrorists."

Betty said she begged to return. He refused. By then, her unit had registered her absence, perhaps even linked her disappearance to his. There was only one word to fit those facts: treachery, *traición*. She was a traitor. There was no going back.

So she stayed. She knew what they did to traitors. And there was another reason. She was pregnant.

IN THE SHINING PATH universe, treachery is unforgivable. Punishment begins with criticism and self-criticism sessions. It ends only with the accused vanquished, undone, destroyed. A journalist friend showed me a secret report written in 1982 by a Shining Path cadre held in a Lima prison who was reporting to the Central Committee on just such a session. The tiny blue ink letters, on small spiral notebook pages folded the size of a matchbook, were only legible with a magnifying glass.

"Comrade Cata" was in charge of punishing three women who had given information to police. In Shining Path lingo, they were guilty of "leaping into the black reactionary mud."

The fact that they had been tortured and raped by police was immaterial. The women wrote self-criticisms and attended criticism sessions. They were beaten and their heads shaved. Another cadre, however, was spared this punishment. She had already fallen "into a crisis" because of torture. According to "Comrade Cata," she had attempted suicide three times and refused to speak or eat.

I had once seen a similar case in Anita, a nursing student charged with sabotaging a state-owned Caterpillar road-grader and held in a small prison in northern Peru. Anita told me the police raped her in gangs, with sticks and a metal rod. When she was brought to prison, she couldn't walk. Blood coated the insides of her thighs. She was three months pregnant. When I spoke with her, Anita no longer talked to the other Shining Path members in prison, even the woman she had been arrested with, whose name was Flor. She spent the hours alone in her cell.

To Anita, my questions were either hilarious or boring—Gonzalo Thought, prison food, the New Society. "There is no war without wounded or dead," she said, the rote answer guerrillas gave to questions about the human cost of the war. Then Anita paused. She let her head tip back to give a low, throaty laugh.

Her companion, Flor, observed Anita laugh. Laugh and laugh. When

Anita fell silent, Flor tugged at her polyester skirt, as if to set an annoying mess in order. "At any moment, the people will rise up to destroy the corrupt government and political parties," she informed me curtly.

After her arrest, Flor said she too was raped. For her, it was the test of a true revolutionary. The rape proved her worth. Her message for the rapists, like a kiss, pressed her mouth into a smile. "With the Party, the corrupt and the torturers will be annihilated. That kind of treatment just makes us stronger. To those police, I will only say that vengeance is sweet."

NIGHT IN HUAMANGA is full of marvels. *Nakaqs*—fat-sucking vampires with the smooth-shaven faces of gringo tourists—hunt the lonely trails. Flying heads fly and chivatos stalk the low hollows. Unlike in Tunnel Six, where Pancha's children could scare the chivatos away, in Huamanga they and the soldiers and the secret senderistas ruled the night. In the Hotel de Turistas, the sound of soldiers billeted in rooms once reserved for visiting dignitaries came in snatches of salsa music and the thud of boots and rifles. People called it the Tourist Barracks, Cuartel de Turistas.

I had a dream like Betty's, of Guzmán. But in my dream, Guzmán paced goat-bodied beyond the yellow print of a kerosene lamp. I woke suddenly. From my bed, I heard the two foxes imprisoned in the hotel's inner garden. Trapped on the puna, the fox cubs had been sold by a peasant to the manager. By then full-grown, they threw their bodies each night with a boom against the glass walls that were their bars. In the morning, I ate breakfast beside the garden. The only clue to their presence was the shit and marking scent smeared on the lowest panes.

In Ayacucho, bodies appeared and disappeared, but on tight schedules. The Shining Path, I was told, only murdered or bombed between 8 and 9 P.M., or just after dawn. Other bodies and explosions were the work of the army, trying to confuse the population by applying what one friend called "psychosocial softening up." No one seemed to be fooled. One morning, five headless bodies appeared on the outskirts of a nearby village. Who killed them? The answer depended on whom I asked.

At the new orphanage, over one hundred children lived in a compound built for four times that number. Banks and export firms had donated huge sums, but only for buildings with brass plaques featuring their names. Meanwhile, the children wore rags, ate mush, and played in a weedy field that the administrator told me was supposed to be a model farm. One problem, he confessed, was that officers kept coming to the orphanage to "adopt" young girls, a cheap way to get a maid.

"They aren't children," one officer had told him. "They're just little peasants."

A public prosecutor who worked in Ayacucho told me he used to keep human heads in his freezer. They were evidence against the army, which had blown up the bodies that belonged to the heads. His office budget didn't cover equipment, so he brought the heads home in a plastic bag. But one night, his daughter, looking for a snack, opened the freezer door. She never spoke of what she had seen. But over the next weeks, her long, glossy, exquisitely curly black hair fell out in clumps. He had the refrigerator moved to his office, and from then on kept it padlocked.

One morning, a guerrilla tossed a grenade into an open-bed truck carrying peasants to a market. The men jumped off and were unhurt. The women, made to sit cross-legged in the middle because women are thought to be weaker and need protection, were massacred, body parts all over the highway. When I made a tally of all the men who are said to have made love to Edith Lagos, I came up with more than fifty names.

There seemed to be bodies everywhere, in various states and poses. Yet one body particularly drew me, perhaps because it proved so elusive. It was the body some said inspired the studious Dr. Guzmán to become the fire-breathing "Gonzalo." Augusta La Torre's passion, I was told, awoke Guzmán's political will. Like Lagos, Augusta La Torre was a local girl. Carlos La Torre, her father, worked in the state bank and was head of the Communist Party in Huanta, an hour north. La Torre was said to be impressed by Guzmán, so cultured and self-assured. When Guzmán visited the La Torre home, Augusta would serve cups of a potent fruit liquor. Guzmán couldn't help but notice her. She had a milk-white complexion, huge, doelike eyes. She looked, some told me, like the Italian screen star Claudia Cardinale, but was *narigona*, big-nosed.

By all accounts, Augusta was a mediocre student, instead devoting herself to her family and the romance novels she hid under her pillow. Her father had taught her about injustice. But her idea of righting wrong was to teach grade school. She chewed her nails. She had no interest in clothes or makeup. Although she loved music, especially Ayacucho huaynos, she was tone-deaf. When she sang, her family was roused to gales of laughter. Augusta was a *buena moza*, people say: a handsome girl.

Then she met and fell in love with Dr. Guzmán. When they married in 1964, he was twenty-seven, she eighteen. This was the way their former friends described them to me: a young man, brilliant and full of ideas, marries a beautiful but naive girl, whose notion of love meant embracing her husband's interests. If Guzmán had been a doctor, she would have run his office. An architect, and she would have schooled herself in design. Because he was, like her father, a Communist, Augusta buried herself in the readings he assigned, his eager disciple.

They lived first with her parents, then moved to the Kremlin. Augusta abandoned her teaching career and became a university student. A terrible cook, she and Guzmán ate at her parents' house or in local restaurants. After visiting doctors, the couple learned that Augusta had underdeveloped ovaries and would never have children. Although a childhood friend of Augusta's told me the news was a great disappointment, it also meant the pair was free to dedicate themselves to revolution—not the weak-willed efforts of the past, but something Guzmán vowed was guaranteed.

The friend painted an idyllic picture: a normal couple, left-leaning but no strangers to the good food, wine, and Saturday-night dance parties that entertained the academic elite. For a laugh, the young couples would cajole Augusta into singing. From his trips, Guzmán would bring her fine chocolates and flowers and occasionally a new dress. She would wear it to please him, but under a baggy wool sweater. "Abimael would say to her, 'Take off that sweater, you look pretty in the dress!' And she would just smile," her friend said. "Perhaps he protected her too much, overprotected her. In some things, she was a bit silly, even foolish. But they loved each other so much."

Guzmán made her director of the Popular Women's Movement. At rival political meetings, she would sit in back taking notes, his eyes and ears. Later, she joined him in China to study revolution with a Long March veteran. They learned about ambush tactics, assaults, column movements, and the preparation of demolition devices. "When we handled very delicate chemical elements," Guzmán told his *El Diario* interviewer, "they recommended that we always keep the ideology in mind, this would make us capable of doing everything and doing it right." In a Huamanga street protest, Augusta was caught and beaten by police. Guzmán, nearby, didn't intervene. Later, he told his followers his behavior was "natural" in the day-to-day of politics.

In 1979 Augusta called her friend for the last time. She and Guzmán were about to disappear underground. Although the friend and Augusta had very different lives—Augusta with her meetings and political allies, her friend with babies and a comfortable house with a television and a maid and a little car—their childhood bond remained strong.

"She was the same Augusta," her friend said. To their rendezvous, Augusta wore a skirt and a baggy sweater. Her nails were bitten to the quick. Augusta promised they would meet again. "I'll always know what is happening to you," Augusta told her friend.

"That's how we always parted, I thought I would see her again. But she didn't keep her promise."

I asked about the Augusta who in 1982 tried (and failed) to execute her aunt and uncle for refusing to sell her weapons. Was this the same girl, I wanted to know, who had given her such a tender farewell kiss? For the friend, it's as if Augusta stepped out of the world and into a place where her past, even her given name, no longer had meaning. "I knew Augusta," the friend told me sadly, "but I never knew the woman who called herself Comrade Norah."

Despite her early prominence in the Shining Path, over the next eleven years, Augusta was rarely mentioned in news reports. Occasionally, police swore to be about to capture Guzmán (though not his guerrilla wife). Other women—like Edith Lagos—got more press. In 1991 police released a captured Shining Path video of a woman's body draped in a red hammer-and-sickle banner. It is Augusta. Police believe she died on November 14, 1988. She was forty-two.

In the video, Guzmán is alone by the bier. His voice distant and garbled, he speaks of her passion, feeling, and bravery. Between pronouncements, he directs the camera: closer, this angle, pull back. He wants this for the record, perhaps some future Revolutionary Museum. Guzmán seems to argue against "some comrades" who doubt a point related to Comrade Norah's death. He says something about a soul, then faith. She was a comrade, he says, "capable of liquidating her life so as not to raise her hand against the Party. . . . In the unfortunate confusion of her nervous solitude, she preferred to annihilate herself."

As he bends to kiss her forehead, this is what he says: "Me acercaré despacio. Sale?" [I'll approach her slowly. Does it come out (on tape)?]

For weeks, the press played with theories. Did Augusta commit suicide? Or was she murdered before she could leave the Party, betray Guzmán? Reporters compared La Torre to Jiang Qing and Krupskaya, Lenin's wife. Few knew their Communist history well enough to mention He Zizhen, Jiang Qing's predecessor. He Zizhen began living with Mao in 1928 (his first wife, Yang Kaihui, was captured by the Nationalists and reportedly tortured to death in 1930). By all accounts, she was a faithful and loving wife. She bore him five children. But He Zizhen could not bear Mao's infidelities. He dealt with her anger by packing her off to Soviet mental hospitals.

Jiang Qing was careful not to make the same mistake. "Sex is engaging in the first rounds," she once said, "but what sustains interest is power."

Even within the Central Committee, there was unease over La Torre's death. Captured documents showed that some members questioned Guzmán's role and for it were severely punished. To date, police have not found La Torre's body.

What became clear to me, however, after watching the video of Guzmán beside Augusta's bier was that he was transforming her death into a powerful message for other cadres. Augusta became a symbol of unconditional support. In her body, Guzmán located the ultimate Shining Path virtue: sacrifice to his cause. Although he asked it of all cadres, I think Guzmán saw sacrifice as an inherently female virtue.

In another sequence of the funeral video, Guzmán stands against a blank wall. He is portly in his tailored Mao jacket. His cheeks are grizzled and softened with wine. Cadres approach to have their pictures taken with him. The men sidle close, almost servile. A bit afraid. But the women join him eagerly, and stand so close to him that their upper arms touch. The effect is not sexual, but reverential. They are his congregation.

To spin out a religious metaphor (appropriate for Guzmán, who one colleague said "was a profoundly religious man who does not believe in God. That's why he forged a clear political line . . . that demands absolute faith"), he was like a pope who feels no fear of women as competitors. They are his loyal handmaidens. Does the pope compete with nuns? The thought wouldn't occur.

As I mulled over the video images, I wondered: what secrets would Comrade Norah have divulged? I thought of her bitten nails, her sweaters, what her friend called "foolishness." When she met Guzmán, she was Betty's age. What did Guzmán mean by "nervous solitude"? How far did Augusta wander before she was reeled in on the line of revolutionary duty?

As I prepared to leave Augusta's childhood friend's house, she asked me: "¿Y Augusta dicen que ha muerto, no?" [They say that Augusta died, don't they?].

"They" means rumor and what passes for reporting in the magazines. There, Guzmán was portrayed as a madman, a drunkard. I asked if she saw the video. Not the scenes of Guzmán by the bier, but the dancing, the wine, the embraces. The woman he danced with, some were saying, was Augusta before her death.

"That was not Augusta," the woman's husband volunteered. "Not her. Only if she has changed so much she is unrecognizable. We saw it just like everyone has on television. And we've read the articles in the magazines. But more than that, how can we know it is true?"

"Can it be true?" asked Augusta's friend.

"Is it true, or is it not true. Well," her husband ended, emphatically.

They told me Augusta was tall.

"As tall as I am?" I asked.

"Let's see."

I stood. They looked at me appraisingly. "She was about that tall," the husband concluded. "Buena moza." A handsome girl. Cara lavada, just her washed face, no makeup. "Like you," he finished.

They served me homemade wine, flavored with herbs. In the dining room, a daughter bounced a baby. The daughter was Augusta's favorite, I was told. They laughed and told jokes. Someone flicked on the radio, and the chords of a huayno enlivened what had gradually become a family party. I thought of those long-ago jaranas, the dancing. I had the feeling that Abimael and his pretty bride could just have departed, their kisses and promises to return still in the air. Were such partings ever so final?

Augusta's friend walked me to the red Toyota, parked at the corner. She squeezed my arm. She wept. But her voice betrayed no tears. I felt wide as the dark night, and as remote. Augusta was not my friend.

She speculated again about what had happened to Augusta.

"No one really knows," I volunteered, referring to Augusta's death. The friend smiled, nodding. If Augusta were my height, I thought, she would have seen her friend this way—her face tipped up toward mine and lit by stars like a pane of wet glass. I could still hear the radio—faint, metallic, full of joy.

GUZMÁN'S FACE WAS everywhere in the Shining Trench, the name its residents gave to the prison cell block where women accused and convicted of belonging to the Shining Path were held when I visited in 1991. My reasons for going were simple. What where these women like, I wondered, in a group, at their strongest? It had to do with official versions, not press fancies or Betty's tragedy. How would they choose to present themselves?

In the prison, most journalists visited the men. But for me, the women were the mysteries: Sybila Arredondo de Arguedas, the wife of the late Peruvian novelist José María Arguedas, the German Renata Herr. At the time, the highest-ranking cadre inside was Laura Zambrano, convicted of having ordered six murders and at least twenty-eight bombings while she led the military committee responsible for metropolitan Lima.

I had seen a photograph of Zambrano in El Diario, along with an interview. Her face square and jowly and dug with frown-lines, she looked uncannily like Jiang Qing, not as she cavorted with Mao in Shanghai finery but much later, after she adopted the severe black suits that stood for ideological purity. Zambrano's no-nonsense hair, slicked with water, was knotted at la nuca. She was the opposite of Edith Lagos—not sex queen, but dominatrix, conviction coiled and ready as a whip.

"As part of the iron legions, we maintain our invincibility with all-powerful Marxist-Leninist-Maoist-Gonzalo Thought and under the absolute leadership of the Party," she had told the El Diario interviewer. When asked about the role of love in the Party, Zambrano had replied: "Love is for class and serves the function of the people's war."

Getting official permission to enter the prison was not difficult. Getting permission to enter the Shining Trench was another matter. The women themselves had to decide.

The photographer, Vera Lentz, and I chose visiting day for women to try to get our interviews. Our driver picked us up in his black Mustang, which carried us through the already hot stink of central Lima. Heading east, the horizon opened after a bend around Acho, the bull ring. There, Lima's true nature was exposed: desert and the forbidding foothills of the Andes. When we pulled up to the prison, a long line of women carrying heavy baskets of food and clothing curled around the prison's outer perimeter. Nearby shacks sold last-minute gifts: plastic bottles of Inka Cola, cigarettes, crackers. One woman rented skirts by the hour, for visitors who forgot the rule and wore pants.

Vera and I were nervous, elated. It felt like bracing to touch an unpredictable animal. Would it prove soft or sting unexpectedly?

The prison security chief was in high spirits when he greeted us in his office. With my tape recorder and Vera's cameras and our anxious faces, we were clearly an amusing diversion.

"I can't promise you anything," he said, guiding us to his office. Every time he chuckled, he patted his belly, round and firm as an egg. He wore a red "Florida" baseball cap. "I'll take you right up to the door. If they say no, nothing I can do. If they agree, well, you're on your own.

"As far as the Shining Path goes, they are a lot calmer than your regular prisoner," he continued from his desk, lacing his hands behind his head. "No drugs or alcohol. And they don't kill each other over a glass of home brew," he added, referring to the rice mash prisoners fermented in plastic buckets.

The security chief impressed me as a practical man. Most Peruvians would have preferred to see the Shining Path guerrillas marched out and shot. But he treated them well. On the other hand, he had to. They knew where he lived, his wife's name, his children's school. The prison's formal name is Castro Castro, after a former director who was gunned down on his doorstep in 1985 by a Shining Path assassination squad, a woman and a man. His crime was to agree to a proposal to move the Shining Path from the island prison of El Frontón to the newly built Castro Castro. The Shining Path believed the police planned to kill them en route.

A year later, when the move was imminent, the security forces suppressed a Shining Path–led protest by bombing El Frontón into rubble. Hundreds of prisoners, including three women held at another prison, died or were executed. In 1991 a police official implicated in the massacre cover-up was murdered by the Shining Path on his doorstep.

Two policemen escorted us through a concrete causeway. I could tell the security chief was enjoying himself: Vera and I, pale at birth and getting paler by the second as we entered the prison's huge, filthy, cacophonous rotunda. The six cellblocks of Castro Castro are built like the rays from a child's drawing of a sun. The sun is the rotunda, a glass-enclosed pod overlooking a circular plaza. The rotunda was built as a surveillance tower for the guards. But that morning, I saw that the panes of gray-tinted glass were cracked and broken. Instead of watching others, the guards felt watched. They also felt like excellent targets. During our visit, they kept to the roof and their tiny shacks of scrap wood, from where they did the daily prisoner count.

Each cellblock was a world unto itself. There was the narco cell, with its satellite dish and antennae thrust out like a sea creature's appendages. Next door were the corrupt police, their building as piss-stained and stinky as a Lima bar. The murderers, kidnappers, and thieves lived in a building scribbled with graffiti. The two guerrilla blocks were tidy and ordered. The men even had bamboo blinds, rolled up or down depending on the weather. They had painted a red hammer and sickle on the rooftop water cistern, which the guards used for target practice.

Because it was visiting day, common prisoners and guards and their female visitors milled beneath the rotunda. Inmates hawked straw baskets they had woven, and the jewel-like colors glowed against their rags and grimy limbs. Some did better financially on the inside than they did while free. Others died of starvation. Everything was for sale. Occasionally, Lima dailies reported with horror that a prostitute had spent the night going from cellblock to cellblock. An enterprising prostitute could make her fortune working the pen, especially if she appealed to the narcos.

At the gate to the Shining Trench, a delegate from inside came forward to speak to the security chief, who had accompanied Vera and me. They shook hands. For a moment, they looked like business associates. Over the noise, I explained that Vera and I were journalists. The delegate was short and stout. Her small brown eyes swam behind thick glasses. The doorway was hung with red hammer-and-sickle flags, which brushed my arms. I could see inside, a long, narrow room that ended with a curtained doorway. To one side were picnic-style tables and benches made of concrete. Sparkly red-and-gold party decorations pasted with letters swung from the ceiling: EGP (Ejército Guerrillero Popular), for Popular Guerrilla Army, and CPA (Comité Popular Abierto), for Open People's Committee. To my right were the stairs leading to the cells on the two upper floors.

The women looked as if they were dressed for a party, which in fact they were. Visiting day meant not only the arrival of families and the children they cared for, but also special events, like music and speeches. Only on holidays, like Guzmán's birthday, did they put on the red shirts, black skirts or pants, and black Mao cap that were a kind of official uniform. For visiting day, it was heels, freshly painted nails, and skirts. They looked young, fit, and scrupulously clean, no mean feat, we later learned, since the only water for ninety people came every other day from one faucet and one toilet.

The delegate declared that further discussion was necessary to agree on the terms of a tour. We were shown to a table. What brought us, who sent us? she wanted to know. Whom did we work for, what was their stand on the People's War?

I answered honestly, though not in much depth. There was too much to argue about. One of the questions had to do with *negros*, blacks, in America.

"African Americans," I suggested.

Aren't they oppressed? the cadre insisted. She was small and eager. She stood so close I could smell the laundry soap she used for shampoo.

I answered that racism was a problem. But it wasn't simple. "Do you know who Gen. Colin Powell is?" I asked.

She did. Every month, she said, they smuggled in a summary of international news. She knew he was a negro running the imperialist action in Iraq, then in its second week. When I probed, she confided, proudly, that the summary was called *Selecciones*, the Spanish *Reader's Digest*. The women were as well-informed as U.S. retirees.

Returning to Powell, she concluded that in every class there are traitors.

Only three cadres spoke to us. Other women looked our way, curious, but not allowed to join the conversation. The cadres questioned us in relays, then ran upstairs to deliver the answers to Zambrano in her cell. They returned with new questions.

After two hours, rolled-up pancakes dribbled with honey were set before us. We had been approved. Delia, the cadre who met us at the door, became our guide and chaperon. She ticked off the rules on one hand: only authorized pictures and interviews, no photo close-ups, no taping of unapproved conversations.

First on the tour were songs. Delia gathered a group of thirty women, who lined up in military formation. They looked like a representative sampling of Peruvian society: mostly brown, but sprinkled with white, Asian, black. I recognized one cadre from the newspaper, a chestnut-haired dance student from an exclusive private university. They sang four anthems: the International, "The Continuism of Marxism-Leninism and Mao Thought," "Long Live Mao Zedong and the Chinese Communist Party" (sung half in Spanish and half in Chinese), and "Our Chief":

> Our Chief is Gonzalo
> he of the brilliant thought and action
> inspired by Marx, Lenin, and Mao he develops
> our powerful ideology
> when before the flaming world is brought
> the invincible people's war.

With flags, they marched to the outdoor patio. Policemen watching from the roof were black slivers against the noon sun. Behind the women loomed a huge mural of Guzmán, his moon-face with its bracket of cheap plastic glasses sweeping like an avenging angel out of a scarlet sky. The women shouted slogans and clapped. Only one did not raise her fist to punctuate the words. Her face had the droopy look of a stroke victim. Later, I learned that her right arm was destroyed when the bomb she was making exploded. Doctors were able to replace her left arm with a metal hook.

The scene was precisely what Vera and I had hoped for. There they were, arrayed like soldiers. Their words were crisp and practiced. Their shoulders were squared, their faces fierce. This is what they wanted me to see: courage and resolve. Revolutionary fervor. There were their own iron legions.

Nevertheless, I felt an urge to smile. It was so fastidious, so squeaky clean. It was like an advertisement for revolution, done on the same principles as one for a cleaning fluid. Strong, fast-acting, and handy against those tough stains (world capitalism). These were Guzmán's children, it occurred to me, the ones he and Augusta had never had. Like an overprotected family, though, they seemed incubated in a

A Shining Path guerrilla in Ayacucho's
Women's Prison. © Robin Kirk

space strangely outside history: the space shuttle, Venezuelan soap
operas, I (heart) T-shirts, plastic saints, the fall of the Wall, and interac-
tive TV, which, I imagined, would instant-replay my mental footage of
them from different angles and with a pull-down scorecard of murders
and bombings linked to each scrubbed and shouting face. Of course,
history runs in their blood as much as it does in mine. But what history

99

is this? I thought. Is this all the choice life gave them, one shallow bowl empty of doubt?

"Gloria" (she refused to give her real name) was waiting beside her cell to be interviewed, the third stop on the tour. She looked like someone about to get a double root canal. Beside her was Fiorella, second only to Zambrano within the Shining Trench. In the dank gloom of the inner cellblock, Fiorella wore a flounced top of polyester eyelet lace and cheap sunglasses.

On Gloria's cell wall was a newspaper photo of Guzmán pasted to a square of red construction paper. There was an overpowering smell of shit. Delia explained that the prison authorities were dumping the shit of common prisoners to one side of their cellblock, to annoy them.

In her mid-thirties, Gloria looked like a lumpy pillow under her faded brown dress. Fiorella's level stare coaxed beads of sweat from her thickish upper lip. Gloria was being tested, I realized. I was the test. Was this a punishment, I wondered? Or a step up, a new merit badge for Party service? Gloria and Fiorella settled on the lower bunk. I was given a chair.

The Party, Shining Path guerrillas say, has a thousand eyes and ears. The Khmer Rouge used to say the Angkar, the Organization, had as many eyes as a pineapple. Gloria's two fixed on mine while Fiorella's, veiled, flicked between our faces.

Gloria gave me the standard line: women are oppressed by society and the family, so are more revolutionary than men. "In our country, who is it that suffers the worst of the crisis? Necessarily she begins to see the solution—revolution."

But what about her? I insisted. How did she see the solution? Her mouth puckered with annoyance. Personal details, Gloria said, do not aid the People's War. Fiorella folded her arms triumphantly. Clearly, Gloria excelled. Our interview went downhill. An excerpt:

Q: Do you have children?
G: That is secondary. It is secondary where my children are, too. (She finally allows that she has four children.)
Q: What do you think you are leaving your children by joining this war?
G: The greatest inheritance one can leave—a new society. That's what makes us happy. We not only fight for our children, but the thousands of children who will benefit from the New Society.
Q: Will we have to wait a long time for this New Society?

G: Not very long! The Party has given us a brilliant perspective. We are preparing to finish off democracy and take power, thus beginning without hesitation the socialist revolution, then the cultural revolutions that will eventually lead to Communism. The conquest of power is a reality! This makes the reaction shake with fear!

Q: Do you want your children to join this war?

G: That is secondary! That will be decided by history.

Q: But if they decided not to, could they still see you?

G: That is not a problem. That is secondary. You have to analyze these problems politically. (Fiorella ends the interview.)

How will marriage change? Will there be day care, abortion? Gloria had heard something about day care in Soviet communes. Maybe it would be good? But her contract with the Party was not one of specifics, but glory, sacrifice, the heaven of the New Society. Was there day care in heaven? For Gloria, the question was ridiculous.

Gloria posed for her authorized picture reading at her Gonzalo shrine. Fiorella picked a book from an orange-crate library. Behind her was a velvet wall-hanging of Lenin. As Vera focused, Fiorella pretended to study the book intensely.

"It's Agatha Christie," Vera whispered to me, "but I can't tell which one. Is it important?"

I told her I wasn't sure.

A dance was in full swing as the tour of the Shining Trench ended. Women in a *banda típica*—drum, pan pipes, and flute—played huaynos. The women swung and stomped and grabbed each other by the waist. Children brought in to visit their mothers and sisters and aunts whirled in their midst. Tapping my foot, I flipped on my tape recorder. I tried to follow the words. There was something about hills, and a flaming sun. Then there was blood—the purifying blood, the blood of the masses, which fed revolution.

One of the cadres invited me to dance. She had a narrow face and eyes as slanted as a cat's. She tried to make it look spontaneous, but it wasn't. Zambrano evidently wanted a gesture of sympathy before we left. She wanted a convert. Even as I said no, I knew that I should dance—if I wanted to return, if I wanted to get to know them, if I wanted to get past the pat answers.

But I couldn't. The cadre tried again. "Dance," she said. She pulled at my arm. I let her. She let go, peeved. "Everyone wants you to." Her look was the same one that Fiorella gave Gloria—like someone being tested. It was time to leave.

Women lined up with drums to bid their visitors goodbye. Visitors packed up their baskets. Delia pulled the iron bars shut behind us. A policeman waited for us, sleepy from a long day of sun and beer. The cadres withdrew into the shadow of the inner cellblock. Even from outside the prison walls, we could hear the rolling of the drums that marked the end of visiting day.

SOON AFTER MY VISIT, Laura Zambrano completed her sentence ("good behavior" whittled it to seven years, eleven months, and fifteen days) and was released. According to the judge who signed the papers, she was a model prisoner. A former high school teacher, she told him she would resume teaching. She also showed an aptitude for weaving rugs, he noted.

The fact that the rugs featured President Gonzalo leading the armed masses away from a city in flames didn't seem to bother him. The judge's allegiance was to law, not sense. The day of her release, Zambrano walked out the prison gate to a waiting car, and she vanished. Some say she went to Europe for a time, then slipped into Peru from Bolivia to resume her Lima post. In 1992 she was arrested once again, this time with Abimael Guzmán.

MY REFUSAL TO DANCE was something I tried to explain to others. How I felt, that mixture of fascination, horror, and pity. Why couldn't I play along? I asked myself.

I heard it in my voice when I spoke to a friend I will call Ruth. It was a typical winter afternoon in Lima, grimy and damp. Ruth was buried in a shawl on the other side of the table. Her cats, excited, prowled the perimeter. Ruth smoked. I drank Chilean wine poured from a Tetra brick box. Usually a frenetic talker, Ruth was silent. I heard myself and didn't like my voice. It sounded too young, and foolish.

Ruth's parents were Europeans who had moved to Peru after her birth, then divorced. Ruth was raised on the estate of her stepfather, one of the richest men in Peru. Ruth grew up in half—European and Peruvian, loving her beautiful mother and hating the ogre who was her mother's husband. Don Enrique's oranges, big as softballs, were world famous. As a hobby, he raised *caballos de paso,* Peruvian show horses. Although he never fed them or brushed them, broke them to the bridle or helped the veterinarian when they were ill, he boasted of their beauty as the product of his superior care, his eye for horseflesh.

Once, David Brinkley and a CBS camera crew filmed Don Enrique. It was 1962, and they wanted to know what the Latin oligarchy was up to now that Castro ruled Cuba. They found out it was up to no good.

In his flowing poncho and wide-brimmed hat, his caballo tossing a heavy silver bridle, Don Enrique talked about "his people," the families who lived in genteel slavery on the estate. He looked like an aging movie star: a long, narrow face, a wisp of a moustache, a snowy white cravat under his chin. It could have been 1862, or 1562.

Six years later, Don Enrique lost everything to General Velasco's land reform. The same event that gave the people of Tunnel Six dignity ruined him. In disgust, he and Ruth's mother moved to Madrid, where they rented a windowless flat filled with other people's worn furniture. The final blow came when Don Enrique ran into a woman who had once sold vegetables near the estate. She was just getting into her chauffeured Mercedes. Graciously, she invited him to swim at the mansion she was renting for the season from the Duchess of Alba.

Until that moment, Don Enrique had not fully realized how much he had lost. However, the experience did not make him a better man. Ruth told me that he remained full of hatred. If he could have, Ruth believed, he would have taken it all back, every inch of ground, every orange, and made even the innocent vegetable seller pay dearly for her invitation. But during a visit to Lima, he died in a car accident, "crushed," Ruth clarified, "like the cockroach he was under seven tons of cement on the Panamerican Highway."

Ruth showed me the CBS tape for a reason. She wanted me to see what it was she thought women like Gloria and Fiorella and Betty and Laura Zambrano thought they were fighting against. The precise person they wanted to make kneel. In the tape, Don Enrique repeatedly doffed his wide-brimmed hat for the visiting Americans and called the people milling in the background his own.

We returned to the dark patio. There, Ruth told me another story, this one about Lydia, a senderista commander Ruth had once met. Several years earlier, Ruth and two television reporters had gone in search of the Shining Path. One part curiosity, eight parts bravado. No television reporter had ever traveled with the guerrillas. In a jungle hotel, they waited a week, then two for their contact. Finally, frustrated and bored, they drove away. Seven hours later, their contact tracked them down, drunk on Peruvian brandy, in a luxury hotel in the Andes. He told them they had no time to lose if they wanted to find *la columna,* the column.

In Peru, the column was a unit within the People's Guerrilla Army. It contained from twenty to one hundred armed and trained militants, and was the principal combat force. La columna operated in a defined region, but true to its guerrilla nature had no fixed base. It was constantly on the move.

To Peruvians, the column had other meanings as well. For instance, when the column came, people hid. But the column could drag them from their homes and administer a "popular trial." The column could shoot them or hack them to death with machetes or stone them as they begged for mercy. Or the column could force a daughter to kill a father, a husband his wife. La columna could force an entire village to march before them, forming the vanguard of an attack. It burnt the houses of those it deemed traitors. It took those, especially the young, it found useful. The column called itself the "people's wrath." Its appearances could be as sudden as a thunderhead cresting a ridge. Its departures were scored by the slow, measured sound of grief.

Ruth and her friends made the rendezvous. It was a stroke of incredible luck. The leader of the column was willing to entertain the possibility of having reporters along. By the next night, they were installed in a house the column had requisitioned from a peasant family. The reporters were to be treated as prisoners of war until the Central Committee decided whether they would be granted an interview, something the Shining Path had never done. If the reporters had lied about who they were, however, they would be killed. Their credentials were collected and sent to Lima for verification.

That night, Ruth met Lydia—Comrade Lydia—the column leader. Lydia, Ruth explained to me, was exceptional. She was nineteen, a high school graduate, whose fondest wish had once been to get a job as a bilingual secretary for a U.S. oil company with wells off the north coast, near Lydia's home. Hundreds of girls showed up for every opening. Lydia was darker than most. The darker girls rarely got called back. Instead, Lydia drifted, then joined the Party. Within a year, she had risen to one of the most important positions in the People's Army.

Ruth spent ten days with Comrade Lydia's column. They marched at night, dressed in black. By 4 A.M., the militants were up and exercising. They practiced ambush, attack, retreat. In the afternoons, there were classes on Gonzalo Thought. Ruth's notes were checked, and she was prohibited from writing names, weapon types, or locations. At meal times, the reporters were treated as honored guests and given huge bowls of noodles. One boy was charged with going into town periodically to buy Ruth cigarettes. "I told them if I couldn't have my cigarettes, then no way, nothing, *se acabó* (it's finished)," Ruth said. But they wouldn't take her money. They warned the European comrade that it was a *vicio*, a sin, but that she would be allowed to smoke *por el frío*, for the cold. A militant who asked to take a drag on her cigarette idly drew a red hammer and sickle on her forearm. "Don't worry, comrade," he told her, smiling. "It washes off."

At twilight, Lydia would organize volleyball and soccer games between la columna and the masses, area farmers. From the hilltops where they camped, Ruth could see the police and army helicopters, gun doors open, buzzing the valleys below. Once, bathing at a stream with Lydia, Ruth said a U.S. Drug Enforcement Administration helicopter swung by so close she could see the gunner, his face antlike with its protective goggles. Lydia's gun was behind them in the grass. She didn't even reach for it. "Don't worry," she told Ruth. *"Nos tienen miedo"* [They are afraid of us].

Ruth never doubted that if the Central Committee had ordered them killed, they would have been killed. Yet, as she talked on her patio, the memory of Lydia undid her. Every morning before leaving the hut, Lydia would adjust Ruth's blanket, tucking her in. The column, its frozen logic, existed, Ruth had no doubt. Yet it did not preclude a tenderness Ruth had not known even as a child. Would Don Enrique have done the same?

"There was something so admirable, yet so frightening about what Lydia had chosen to make of her life," Ruth told me. "In some ways, these young people are the best Peru has to offer. And this is what they have chosen. On one level, it requires great respect. On another, I can only contemplate it with fear and repulsion."

They were never granted their interview. After ten days, Lydia left them on the highway. Although they were given permission to write about their experience, Ruth has never written a line.

Ruth told me one more thing. The night she and her two friends returned to Lima, they wanted to celebrate. In a bar, Ruth saw a poet she had not spoken to for years. As they chatted, Ruth realized he knew all about her trip. Without saying so outright, he let her know that he was one of the people who had verified her credentials, thus saving her life.

And he was still checking up on her. His report would make it back to Lydia. Was Ruth behaving? Lydia might inquire. A thousand eyes, a thousand ears. The shiver Ruth experienced was with her still.

ONE AFTERNOON, I went to Villa El Salvador to interview the vice-mayor, María Elena Moyano. I was doing a story about a new generation of Peruvian politician—not white, sometimes female, with a solid constituency in the impoverished neighborhoods their families had helped build. A black woman with an electric, gap-toothed smile, Moyano was twelve years old when her parents took part in the land takeover that led to the creation of Villa in 1971. As a girl, she had been part of a church-organized youth group heavily influenced by liberation theology. After finishing high school, she held a series of posts until being elected president of the Villa Women's Federation. In 1989, at thirty, she won the vice-mayor's seat on a ticket sponsored by the United Left coalition.

Although both men and women built Villa, it could be said that women raised it much as they raised their own children. Women defended their *iglus* from police while the men were at work. Even as they spent long hours as washerwomen and market vendors and maids, and caring for their own families, they devoted time to getting electricity and water, establishing bus routes, grading roads, building schools, establishing cooperative businesses. By the time Moyano took office, Villa was considered a model city. Every time American politicians came to visit Peru, Agency for International Development vans ferried them to Villa, where they were received in busy workshops, fed in communal kitchens, and shown new project plans. It was a tour designed to showcase hard work, perseverance, and the essential goodness of the poor. The message was simple: release them from the bondage of dependency and they will help themselves. *Autogestión* (self-help) was the key. The Americans inevitably came away impressed and showed it by directing more development cash to the Villa accounts.

There was truth to the message. There was also careful editing. By the time Moyano was elected, the Shining Path had mounted a determined campaign to win Villa. The leaders of the United Left dismissed it, sure that Villa's heroes, those noble cholos, were already theirs. But not all of them were. In community meetings, senderistas would stand and say their piece, identifying themselves as clearly as if they had worn a conventioneer's hat. They also set off bombs, pressured drivers to honor armed strikes, and slipped death threats under doors. For them, all of Villa's advances amounted to a gigantic trick. The goal of the dark forces behind it—the political parties, the pope, the imperialist U.S.A.—was to keep the masses in misery and exploit their labor.

Moyano was one of the few leaders on the left who recognized the strength of the Shining Path message. Unlike others, what she saw was that it was not directed at the noble cholos who had built Villa, but their children: the ones who didn't have jobs, the ones crowded into the inadequate schools, the ones who saw their futures opening before them like the vast desert south of town. Villa was failing them not because of an internal flaw, but because Villa was no island. Villa was part of Peru and Peru was a mess.

"Our youth are rebellious, impulsive," she once told an interviewer. "In the Shining Path, you see expressed their doubts and frustrations about their lack of a future. It is a mystique, a total commitment, that seems to answer their hunger for complete change."

Moyano made the Shining Path crazy. After guerrillas blew up the warehouse that supplied ninety-two Villa soup kitchens and killed and threatened local leaders, Moyano led the first-ever march against them. They vowed to annihilate her. She gave the press long interviews in which she rejected their terror tactics. Guerrillas called her leftist beliefs "revisionist" and claimed she had stolen soup kitchen money. Moyano made the soup kitchen accounts public to show there had been no wrongdoing. To keep guerrillas from attacking soup kitchens and individual leaders, she supported organizing neighborhood watch committees to walk the streets at night. The Shining Path accused her of joining forces with the army. She replied that to defeat the Shining Path, "we must root out fear."

Moyano never showed up for my interview. Protected by four bodyguards, she had been varying her schedule so much, to throw off a potential attempt on her life, that it had escaped her control entirely. As I waited that gloomy morning, her secretary pointed out for me the rickety shacks, high in the dunes, where the guerrilla columns moved at night. "The poorest of the poor," she said.

On February 15, 1992, Moyano was shot as she chatted with people attending a chicken barbecue fund-raiser. Some inside knew what would happen, but no one warned Moyano. They were too frightened. The assassins had been there for hours, eating chicken, waiting.

Among her attackers was another black woman. I would bet Moyano knew her as the woman forced her down, then shot her in the temple and dropped five pounds of dynamite in her lap. To me, this encounter is fully as mysterious—and charged—as another encounter commemorated in 1992, that of the Inca Atahualpa with the conqueror Pizarro almost five centuries earlier. As they stood face to face, Inca and Spaniard, they must have been impressed by their physical differences. One was burned red and covered with hair. The other was dirt-brown, smooth as an egg. They gazed across culture, indeed a kind of historical chasm. But Moyano and her attacker could not have been other than struck by their similarities. Both black, both female, both poor. They lived the same culture, shared history. Yet the political choices they had made turned them into enemies to the death.

Four years after killing Moyano, to commemorate International Women's Day, the Shining Path killed Pascuala Rosado, the former mayor of another Lima shantytown. Rosado had recently returned to Peru after several years away, a precaution against their threats. They shot her as she was leaving her home. Just so no one would have any doubts about the message they intended to send, they killed her as they had killed Moyano—with a bullet and a lapful of dynamite.

We'll get you, no matter how long we have to wait, they meant. We are waiting. And we see.

BETTY HAD MADE A pile of teary pink tissues between us. Despite the guerrilla promise of equality, in the end a man was her downfall. He wooed her, beat her, then left her. It was the old story.

Before the baby was born, she bought a bus ticket home. For two years, she said she never left a cousin's house. She thought about making contact again with the guerrillas. But how could she explain! Her weakness was inexcusable. They would never believe her.

And there was her son to consider. Who would care for him if she died? Gradually, she began going outside again. People talked. She shrugged them off. She lied that she had been away working. Her partner was in Lima, she said, where they would soon join him.

To her surprise, he did come looking for her one day. He offered to marry her. "I didn't want that," she said, lifting her chin. "He promised to send us money, but after the first time nothing arrived. We do better without him."

She got a part-time job. But rumors caught up with her. After a guerrilla bombing, she was picked up by the police. In the police pickup truck, lying face down under a policeman's knees, she thought she would never see her son again. They took her to a place where many people had "disappeared." When the police questioned her, she cried. She had been forced to join the Shining Path, she lied.

The police made her take her clothes off. They hung her from her wrists. They clamped cables connected to a car battery to her nipples, earlobes, and labia. She repeated her story. She had been forced. Then they raped her. As she tells it, the rape was kind of an afterthought, not intended to force out any confession. It was what they did to unwind. Hers had been a long and not very productive session.

In the years that followed, Betty was picked up by police several times. They had a routine. The trip to the spot where they questioned her. Then the rape. Over time, the questioning became less harsh, almost chatty. Betty never knew when one of the policemen who had raped her would pass her on the street and smile that special smile of knowing.

On the other hand, maybe some guerrilla will kill her as a *soplón*, a snitch. "We will find you wherever you hide," says the Shining Path to those who waver. "Even if we have to drag you from your grave." Although she was only twenty-seven when we spoke, Betty no longer felt young or hopeful. She earned the equivalent of fifty-five dollars a month, minus teacher union dues and health insurance. What was left bought two pieces of bread a day, a school uniform for her son, and three plucked chickens. She and her son were back in her aunt's house.

"We tolerate each other," she said, smiling weakly.

Someday, she told me, someone who remembers Comrade Rita will wander by. Maybe, she mused, it would have been smarter to have stayed in. Then, like the other women she knew, she would be dead.

That was her only regret, that she was not dead. The rest, she said, she would do again if given the chance.

AFTER GUZMÁN'S ARREST, there were rumors that a woman would assume command of the Shining Path. The name of Teresa Durand was mentioned, jokester Techi. Or Martha Huatay, who once defended Shining Path members in the courts. Of the two, Huatay was the stronger candidate. Techi, I'm afraid, still trailed behind her the reputation of a *palomillera*. But then Huatay—square-faced, brilliant, a natural leader—was arrested. She was tortured so badly that even the government officials who announced her conviction while displaying a photograph of Huatay's swollen, bruised face seemed chagrined.

It would be an exaggeration for me to conclude that the Shining Path holds some special message for the future of women in Peru. Most women were never cadres, but led soup kitchens, mothers' clubs, human rights groups, and Protestant churches, and shunned violence.

For me, the message is disturbing enough for the present. Despite all, this place in Guzmán's "war machine" was what some women chose. The yearning for a more just society meant that Betty and Gloria and Laura and Lydia and all the rest spent their youth singing the praises of Gonzalo in garbled Chinese, under a flag that for the rest of the world has come to mean a time past. Now that the Shining Path itself fades in importance, I ask myself what they won. What, after all that sacrifice, did they get? There are places on this earth where the passage of time does not bring better, but worse, not easier choices but harder ones, and harder to give up. That was where hope left Betty—cursing life and loving death, a believer who no longer believed, but whose only regret was that she had lived to have one.

5

Señoras

Es que todo tiempo pasado fue mejor, Estela.
Qué linda era Lima entonces, ¿no, Carmela?
Preciosa. Era una ciudad realmente preciosa."
[Those were the good old days, Estela.
Lima was pretty then, wasn't it, Carmela?
Beautiful. It was such a pretty city.]

Dos señoras conversan,
Alfredo Bryce Echenique

MY FIRST LANDLADY IN Lima was named María. She was cigarette-thin and read her Bible by candlelight to save on electricity. Poor eyesight made her push the candle so close to the book's yellowed pages that holes had been seared in her favorite passages. Every day, she wore the same outfit, polyester pants with an elastic waist and a pullover sweater, a scarf wrapped turban-style around her head. It was her attempt, I thought, to evoke Barbara Stanwyck, the actress she told me she had resembled as a girl. At night, she either read the Bible or watched the news and soap operas, Brazilian if she were lucky. The Brazilian ones had better kissing than Mexican or Venezuelan soaps, and the plots were inventive and incorporated real-life themes like hyperinflation and graft. Occasionally, María would stop me on my way out and mention some political scandal, and it usually took me a moment to figure out whether she was talking about the day's news or a soap opera twist.

For instance: Tania, kidnaped, discovers she is pregnant with her ex-husband's child, and though he was killed in a bank robbery, a man of his weight and stature has been shadowing the house where Tania's sister has launched a fashionable boutique with her maid, who has a wasting disease. A Nisei agricultural engineer who once hosted a television issues program that no one watched and has no party, supporters, or platform mounts a bruising presidential campaign against a world-famous novelist who has said, for the record, that he considers the country an "incurable disease" and wants to make it into a Switzerland, which in the primal fear of the moment is refracted into a Frankenstein-like vow to perform unnatural acts on the populace that will erase their very souls.

The worst drought in fifty years had robbed the Rímac River of its spring torrent, which meant water was piped to the house infrequently and never according to the schedule published in the newspaper. Its arrival was announced by a low creaking beneath the foundation and the clanging of the pipes as they contracted against the water's coolness. Sometimes it happened at five in the morning, sometimes at eleven at night. I would run to the tap with my bucket. There was no telling how long the flow would last or when it would return. Water became such a precious, coveted commodity, the subject of intense speculation and desire, that journalists came up with new and elaborate phrases to mark its specialness: *líquido elemento,* for instance, or *precipitaciones lluviosas* (rain-like precipitation), for rain.

All of this María watched and worried over in the one room she reserved for herself in her mansion, divided into sections for renters like me and the Frenchwoman who occupied the apartment over the garage. Like other widowed señoras in Lima, necessity brought her to it: dividing up what was once a gracious home to wring out just enough money to pay the utilities, keep her aging Saab running, get a cholo to cut her sooty grass once a month, and buy the vegetables for her once-daily bowl of soup. María had long ago sold off her best furniture, leaving the pastel blue walls of the first floor bare and scuffed. The Frenchwoman and I paid our rent in dollars, which she kept in a roll hidden in her room. Her eyes were clouded, but she saw well enough to demand newish bills, not the ones that came creased and stained with purple or red ink and were worth less on Ocoña. Dawes brought them to me fresh from the jungle.

There was nothing genteel about María's poverty. She was conniving and hardhearted. To clean and do laundry, she hired the dark-

"Carmen," a Lima maid. © Robin Kirk

skinned girls who came knocking at the door desperate for work, and drove them mercilessly for a week or two until they realized they'd never be paid. When their fathers or brothers or uncles came to collect, María would bar the door, call the police and accuse the girls of thievery. She got away with it every time. When I was out, she occasionally crept upstairs to my three rooms to inventory the cracked plastic dishes, convinced I was secretly profiting from them in a way that cost her personally. We shared a telephone, and it wasn't long before she began listening in on my conversations, unaware that her raspy breathing and the babble of the soap operas gave her away.

For the few months I lived there, I was convinced it was my bad luck. Out of all the apartments in Lima, I thought, I had chosen the one with the crazy señora. I had been seduced by the patio outside the kitchen, where I dreamed of setting up an umbrella table like the one in the Inka Cola ads, Peru's national soft drink, where bronzed yet clearly Caucasian youths cavorted on beaches. I saw myself lounging with coffee in the mornings and pisco sours in the evenings, after a hard day gathering news. On his visits, Orin, who was then living in the north of Peru, would laugh at my folly, the sweep of his arm taking in the dark puddles collecting on the patio tile, left by the dirty fog that embraces Lima nine months of the year. Occasionally, María would use the patio to heap abuse on a maid who had finally got wise and was walking out the front door or the relative who would show up a day or two later, trying reason. It was hard to do with María shouting from above like some vengeful wight.

The problem was that she was willing to do anything to save the equivalent of ten dollars. And even the maids who needed that ten dollars desperately, sometimes enough to come back two or three times, weren't willing to go to jail for it. So María won again and again, and took her raw pleasure from the game, the only thing, beside the soaps, that made her completely happy.

BEFORE THE VOTE FOR president in 1990, I attended a briefing for journalists at a Western embassy. Most were from elsewhere, flown in for the election. The auguries were dire: rates of unemployment, malnutrition, and infant / mother mortality were sharply up while key industries, like fishing, were shutting down. The message was that Peru was on the verge of collapse. Although we were safely in the back of the bunkerlike embassy, I had the giddy sense that the briefing room itself was pushed to a brink.

What happens to countries that tip over the edge? Was there an edge? The journalists traded stories about Somalia and Cambodia, and one referred to Weimar Germany.

An embassy official chose that moment to comment. Rescue was at hand, he said, in the guise of Mario Vargas Llosa. After assuming the presidency, there would be problems and an economic "shock" was inevitable. But happier times were on the way.

"What about Fujimori?" I asked, having arrived with a taxi driver who had emblazoned his cracked dashboard with El Chino's campaign handouts.

"Someone to be watched," the official noted. But he attributed the candidate's rise to a cynical maneuver by the Apra to leak votes away from the novelist. "That balloon will be deflated," he predicted.

I SPENT THE NIGHT before the election in El Agustino, a Lima slum. My idea was to see how a sampling of the largest single block of Peru's voters—the urban poor—went to the polls. Some nuns had agreed to lend me a bed in their house. In the morning, I planned to visit the local mesas, where the votes would be cast.

After I arrived, Sister Ana María and Sister María José, habitless, invited me for instant coffee in their kitchen, a luxury since there hadn't been water or electricity all day. Matronly and in their forties, the sisters had come to El Agustino a decade earlier, when the *pueblo joven* (young town) named Huáscar had been established. In Lima vernacular, "young town" means a piece of land that has been forcibly occupied by poor families. Most would have no other way of acquiring a home. Huáscar buds off of a colonial-era slum and is named after the Inca prince killed by Atahualpa, his brother, in the civil war that ended with the arrival of the Spanish in 1532.

Occupations like the one that began Huáscar are carefully planned by a committee of squatters. On the appointed morning, hundreds of people appear on a plot and divide themselves into the lots they hope will one day contain houses. They are equipped with poles and mats of straw to build their iglus, and portable kerosene stoves, blankets, bottles of water and liquor to ward off thirst and the cold, a bit of food, and homemade Peruvian flags. Battles with the police, or the police and hired thugs if the land is privately owned, follow. Although some invasions fail or are forced to move, many, like Huáscar, prevail.

Over the years, the straw mats had been replaced by homes of iron rebar, concrete, stone, brick, and glass. The residents of Huáscar had built themselves a school, and paid for everything except the salaries of the teachers, who were usually on strike anyway since by then the government paid them the equivalent of fifty dollars per month. They had also pestered municipal authorities for water and sewage pipes and electricity, and after years of petitions and canceled appointments and marches on the mayor's office had won them, ironically at a time when most households could no longer afford to pay the monthly bill. Luckily, water and electricity were usually rationed. That morning, Sister Ana María and Sister María José had bought themselves a cylinder of water, about ten gallons, and had heated up a thermos-full on a backpacker's stove for their evening coffee.

From a node that hugged the cliffs overlooking the Pacific, Lima had grown with its young towns, which by 1990 contained over two-thirds of its population. Satellite pictures of the city's growth reminded me of one of those speeded-up films of a rose blooming, except with Lima there was never any withering or diminishment, only more bloom and more and more until the camera's eye itself is enveloped. Lima grew along the length of the Rímac River and those other rivers of sorts, the two highways that divide the city into what demographers call "cones": the Panamerican Highway, laid north-south, and the Central Highway, which cuts Lima into northern and southern sections and links the city to the Andes.

Sister Ana María and Sister María José were quick to point out that Huáscar's relatively prosperous look—two- and three-level homes under construction, street lights, bus service—was deceiving. "What you will find, once you go inside, is that there is nothing to eat," Sister Ana María told me. "All of that rebar and sacks of concrete you see have been that way for months and months, since no one has the money any more to finish."

When Huáscar was still iglus, Sister María José had helped set up a soup kitchen. Although they were never insistent about it, the sisters' faith was clearly shaped by liberation theology, which considers the struggle for social justice as important a part of the worship of God as prayer. The parish of Father Gustavo Gutiérrez, who wrote *Liberation Theology*, was nearby, and they spoke admiringly of the gnomish theologian. Several of the parishes that ministered to the shanty towns were led by priests and nuns who followed Gutiérrez; who else would volunteer for those conditions? It wasn't just the relentless poverty, but Lima itself that oppressed, its aggressive squalor, the unlovely streets, the rind of grime that collected on every edge. Truth be told, even Gutiérrez never stayed for long, and was always jetting off to some seminar in Europe or the United States.

But that night, sipping the sweet coffee in the light of a single candle,

A Lima street vendor selling tamales.
© Robin Kirk

the darkness seemed edged with menace. When the sisters started out a decade ago, they had ministered mainly to the very poor, among them recent arrivals to Lima. But over the past two years, more and more working-class families had begun to use the soup kitchen. Sister María José said that families that had once considered themselves comfortable—factory workers, state employees, teachers—were now showing up at the soup kitchen with their pails, to collect the food they would take back to their empty concrete homes to divide and eat. That day, the kitchen had served chopped beets, wheat soup (flavored with bone stock), and a rice-wheat mix. Many people had lost their jobs and now earned their living selling vegetables or batteries or with *cachuelos,* occasional work.

These pursuits were the backbone of the famous "informal" sector: enterprises set up outside formal channels and paying no taxes to the state. A lot had been made of "informals" in the press. Certain Western diplomats saw Peru's salvation in what they called their heroism. But I always wondered: what choice did they have? To be a hero, you have to make a choice, perform the heroic deed or walk away, and the heart of the matter lies in choosing selflessly. How could these Peruvians walk away from themselves? All the informals I ever spoke to wanted to be formal, so the police wouldn't destroy their little table, so they could get a loan, trade their spot on the sidewalk for a market stall. Certain intersections, even in impoverished Huáscar, were choked with informals selling the same things, even arranged the same ways on their tables, to people without much money to buy. Certainly, informals were admirable and worthy of the "microenterprise" loans Western diplomats said they were making. But when I visited young towns, I never felt like I was watching heroism but rather dignity in the face of slow disaster: graying the clothes, emptying the cupboards, stifling hope.

Those who could, left for Colombia, Argentina, Chile. Shady travel agents sold thousands of "tours" to Nicaragua, where, it was understood, connections would be made for Japan or the United States. It wasn't heroism that kept the rest there, but the lack of a three-thousand-dollar stake. A poll found that 71 percent of the Peruvians interviewed would pack their bags tomorrow if they could and leave the country. One English language school advertised: "El que no sabe inglés, no es" [He who doesn't speak English doesn't exist]. One study in a young town similar to Huáscar showed that school-age children had simply stopped growing in 1988, cold-cocked, stunned like birds after hitting a pane of glass.

It was precisely this situation that Mario Vargas Llosa promised to rectify. Catapulted into politics by his opposition to the bank nationalization, Vargas Llosa had built his party, Libertad (Freedom), and campaigned on the promise to "modernize" Peru, which meant reduce government, open Peru to the global marketplace, sell off state enterprises, and encourage entrepreneurship by getting rid of red tape. He never minimized the obstacles. First, he said, he would have to right the economy, which meant stopping the inflation that had reached 7,000 percent annually. To do it, he would shut off García's maquinita, end subsidies, and raise prices without touching wages, measures that would hit hardest at the poor.

In Peru, such drastic economic measures, bundled into one big package, are called *paquetazos*. The last one had been in 1988, when García had made a halfhearted attempt to shore up the failing economy. But by election time, it was rumored that the Apra had spent every dollar of the country's reserves and was considering raffling off the gold and silver ingots that were the last anchor for the nearly worthless currency. Speculation had reached such a peak that García's spokesman had to publicly deny that "Crazy Horse" would sell off the antiquities stored in the National Bank, those few pre-Columbian gold pieces that had escaped Spanish foundries.

No one doubted that Vargas Llosa's paquetazo would be harsh. People began calling it "the shock," like some evil, addictive dance step. To his credit, the novelist was honest, and he had announced his intentions early and often, to underscore, he believed, the scope of the calamity left by the Apra. Of course, the Apra neatly capitalized on his statements by portraying Vargas Llosa as the economic grim reaper.

Over the weeks before election day, Vargas Llosa kept a frenetic pace as he hopped from city to city, holding rallies and making lightning visits to shantytowns. Occasionally, he was stoned, and búfalos paid by the Apra roughed up his supporters and drowned out his words with shouts and slogans. To many of the foreign journalists, Vargas Llosa was heroic, a truthful man tilting against the corrupt and self-serving demagogue that García had become. But I saw in his candidacy something doomed, almost grotesque. For a writer so attuned to nuance, so perceptive of the drifts in human nature, Vargas Llosa seemed oblivious to the effect of his campaign on poor Peruvians. Even as he preached the virtues of independence, he surrounded himself with the *viejas glorias,* the old glories, of past political debacles—those scrubbed pink faces that had led Peru step by step into the predicament he believed he could rescue it from. Although he touted himself as the champion of the informals, his political allies were the same mayors and prefects who sent police to evict the informals who surrounded established businesses and blocked streets. Some of his supporters called him a "luxury" candidate, meaning that Peru was lucky to have a man of his intelligence and dedication; yet once made, the phrase came to mean a candidate Peru could not afford. Others, less charitable, called him "Café Mario," alluding to the many years he had spent abroad pursuing a literary career. While he extolled the free market and the lifting of unnecessary regulations, his political coalition drowned the airwaves in political ads, proving eloquently that in a society plagued by inequality, the rich and powerful take what they want. An agnostic, Vargas Llosa yet became the champion of the most conservative wing of the Catholic Church, which was identified not with people like Sister Ana María and Sister María José, but the wealthy parishes in Miraflores and San Isidro, where my landlady lived. The political schemers he denounced with righteous fury schemed their way onto his ticket. Massive giveaways in the young towns of cheap toys and chocolate repeatedly turned into riots and burnished his image as a rich man who let crumbs fall from between his fingers. Even as he imagined himself as the symbol of change, most Peruvians saw him as dramatically, even stubbornly the same, the white patrón who would turn deaf and dumb to the entreaties of the poor once he moved to Pizarro's mansion.

For me, it was like watching a slow-motion film of a car crash or a collapsing bridge or a train wreck: a tremble of trouble propelled as much as anything by its own inertia finally busting the screen apart. As I sat in the nuns' kitchen that night, his coming defeat was palpable to me, like grit in the air. And it was clear who would do it: El Chino Fujimori, a man no one knew much about, but who had suddenly burst upon the scene as Vargas Llosa planned his last and seemingly triumphant campaign rallies.

The nuns liked him. El Chino, the Chinaman, was an affectionate term, like Shorty, Skinny, or Blackie, all common nicknames in Peru. Alberto Fujimori had visited Huáscar in a borrowed tractor, called the Fujimobile. The name of his hastily convened political party—Cambio 90, Change 90—was a direct rip-off of Vargas Llosa's campaign slogan, "The great change, with freedom." But with Fujimori, the meaning didn't twist in on itself. Although Fujimori was clearly supported by the Apra in a cynical attempt to derail Vargas Llosa's victory, he came off as stubbornly independent. For weeks, the taxi drivers and market vendors—the very same informals that Vargas Llosa had hoped to capture—had been insistently promoting him as the antidote to the Vargas Llosa paquetazo. Fujimori had one campaign pledge, and he made it simple: no shock.

What the no-shock meant was never explained. It was enough to assure voters, as he did, that "Honesty, Technology, and Work" would save Peru. A vote for Fujimori was a leap into the unknown. Was he just a mask for the Apra; would the army mount a coup if he won; would the few remaining solvent businesses in Peru simply pack up and leave? My conversation with the sisters that night left me troubled, unable to sleep. Upset was in the air, like dynamite residue. Vargas Llosa's supporters had packed the Sheraton, their ritzy perch from which to watch the masses swirl in the streets below them. Again, Vargas Llosa had chosen precisely the wrong image to define his campaign. By I A.M., the results were clear. Mario Vargas Llosa had failed to win the majority needed to avoid a runoff. The Sheraton buzzed with disbelief. In Huáscar, the lights came back on. And there was jubilation in the streets. The cholos, with their chino, had carried the day.

MARÍA KNEW WHO was to blame for Peru's troubles and she was never shy about telling me: the cholos. The cholos had tainted the capital with their filthy ways, their exploding families, their wife-beating, and bad manners. The cholos were draining the city of its charm, its resources, its líquido elemento. For María, the shantytowns were the outposts of a barbarian tribe, biding its time. The *gente decente*—decent people—were surrounded.

Gente decente—this was a phrase I heard often, usually from señoras of a certain age who were cramped into corners of their concrete-block mansions. They weren't wealthy enough to have pulled up stakes and moved to Miami. Their children visited, grumpily, on Sundays. Nailed down by age and infirmity and fear of the unfamiliar, they had few options. So they complained. When María said to me, peering up from her self-imposed darkness, that Lima was not always like this, I couldn't imagine what it used to be. By then, the present had destroyed my ability to perceive fossils of grace. What little I imagined was gleaned from books, like this passage from a 1936 travel memoir:

> [The bus] conducted me along a broad boulevard with trees in rows of lavender flower, past villas dripping with bloom, like the houses of southern California. . . . Then, suddenly the avenue had led us into narrow streets of two-story houses, with latticed Moorish balconies on their upper floors. Often these lattices were beautifully and intricately carved, and sometimes a shutter stood open, and through the aperture a dark head regarded the world. But the head did not wear the high comb and the mantilla implied in the Spanish-Colonial balcony; for the head was bobbed in the manner of the moment. . . . It seemed as though New York had moved into Lima.

María told me there was no garbage or grime or streets choked with vendors. Lima was marvelous, *una maravilla*.

And here was where the monologue always got tiresome, since what she meant was that everyone knew their place then. The cholos kept to the fields or the chores, where they belonged. Maids didn't demand raises or to go to night school. Cholos kept the city streets practically scrubbed instead of spitting on them. On car trips to Chosica, just outside Lima's cap of fog, cholos would prepare them *pachamanca,* guinea pig and potatoes and fava beans roasted over buried coals. Not like now, when pachamanca is practically a franchise and the portions are not as big and the taste not the same and instead of looking at her with gratitude and respect, their cholo eyes have the unmistakable glint of U.S. dollar bills.

María believed the cholos didn't know their place anymore. Unlike Don Enrique, who had lost his land to the cholos, María had lost nothing of tangible value. What she believed the cholos had taken was her culture. For her, the ultimate expression of her loss was public urination. In parks, against walls, against yard shrubbery and car tires, cholo men peed with their members grasped casually in their hands.

María was not alone in her opinion. For weeks, *El Comercio,* the leading newspaper, had campaigned against public urination. Photographers sneaked up on men to snap their likenesses in the act, to be displayed in the metro section the next day. Since *El Comercio* supported Café Mario, public urination was generally framed as yet more proof of the bankruptcy of the Apra party and particularly its leader, Crazy Horse.

But it was also much more. For María, as well as for *El Comercio,* public urination was a manifestation of generalized decline, a loss of respect, values, and national pride. Little was ever said about ways to solve this problem: public restrooms, for instance. Instead, the solution seemed to be instilling "culture"—or, since that appeared impossible, finding some way to cut down on an overpopulation of cholos.

"Limans," *El Comercio* lamented with more than a hint of bitterness, "have become a small colony in their native land."

IN A WAY, MARÍA and *El Comercio* were right—the cholos were draining the líquido elemento, the electric current, public services, and the buoyant privilege that had once belonged to the light-skinned middle class. Migration to the cities, particularly Lima, had so outgrown city services that everyone suffered. While drought and guerrilla attacks certainly hurt, the main culprits were the more than 2 million people who had arrived in the capital since the last power station was expanded in 1982.

One afternoon, I went with a photographer to see a new occupation near the Central Highway. Unlike Huáscar, which was near downtown Lima, the new invasion was several miles out, amid the fields that had once supplied Lima with vegetables. The landowner, who knew his farming days were over, had already begun to sell off his fields to a developer who had quickly put up new homes. But a few fields were still under cultivation. It was there the occupiers had congregated. Their task was formidable. They not only had to force the landowner to sell them the land at a discount, but also mount the occupation without help from the neighbors, the newly installed middle-class families who had no wish to see a pueblo joven spring up at their feet.

We found the occupiers milling at the edge of a large tilled field, where the remains of their straw huts still smoked from the fires the police had set that morning. With sharpened cane staves in hand, some still bearing Peruvian flags, they were preparing to retake the ground. Muddy and wet, they were in an ugly mood. A rumor circulated that during the dawn raid, police had captured and raped a woman. Some favored standing up to the police, not running away. But cooler heads counseled patience.

"We only want a place to live, we are willing to pay something," said a young man to me. His T-shirt was torn across his bony chest. The ash on his face made him look like a coal miner. A band of children, equally ragged and grubby, followed him like ducklings. As an afterthought, he added, as if it needed saying: "We're not doing this for fun."

Across the field, a police troop carrier inched down the dirt track that followed an irrigation canal. Its sides were cut into three openings. I could just make out the green knees of the officers and the glint of the guns they carried upright with the stocks resting on the floor. The carrier stopped. Slowly, policemen in riot gear descended and formed a line at the field's edge. Some of the occupiers had already penetrated the field and were rapidly building their iglus, half-burned sheets of straw on charred cane poles. With a shout, the police charged. I heard the hollow poof of tear gas guns, though the canisters fell harmlessly to the side. With their night sticks raised, the police neared the crowd, scattering it. Some women stood behind me warily, testing if police would attack a gringa with a camera. Apparently, they wouldn't. My entourage grew. Others took to a low hill, which I learned later was an Inca temple, its lower walls already scavenged by these same families for bricks to hurl.

Perhaps it was the hour, so soon after lunch, or the fact that there was apparently no senior officer present to urge the police on. But their charge looked almost languid, with their night sticks half raised and their expressions detached beneath the plastic visors of their riot helmets. They milled for a while at midfield, kicking at the hut remains. Then, they withdrew to their carrier. Later, the photographer and I found the carrier parked at one of the new houses nearby, where the owner had set up a small sundries store. Because of the occupation, she had the bars of the store down. Through them, she had treated the men to a large bottle of Inka Cola.

There was an air of defeat about them. They would run the people off a couple more times, then call it a day. If the farmer didn't succeed in selling off the land to a developer with more huevones, who would hire an army of private thugs to really lay waste to the occupiers' plans, within a couple of days, an entire neighborhood would be up, complete with streets and a block association. By then, some of the officers might even have told their relatives: hey, get yourselves a lot, this one's about to fly. They were cholos, too. In their lackadaisical charge across the field, I saw it in their faces. They could see themselves on either side of the riot shield: wielding it or taking careful aim.

AT ABOUT THIS TIME, Orin and I returned to Tunnel Six for a visit. There were new babies—Bárbara had a boy, Ronald, and Pancha had two girls, Cristina and Luz, who was a month old. Pancha's eldest, Profelinda, had changed from a reed-thin girl into a stocky adolescent, and there was a new power in her shoulders and arms. The teeth that had once plagued her were gone, replaced by dentures that featured one lustrous tooth framed in gold. That night, the musicians who had played for Marco's funeral returned, and there was drinking and dancing on the pampa.

The economic crisis had turned the Tunnel Six economy in on itself. Families ate what they grew and what little they bought by selling a bit in town. Víctor and Pancha were thinking of moving to Sullana, where they would help José, Pancha's brother, buy a stall in the market. He

The Córdova-Paz family in 1990, after
moving to the city. © Orin Starn

had left Tunnel Six after Marco's death, and tried his luck farming corn
in the jungle. But his body couldn't withstand the punishing routine.
He briefly considered trading the corn for coca, since it was the only
crop that made a consistent profit. But that meant siding with the
Shining Path, which controlled the area. Instead, he went to Sullana,
where a sister was selling clothes from a stand in the market. Since she
was an informal, the police would evict her occasionally and ruin her
stock. She needed help, especially to pack the stock quickly and run.

Víctor, Profelinda, and Santos accompanied us on our return from
Tunnel Six to Sullana, where we spent a night in José's adobe house.
Santos is Margarita's youngest daughter and technically Profelinda's
aunt. But Santos and Profelinda were only a couple of months apart
and had become inseparable. Margarita had moved to Sullana to cook
for José. In the evenings, she still liked to sit outside, as she had on the
pampa, and discuss the day's events. But she no longer had her loom.
And it wasn't the same, looking over the thicket of television antennas
instead of the fields below the canal, where the neighbors perhaps were

up to no good. The no-good things happened behind closed doors, drowned out by the sounds of radios and TVs and passing trucks.

For the family, the move to the city had already worked a subtle though apparent change. Margarita remained gruff and generous, and José was still their hardest worker. But the city around them, low and brown and pressed by the relentless heat, seemed to make them physically smaller. Their dreams and aspirations were no longer the mysteries of ronda justice, but a decent concrete floor for the house, chairs, and a television. Although Margarita missed her goats and pigs, she had developed a new fascination for the pills and salves available at the local health clinic. What Profelinda and Santos wanted was simplest of all: ice cream.

Orin and I took them to an ice cream parlor in downtown Piura. They wore their finest dresses, frilly pastels a bit limp from travel and sleeping and the chores Margarita demanded.

"Guaaaa," Profelinda said as a tall sundae crowned with whipped cream and a neon cherry was put before her. She looked at Santos. They laughed low, conspiratorial laughs, as if all the time Orin and I had spent in Tunnel Six had been part of their grand and secret plan to end up precisely here, before these huge sundaes.

Showing on the television suspended above the room was *Natacha,* at the time the most popular soap opera in Peru. The story was of an orphaned country girl, Natacha, who goes to Lima. She finds work as a maid and falls in love with Raúl, the eldest son of the señora who hires her. Horrified, the señora does everything in her power to foil the budding romance. But love prevails. Raúl marries Natacha. The señora learns to love her sweet daughter-in-law.

The script was based on a production done in the 1950s that had also been a hit. But in the updated *Natacha,* the cast featured a well-known Venezuelan actress as Natacha. Unlike most of the maids I knew, this Natacha had plenty of time to brood and weep in her cozy room. The señora was mean, but she paid a steady salary and gave the girl time off and kept the youngest son out of Natacha's room at night. The señora never beat her or called her a dirty chola. Of course, she wasn't a chola. She was blond and blue-eyed, and did nothing to mask the distinctive Caracas roll and clip in her voice. Natacha was *cama adentro* (live-in), but since she spent most of her time mooning over Raúl, it didn't seem a hardship that she had few outside interests and friends, and was completely fulfilled by her vocation.

The choice of a white woman to play the maid, as mediocre and fearful as it was, turned *Natacha* from social commentary into a fairy tale, where race and class were erased to make way for destiny. It was destiny that determined Natacha's future with Raúl, the divine will to favor the good and punish the bad. At that moment in Peru's history, it seemed that fate again was also in the lead, punishing the proud, the Café Marios, and favoring the good, El Chino, the quiet, industrious and God-fearing one. Or perhaps fate would throw down the presumptuous Chino, wily pretender and fake, and anoint the man who would save Peru, Don Mario. When *Natacha* came on, all the eyes in the ice-cream parlor turned to it, hushed and attentive. Even the señoras, perfumed and dressed in Sunday finery and with their children and the maid in tow, were transfixed. Everyone rooted for Natacha, whose love for Raúl emanated from every pore.

Profelinda and Santos methodically moved ice cream to their mouths. It was if they were spooning up hope—sweet, creamy, deliciously improbable in the heat still radiating from the streets and sidewalks.

Raúl, oblivious, asked Natacha for a coffee. In the parlor, there was an intake of breath. Natacha served it, trembling, wide-eyed.

A spoon of ice cream hung before Santos's mouth.

"Guaaaa!" said Profelinda. Santos looked at her, joyous, and popped the spoon into her mouth.

IN THE WEEK LEADING up to the runoff vote, María would go to mass in the church a block from the house to pray with other señoras for El Chino's defeat. Some señoras had devised a way to "freeze" the Nisei candidate in his seemingly unstoppable roll to victory: by cutting up a photo of him, dropping it into a glass of water, and sticking it in the freezer. Perhaps it would have worked, if there had been enough electricity to power the refrigerators. But like everything else in Lima, the electricity—drawn from the turbines that no longer had water enough to turn them—was no longer reliable, leaving the líquido elemento still liquid in its glass and Fujimori's momentum unhampered. María claimed she had relatives somewhere in Florida who would take her in when the country, as she expected, collapsed. They never called, though, or wrote. I think she expected a cataclysm to occur if Fujimori donned the red-and-white presidential sash, a tidal wave or perhaps a hurricane, unheard of off the Pacific but entirely as improbable in her mind as a Chinaman leading her country.

The peasant girls who had once flocked to the door when María put her sign in the window had somehow pooled their knowledge and began avoiding the house. María was forced to hire Juana, who demanded pay in advance. Juana had worked for María and her husband as a maid in a hotel they used to own. María may also have preferred her because she had heard that the Shining Path had planted spies among the younger maids and they were dutifully reporting to their maximum leader. What he would want with María was unclear. To her, it was enough that there was something to be had.

Vargas Llosa tried to drop out of the race in exchange for promises from Fujimori that he would adopt a part of Libertad's platform—sell off state industries, lift price controls and subsidies, impose an austerity program that would allow Peru to reopen negotiations with international lenders. But in the end, Vargas Llosa's friends and advisers convinced him that to drop out invited a coup d'etat. Instead of buying more television advertising, Vargas Llosa opted to increased funding to the Program for Social Aid, which he described as a model of the emergency aid program he would carry out to mitigate the worst effects of the coming "shock." Perhaps he believed it; but to many Peruvians, the food giveaways and sudden construction projects and blueprints for piped-in water and electricity looked like yet another clumsy attempt to buy votes. One editorialist derided his "aristocratic conscience." In the pueblos jóvenes, Fujimori enthusiasts would drown out his supporters with cries of "El Chinito" and pull at their eyes to simulate epicanthic folds.

The newspapers that opposed Vargas Llosa—*Página Libre,* which he called "a scandal sheet," and *La República*—liked to contrast the candidates by photographing their supporters, usually a señora for Vargas Llosa, looking as if she had just discovered the dirty laundry the maid had failed to do, and dancing cholos for Fujimori, what the maids would like to do once they finished those chores. One of Peru's best cartoonists, Alfredo, based an entire series on the señoras, which he

Woman with incense following the Lord
of Miracles. © Robin Kirk

called *las viejas pitucas* (the old snobs). Every day, the polls brought bad
news for Vargas Llosa. Fujimori was pulling ahead.

Before the scheduled debate between the candidates, the Lima archbishop took the unusual step of calling out the Lord of Miracles. An
image of a crucified Christ painted on a wall by slaves, the Lord of
Miracles miraculously survived a devastating earthquake in 1687 and
has since become the most popular religious image in Peru. For students of pre-Columbian history, the image was linked to Pachacámac,
a deity whose temple marked Lima before the Spanish arrival. Each
October, the beginning of Lima spring, a copy of the image is paraded

through Lima on a giant litter carried by members of "the Brotherhood," male devotees who wear a distinctive purple habit. Women precede and follow the litter singing hymns and carrying burning incense.

It was only the sixth time in Peruvian history that the Lord of Miracles had been brought out in a month other than October. The archbishop, who did little to hide his support for the novelist, claimed it was to counter the attacks by Protestant congregations—in Peru called evangelicals—against the Catholic Church. At less than 5 percent of the population, Protestants were far from a serious threat to the Catholics. But their numbers were growing, especially in highland areas devastated by war. The fact that some Protestants had unified behind Fujimori and were actively campaigning for him was, the archbishop insisted, beside the point. In his campaign memoir, Vargas Llosa recounted that one supporter offered to "arrange" a miracle during the procession and have the image verbally encourage a vote for him. Wisely, the novelist declined.

A televised debate between the candidates culminated the runoff. For journalists, a seat was a coveted prize, and somehow I managed to get one. The tension in the room was palpable. When he took the stage, Vargas Llosa was visibly weary, whittled down by months of campaigning and his unexpected troubles. In contrast, Fujimori seemed relaxed, healthy, a little rooster.

While Vargas Llosa had clearly chosen to approach the debate as a dignified exchange on policy, Fujimori hit low and hard and personal. He questioned the novelist's patriotism, his faith, his huevones for offering to withdraw to avoid a runoff. Because Vargas Llosa had taken part in a commission to investigate a 1983 massacre, Fujimori suggested that he had in fact had a hand in the killing, or at least the cover-up. He was a pornographer (for *In Praise of the Stepmother*) and a drug addict (because he admitted experimenting with marijuana at fourteen). His impressive achievements—professorships in Europe, his prizes, his world renown—were, for Fujimori, proof that he had betrayed Peru. "You say you want to make a Switzerland of Peru during your government," Fujimori accused, as if the idea cloaked some deeply nefarious final solution.

Vargas Llosa looked as if his world had suddenly turned from full color to uniform gray. His worst nightmare—a provincial technocrat, a man with complex and hidden alliances, a man steeped in the staleness of Peruvian intellectual thought—was besting him with gossip, prejudice, and chauvinism. There was no platform to criticize, no great ideas. It was like battling Lima fog: ubiquitous, penetrating, insidious. By the end of the debate, when Fujimori held aloft a pro–Vargas Llosa newspaper that had already published an issue proclaiming the novelist the victor (a photograph that was faithfully spread across all the pro-Fujimori newspapers the next morning), the outcome of the runoff was clear. Fujimori would be Peru's next president.

Later, Vargas Llosa accepted some responsibility for campaign mismanagement—the torrent of publicity, his fatal alliance with the *viejas glorias,* his own profound ambivalence about politics. Yet he blamed his defeat squarely on the voters, who "don't make analyses, those who follow their impulses" and were "uncultured." For many, he thereby embraced the accusations made by Fujimori and confirmed the doubts of those who had not trusted him. Through all the advertising and the promises and the high-concept speeches, they saw the distaste in his gaze and punished him for it.

THE DAY AFTER FUJIMORI'S inauguration, conservative columnist Patricio Ricketts greeted him with grim news. "This is the deepest and most generalized crisis since Independence," he wrote. "If the government lacks the courage to do what is necessary, what awaits is the explosion and final collapse."

Two weeks later, on August 8, Fujimori imposed the shock. He made his prime minister announce the news on television. The prime minister spoke slowly and with precision, as if through calm and logic the measures would somehow seem less catastrophic. The "Fujishock," as it came to be known, embodied María's worst fears. With the stroke of a pen, Fujimori abolished the subsidies that had been keeping necessities like noodles, gasoline, and medicines within her reach. Although the prime minister promised welfare for the poorest, it never materialized and few seriously expected it to. The state's coffers were empty.

While the prime minister spoke, police and army troops were ordered to the streets, to prevent looting. The prime minister announced that the money printing that had buoyed the previous administration would stop. Some prices were doubled. Others increased 2,000 percent. The effect was much like a car hitting a brick wall: family budgets flying out the window, factory schedules shattering, hopes crumpling like metal on stone. "May God help us," the prime minister closed, his hands folded on the pages of his speech.

I turned off my portable black-and-white television. I opened the doors to the patio to listen for a reaction: bombs, I thought, screams, honking, the furious banging of pots. But the Fujishock was a collision without noise. What I heard was the silence of other televisions turned off, other ears searching for sound. It was dead calm in Lima that night, as if the fog itself had conspired with the El Chino.

The next morning, a Friday, I took a walk. Few had bothered to go to work. No one knew what the bus fare would be. No one had the cash for gas. Most stores were closed, their windows sheathed with roll-down metal doors. The only one I found open was a supermarket, where sharpshooters crouched on the roof, their faces hidden with ski masks.

It was strangely warm for winter. I thought of the days after the 1989 earthquake in San Francisco, also unseasonably warm. I had seen that earthquake coming like a set of ocean swells under the asphalt of Twenty-second Street. But the Fujishock had surprised everyone. The two disasters—one financial, the other geological—felt the same to me, and caused a similar dissociation in my mind between thought and action, thinking something and doing it.

There was nothing to drink in the house, so I went to the super-market to buy bottled water. I walked alone down its aisles as the checkers whispered, biting their nails. I remember debating to myself: fizzy or unfizzy water? What about water for washing? Rinsing my hands? I chose a liter bottle of club soda and paid for it, the sheaf of bills in my wallet barely covering the purchase. As I left the store, it oc-curred to me that I had just spent the equivalent of twenty dollars for a liter of water. *Anonado,* the newspapers dubbed the sensation, or *aton-tonado,* knocked silly, bewildered.

Later, I heard that a few mobs descended on fields near Lima to strip them of plants, ripe or not. In Tumbes, on the Peru-Ecuador border, some stores were sacked. Some trucks were stopped, their drivers robbed and stripped of cargo. A friend told me that her bus, traveling north to Lima on the Panamerican highway, was blocked by a mob armed with sticks and stones just outside Nazca. My friend got out her money. But all the people wanted was gasoline to run the town generator. The driver siphoned gasoline from the bus, then embraced each of the men, who turned out to be the mayor and town council members.

When the Ministry of Labor finally set the minimum wage over a week later, one newspaper calculated that the amount, a little over fifty dollars, didn't even cover the cost of a month of bread and coffee for a family of four. As government authorities predicted, prices were eventually forced down since no one could afford to buy even bread. But for most, it was from cloud to cloud—lower, but still beyond reach.

The newspapers filled their pages with new words: *crédito puente* (bridge loan), *deuda fresca* (fresh debt), *arreglo secuencial* vs. *arreglo simultáneo* (a sequential vs. a simultaneous agreement), *capital golondrino* (swallow capital, which comes and goes with the speed of a swallow), *reinserción* (reinsertion), in this case into the debt marketplace. This new lexicon had to do with a kind of rebaptism of Peru by international lenders, pleased by what they saw. Of course, they weren't in Peru, so what made them happy were balance sheets showing that hyperinflation had been knocked cold in the space of the prime minister's speech. Alfredo made his comments with the *Calatos,* the Naked Ones, a series that featured figures living in shacks and without clothes or anything to eat. In one frame, naked figures stand next to a fat man wearing a hat that reads International Monetary Fund. "Just so you know," a naked figure says, "we have $500 million in net reserves in his front pocket."

That María's favored candidate, Vargas Llosa, would probably have imposed the same shock did not mitigate her fury with El Chinito. The Fujishock confirmed María's lack of faith in cholos. Even though Fujimori was Japanese-Peruvian, to her he epitomized cholo ignorance, cholo bumbling, cholo ineptitude. "He can't even speak the language," she told me one night on the stairs, referring to his Nisei accent. "This is who we call president?" Most of her money was in dollars, including my rent, so the effect of the economic changes on her was muted. She talked more frequently, though, of moving to Florida with her nieces and nephews, and leaving Peru to rot.

At the end of 1990, that disastrous year—and not Peru's worst, as it turned out—the flight of a Japanese reporter in a Soviet spaceship over Peru underscored the sensation of a country set adrift. As Lima reporters stood on the roof of the monolithic Sheraton Hotel, peering at the same leaden fog that had hung over the city since June, astronaut

Fujimori holding a vicuña.
© Lucien Chauvin

Toyoshiro Akiyama reported seeing "something a little like a small stream" in the vicinity of Peru, hidden by clouds. A special four-page supplement in *La República* featured photographs of the Peruvian reporters gazing skyward in the dawn darkness. President Fujimori had asked the astronaut to talk about Peru's tourist attractions, and as he did, film of Machu Picchu, the Nazca lines, and the Colca Canyon apparently ran on Japanese television. But as far as the Japanese were concerned, these could have been filmed on another planet, someplace too far away and chaotic and dangerous to ever contemplate traveling. The stunt, meant to display Peru's membership in the club of nations fluent in spacecraft, global telecommunications, and adventure tourism, only seemed to underscore its fatal distance, adrift in a separate solar system of calamity.

LONG AFTER I LEFT María's house, I heard through Juana that María had accused me of theft and was threatening to call the police. Early in my stay, I had cut a length of worn-out wire from the ancient telephone and reconnected it with cord brought from San Francisco. The worn-out wire was the stolen material in question. I had saved the old wire in case I needed to harvest a bit more, and had inadvertently packed the short coil when I left.

I returned with the coil one afternoon, furious before even ringing the doorbell to summon María from her dark room. All her infractions seemed to coalesce in this one moment. With satisfaction, I saw that both my upstairs rooms and the garage apartment once occupied by the Frenchwoman remained empty.

When María opened the door, she was all smiles. "How nice to see you," she said.

"Here is your filthy wire," I replied, throwing it at her feet.

She was paler than I remembered. Her head scarf was missing, revealing the patchy, sparse hair underneath. She claimed she had never accused me of anything. She said she had always treated me with the greatest respect. She was practically a foreigner herself, she said, because of her marriage to an Englishman. How could I imagine that she would think of me with anything less than the greatest esteem?

I heard her words as lies. With a final glare, I left her with what I thought would be a devastating insult, something about cholos and true dignity. Here she was, I thought, in the fortress privilege had granted her, grumbling about a favor I had done her as if it were a crime. I used a new word I had recently learned to insult her, *mezquina*, which I thought meant meddlesome.

"Mezquina," I said, "goodbye."

Later, though, I learned that I had misunderstood the word. *Mezquina* means wretched, forlorn, piteous. At the time, I should have seen this in her pallid skin, those meager soups, her burned Bible. I did not. I was looking for other kinds of stories, about overcoming damning odds, generosity, heroism. Not defeat.

Not long after my hard words, María died of the cancer that had been consuming her, undetected, during my stay in her home. Juana told me there was barely enough left from her estate to bury her. The fabled relatives from the United States did not come to her funeral. Once, I had occasion to pass the house, and saw that its new owner had invested in the iron fence that María had always coveted, painted white and armed with elaborate teeth at the top that would rip the rags from any determined thief. The bars were set so close that the lower level of the house, where María had lived, was difficult to see. But someone else lived upstairs, where I had stayed. They had that umbrella table I had always coveted, though at that moment its bright colors were furled against the fog.

6

The Monkey's Paw

I SHOULD HAVE remembered about the *chifa*. When Cromwell invited me for dinner and asked where I'd like to go, I replied breezily that it didn't matter, pizza or Chinese, whichever he and Carmen Rosa preferred. When we walked into the chifa, a Chinese restaurant—its plastic red-and-gold arch like the gaping jaws of a monster fish, the dark internal compartments connecting off a central passageway lined with red plastic dividers—it was the smell that brought it back to me, sweet and heavy and spiked with enhancers, the Latin relish for sugar melded to some impossible-to-trace evocation of Chinese cuisine, Canton by way of Lima, deep-fried, smothered in red and green sauces, limp vegetables, and the hard, coiled meat of peeled shrimp.

The red leatherette menus were opened for us. A burly Peruvian waiter took our order for the banquet-style meal Cromwell prefers. A vigorous man, Cromwell has a tightly curled cap of black hair over a handsome, square-jawed face. He is neither cold nor slow to laugh, but deliberate in both word and habit. The menu selections pleased him. He ordered for us, choosing meat, chicken, and seafood dishes, sweet and salty, to round out our meal.

As the platters began to arrive, our talk turned to the event that led to our friendship. On October 21, 1990, the Castillo's son, Ernesto, was "disappeared," the term used to describe an arrest that goes unrecorded and often ends in murder. In some ways, it was a run-of-the-mill case. Since the mid-1980s the United Nations had put Peru near the top of the list of countries that forcibly disappear their citizens. Yet successive administrations discounted reports of abuses. In 1985 President Belaunde even bragged that he had thrown an Amnesty Interna-

Carmen Rosa and Cromwell Castillo.
© Orin Starn

tional report into the garbage. The year Ernesto vanished, Peruvian human rights groups registered 246 "disappearances" nationwide. Most involved young men, many students. In Lima, police were in the habit of grabbing people and forcing them into the trunks of patrol cars. In the mountains, military patrols would round up and shoot farmers they considered suspect and dump the bodies in rocky gorges.

In other ways, the Castillo case was unique. Ernesto was middle class and had attended the country's leading private university. Most "disappeared" were peasants. Carmen Rosa is the daughter of an army officer, and Cromwell is a successful accountant and entrepreneur.

Most families of the "disappeared" were poor. The Castillos know how to work the intricate system of personal friendships and family relations summed up in Peru by the word *vara:* clout and the savvy to wield it.

They recognized this, and considered it a strength. "Perhaps through our pressure and dedication," Cromwell told me during our first interview, "we can win better results and awaken a greater degree of compassion in people who can help."

When I first read about Ernesto in the newspaper, it occurred to me that this was a story my editors would love. A promising boy, a good-looking, American-type boy, who studies hard and has his own room and wears jeans and T-shirts and loves his family dog, leaves home one day never to return. His parents dedicate their lives to finding him. The government, convinced that occasional mistakes are part of a successful war on guerrillas, does everything in its power to frustrate their search. Yet because of the Castillo's social status, eloquence, and money, they actually had a chance. It seemed a straightforward and compelling way to talk about human rights.

At the time, my editors had been encouraging me to do stories with American "hooks," like the war on drugs or quirky American ventures (the largest soup pot ever constructed, in a Lima shantytown) or American couples adopting Peruvian babies. A photographer took a picture of Cromwell, with Carmen Rosa behind him holding a photograph of Ernesto as they stood in Ernesto's book-filled bedroom. I put something in about the United States being concerned about human rights, though I had to press the embassy official I interviewed to even mention the theme. The Castillo's normalcy clinched the story. I made the front page.

By the time the story was published, the Castillos and I had become friends. Orin and I ate pizza in the Castillo's austere dining room, the silver service pushed to the back of the sideboard to accommodate pizzas in the style Ernesto and his university friends had introduced to their home. We accompanied them to public events and listened in the audience as Cromwell talked about Ernesto. In our home, we served them the Chilean red wine Cromwell favored, and talked of politics, music, and their travels.

Slim, skin ivory under an elegant black bouffant, Carmen Rosa loved Ernest with the intensity mothers seem to save for their firstborn sons. Against Cromwell's solid and dependable exterior, she was an acute angle, embittered by her loss, but also for that reason implacable. She favored silks and tweeds and heavy perfume. Although I never asked them directly, I had heard that before Ernesto "disappeared," they had separated. But common purpose rekindled their marriage. Over our Chinese banquet, Cromwell looked at her with admiration. While he had mastered the intricate legal issues of the case, Carmen Rosa's memory for each slight they had suffered, each betrayal, lie, half-truth, provocation, double cross, and slander, was stored in exact detail for future use.

On our table, Cromwell had laid an envelope containing the latest news. He waited until the waiter cleared the platters—keeping them level so as not to drip the sauces pooled there—to open it and pull out a sheaf of papers copied and collated with his accountant's eye for order. Over that dinner in 1993, the Castillos told me of their preparations to take Ernesto's case before the Inter-American Court in San José, Costa Rica, the forum of last resort, where Cromwell and Carmen Rosa hoped to find justice. For them, that meant acknowledgment by the Peruvian government and the prosecution of those responsible for their son's "disappearance."

Many Peruvians, even some who lost a loved one in a similar way, disapproved of their quest. What's done is done, the reasoning went. The Castillos pretty much knew what happened to their son. No Peruvian seriously doubted that such things happened. But it was time to think about the future, not the past, they might say. Since the 1970s this debate has taken place in Argentina, Chile, Uruguay, El Salvador, Guatemala, Brazil, and South Africa. Despite the protest of some victims and their families, all these countries have chosen more or less direct paths to something less than justice, either through amnesties for convicted murderers, as in Argentina, or investigations that from the outset are limited to what has become known as truth-telling, the acknowledgment of what happened, but without prosecution and punishment.

For Chilean lawyer and human rights activist José Zalaquett, author of the introduction to Chile's Rettig report, which chronicled five years of Gen. Augusto Pinochet's murderous rule, far from a fatal falling away from what is good and right, truth-telling without punishment can be what he calls "a less striking form of courage. It is the courage to forgo easy righteousness, to learn how to live with real-life restrictions."

Among those restrictions is the fact that the abusers—the officers and government officials who condoned and carried out human rights crimes—remain at their posts, in their neighborhoods, at their churches, and in the markets where they can in the space of a breath cross paths with the Castillos and wish them good morning. By the mango cart, for example, or haggling for a fresh snapper from the fish stand.

Such learning, however, does not tempt Cromwell and Carmen Rosa Castillo. As I sat in the Chinese restaurant, thinking of their lost boy, I remembered a story from my childhood, the one about the magical monkey's paw delivered to the elderly couple who had lost a son and for that reason lived out their lives in grief and longing for what might have been. The paw grants two wishes. So they wish for their son. And soon, outside their door, they hear the dragging step of their son's corpse. Realizing their terrible mistake, the father grabs the paw and uses that last wish to send his son back to the grave.

But I know that if Cromwell had the magic spell, that bony paw that would reconjure Ernesto, he would use it, I'm sure of it, if only to see and touch his boy once more and knowing the truth take careful note so that, with eyewitness testimony, time cards, radio transcripts, ballistics tests, and his son's own words he could build the cage brick by brick and bar by bar that would imprison Ernesto's killers.

ERNESTO HAD NOT registered in 1990 at the university, where he was a sociology major. According to Cromwell, he wanted to take time off, figure out where he was headed. For a twenty-two-year-old, raised in comfort but increasingly aware of the precarious nature of his family's security, it was a hard time to concentrate on school. A year earlier, Ernesto's cousin, Abel, had been arrested by police and killed, apparently shackled before being blown up with dynamite. Cromwell and Carmen Rosa said they did not know if Abel had ties to the Shining Path. But his violent death shocked Ernesto, who considered him a brother. After the Fujishock, the food of necessity for poor city dwellers appeared to be Sublimes, chocolate squares sold out of crates for less than a dime. Meanwhile, a drought in southern Peru sent farmers to the highways to sell to passing motorists stock slaughtered before it died of hunger and thirst.

As I wrote in my journal in August, "The real story is shock and resignation. This is a post-disaster nightmare, where the blizzard, hurricane, or earthquake has occurred, but no international aid has arrived or will ever arrive. August is the month of winds in Lima. Kite makers hang up their cellophane and wood creations at intersections while peasant women mill in traffic hawking their sheep and llamas." The universities were packed with students, but those few who managed to survive employee strikes, the astronomical cost of books, and occasionally murderous fights between the Shining Path and other political groups on campus knew that no jobs awaited them upon graduation.

As the Shining Path moved increasingly to urban Peru, especially Lima, there was serious talk of a guerrilla takeover. Though improbable, it had edged within the realm of possibility. The press flocked to one shantytown known as La Raucana, run by the Shining Path but hidden only, apparently, to government eyes. The rest of us checked in with the guard at the opening in the wall of what had once been a stock yard, and got a guided tour of the New Society of Maoist harmony under the watchful eyes of sentries posted in towers set into each corner of the wall.

One night about that time I treated myself to an American movie, *When Harry Met Sally*. As I walked to the theater, the winter fog was lowering, soon to become the misty drizzle Limans call *llovizna*. It was almost empty, since few could afford the ticket. Besides, going to movies in Peru could be frustrating. The projectors often stopped because of power rationing or the film itself snapped or an entirely different movie from the one advertised was shown or the original movie was presented in a jumble of reels that made even the most trivial of stories a postmodern collage.

When Harry Met Sally went on normally for about an hour. To my eye, trained to pauperous Lima, the actors seemed amazingly clean and well fed as they fell in love in the brilliant glow of New England autumn. Then the floor of the theater trembled slightly. With a second's delay, I heard a distant bomb explode. The projector light dimmed, then regained force, then dimmed again and winked out. Other bombs, simultaneous but miles away, had exploded beneath the high-tension towers that supply Lima. With the fluctuation in the light, I could sense their swaying motion before crashing to the ground. Groaning, the other moviegoers fumbled for their coats in the perfect darkness.

The *susto*—fright—stayed with me, and I took a moment to catch my breath. A good fright, like a bruise, takes time to fade.

Outside, all was dark save for the headlights of the cars and Lima's one ritzy ice cream parlor, Quattro D, patronized by the few wealthy families who hadn't left for Miami. Its lime-green-and-cream walls glowed in the mist, gas generator growling like a spaceship. I crossed the street to avoid the police station where young men rattled their guns nervously. School girls screamed, whether giddy or afraid I couldn't tell. Although I had planned to buy bread, the store near my home had barred its doors. Ski-masked guards with pump-action shotguns crouched on the roof. Bread, I concluded, could wait for morning.

PHOTOS OF ERNESTO taken at about this time show a chubby youth with square-framed glasses under heavy brows and a knowing smile that is all Carmen Rosa. The way Cromwell tells it, he was not a rebellious child. While his sister, Mónica, was good at math and science, Ernesto liked people. Outgoing, Ernesto kept up with his university friends even though he was not enrolled that term. He told his parents he was off to see a friend the day he vanished.

Limans call October the *mes morada,* the purple month, since it is during this month that the devout parade the purple-clad Lord of Miracles through the streets. But the Shining Path had turned it red. On October 21, police reported more than two thousand arrests, many tied to a Shining Path march in Villa El Salvador, a huge expanse of buildings and shanties that is part of greater Lima. Carrying red hammer-and-sickle flags and setting off homemade explosives, youths had filled the streets and shouted slogans in support of armed struggle. A call went out to police, who had mounted a dragnet by 11 A.M.

That Sunday, Ernest, as Carmen Rosa calls him, had left home early. He promised to return for Mónica's birthday party that afternoon. Night fell. Ernest didn't call. Near midnight, an anonymous caller told Carmen Rosa that her son had been arrested in Villa El Salvador.

For four days, the Castillos searched. They went to the morgue and the hospitals and the police holding cells, at least the ones they were allowed to see. With Ernesto's college friends, they scoured Villa El

Salvador for witnesses. On October 25, the Castillos submitted a writ of habeas corpus to a judge. If determined to have foundation in fact, a writ gives the judge the authority to demand that the state produce a detainee immediately and investigate the illegal arrest. Although writs were frequently submitted by anxious families, not a single one had been approved by a judge since the war began.

Moved by the Castillo's plight, Judge Eva Greta Minaya drove to the police station and requested the detainee registry, which is filled out by hand. The duty officer told her it could not be found. When Judge Minaya demanded it, she was told that the statistics department had taken it without notifying the station chief. When she finally tracked down the registry, she discovered that the last page, the page corresponding to the day Ernesto had vanished, had been torn out and replaced with a poor photocopy. The name Ernesto Castillo did not appear there. She declared the writ of habeas corpus founded and ordered Ernesto to be delivered to her immediately.

Nothing happened. The habeas corpus, which held the then-interior minister, who oversees the police, responsible for producing Ernesto, was ignored. Although the Castillos continued to litigate on the government's inaction, the basis of their international case, the hope they guarded for finding Ernesto alive dwindled as the days passed. By mid-November, their lawyer, Augusto Zúñiga, took them aside. "Do you think Ernesto is alive?" he asked them gently. "Ernesto is not alive," he said. Zúñiga's wife, who had a friend married to a police officer close to the case, had passed along the news.

It is a moment that has come to many families. Tenacious hope winks into a pearl-gray nothing. What happened? In a secret jail, the guards, the routine, the very walls tell the prisoner that he is nothing. A "disappearance" makes it so. Carmen Rosa refused to move a single book or paper from Ernesto's room, as if to somehow anchor him there. And it was at Ernesto's desk that Cromwell began to write the letters and assemble the notes and devise the strategy he hoped would snare Ernesto's killers.

Augusto Zúñiga was the centerpiece of the strategy. Zúñiga had successfully prosecuted fourteen policemen for massacring peasants in Soccos, Ayacucho, in 1984, one of only a handful of cases where security force members were held responsible for murdering civilians. In

1986 he worked with a team to prosecute the navy and police for killing three hundred prisoners and "disappearing" some thirty more after an uprising at two Lima prisons. In 1995 the Inter-American Court ordered the Peruvian government to pay "just compensation" to some of the victims' families.

Hours spent smoking over the thousands of typewritten pages that constitute a legal case in Peru gave Zúñiga's skin a yellowish cast. He favored European-style double-breasted suits, quite a contrast to the off-the-rack polyester bell-bottoms worn by most of his colleagues. His rectangular face, heavy jaw under a lifting horizon of forehead, generally wore an expression of frank appraisal, neither friendly nor excessively reserved. Although a stocky man, Zúñiga's fastidious manner lent a liquid quickness to his frame heightened by the two large and pale eyes that floated behind thick glasses.

When I first met Zúñiga years before Ernesto "disappeared," I found him cold and fussy. This impression was heightened by his penguin-like walk, chest thrust forward as if to display downy plumage. How could anyone, I wondered, trust that justice could be wrung out of Peruvian law? Peru's courts follow the Napoleonic model, where judges investigate, hear, and rule on cases without juries. While this model has its merits elsewhere, in Peru, poorly paid and poorly educated justices fall easy prey to political pressure and graft. Peruvian lawyers often begin work on a case by applying vara, direct influence on a judge. Honest judges, like Judge Minaya, can be found. But they sparkle like supernovas in the surrounding darkness. It could certainly be said that the interests of the rich and powerful tend to prevail in most courts. In Peru, it seemed a certainty.

Cases against the security forces were especially difficult to win. Peruvian law is divided into two jurisdictions, or *fueros:* one for civilians, and one for members of the police and military. Unlike the U.S. system, where the People, represented by district attorneys, argue against the accused, in Peru, security force officers enjoy the government's protection, and civilians investigate and prosecute them using their own wits and resources. Military tribunals hear cases against the security forces even when off-duty officers are accused of common crimes like murder or rape, although these crimes are not included in the military penal code, which is restricted to "negligence" and "abuse of authority." The result of these courts martial is usually cover-up and impunity.

Except Soccos. When Zúñiga recounted his long court battle to me, he allowed himself a slight upturning of the mouth, not a smile exactly but a sign of savored triumph. Perhaps it was because the victims had been at a birthday party, perhaps because it involved police, beneath the military in the hierarchy of force and therefore more vulnerable to civilian pressure. After their drunken attempt to join in the party was rebuffed, the enraged officers arrested the party-goers, beat, interrogated, and killed some of them, then marched the survivors to a gorge where they were shot, thrown from a cliff, and dynamited. Forty-seven men, women and children perished.

In his office, Zúñiga took pleasure in examining the various threads of his victory much as a chemist would review a particularly elegant distillation. Fourteen officers received suspended sentences of between three months to a year, although all remained on active duty. While the punishment may seem light, the mere fact that it existed is remarkable. The odds had been against him and he had won. The same challenge drew him to the Castillos.

To find Ernesto's killers, Zúñiga and the Castillos began with the morning of October 21. Since the police themselves would not investigate Ernesto's "disappearance"—rare is the officer who will work a case perceived as political or damaging to the force—they became sleuths, distributing photos, interviewing potential witnesses, checking out anonymous telephone tips. Every weekend, the Castillos went to Villa El Salvador. Friends of friends in the police force asked about the police station.

Tips led them to a street fronting a concrete-block house. After the Castillos returned to the spot several times and won the trust of a young woman who lived there, she told them that a youth fitting Ernesto's description had been stopped by police that Sunday beneath her living room window. They had forced him into the trunk of a patrol car. Eventually, the Castillos collected the testimony of seven eyewitnesses who claimed to have seen the same thing.

Just as they had with Judge Minaya, police denied to the Castillos ever seeing or arresting Ernesto. But a police friend of Zúñiga's told him in confidence that a curious procedure was often followed at these stations. When suspected guerrillas were brought in, a few were immediately commandeered by specialized police units. Unlike the prisoners who remained at the station to be registered and interrogated, these individuals were taken away. Zúñiga knew that despite a decade of brutal war, in which guerrillas routinely ambushed police or dragged them off public buses to shoot them, a low-ranking officer still did not have the power to circumvent procedure so blatantly. Somebody had to give an order. Usually, the local police station commander was in charge. That morning, however, Zúñiga discovered that a higher-ranking officer had been monitoring the frequency used to send the first reports of a Shining Path march. By the time Ernesto was pulled from the trunk, the officer in charge of the operation was Juan Carlos Mejía.

Mejía was a minor celebrity within the police force. In charge of an obscure branch called the Special Assault Forces Training Center (CEFEA), Mejía considered himself an antiguerrilla specialist. His fame, however, came from bombs. He was an expert in explosives, lit with a match or rigged to detonate with the lifting of a telephone receiver.

To bolster their argument that police had never arrested Ernesto, the Interior Ministry released their version of the operation mounted after the first reports of Shining Path activity were broadcast. Seeking to prove that no one by Ernesto's name was in custody, they inadvertently conceded a crucial fact: that morning, Mejía had taken charge of the hunt for Shining Path militants. He had been cruising Lima with three CEFEA officers. When reports of the march crackled through, Mejía ordered all detainees to be taken to Villa María del Triunfo.

Reporters who later interviewed police officers present that morning were told that when Mejía arrived, Ernesto was just being pulled from the trunk. Mejía was impossible to miss. Burly and bullnecked, he favored green camouflage even while working Lima's brown desert streets. Already well *abollado* (literally, dented), Ernesto's glasses were gone and one eye was swollen shut. Because police attempted to hide the registry from Judge Minaya, Zúñiga believes his name was noted down. Mejía grabbed Ernesto by the collar and shoved him into his pickup truck.

From there, the trail grows dim. Ernesto may have been taken to CEFEA headquarters. A CEFEA officer later told journalists he saw a man fitting Ernesto's description brought inside. He "heard" the interrogation, which apparently lasted through the night. Other officers, the man recounted, later told him that at dawn, the man had been taken from the building and loaded into a pickup. Although the CEFEA officer did not witness the departure or what happened next, he said he was told that they took the prisoner to a beach south of Lima, where he was blown up with four sticks of dynamite.

ALL THIS, THE Castillos knew within a month of Ernesto's "disappearance." Still, walking the streets of Lima or driving their sea-green sedan, Carmen Rosa told me she has seen Ernesto's ghost. Once, Cromwell's sister says her car hit a young man of Ernesto's size and complexion. But when she searched the pavement where the collision had to have occurred, there was nothing there but air. One morning, a woman came to the Castillo's house to thank them for saving her son. The infant had been on the brink of death until she prayed to the spirit of Ernesto, whom she had read about in the newspaper.

At first, the Castillo's telephone was constantly busy. Friends called, reporters called, Ernesto's college friends called. Tips seemed to come in thematic groups. One week was for reports of bodies found resembling Ernesto; another week was for secluded spots at the beach rumored to be still in use by police to kill their prisoners. Together, they viewed corpses, sifted beach sand for bone fragments. It was the government's staunch position, voiced by the interior minister, that Ernesto had simply gone underground to practice terrorism full-time. According to the minister, the death of Abel, Ernesto's cousin, confirmed Ernesto's and therefore his family's allegiance to the Shining Path. The government openly described its new antiguerrilla policy as "intelligent repression"—identifying the bad guys and eliminating them, without harming the innocent.

When Cromwell went on television to talk about his son, as he did frequently in those days, he addressed the minister directly. He did not believe his son was a guerrilla. But if Ernesto was a guerrilla, Cromwell said, then it was the government's responsibility to capture and prosecute him, not "disappear" him.

It was a simple argument, and to me compelling. Nevertheless, in Peru, it had the effect of an admission of Ernesto's guilt and a justification of what had happened to him. In this, the case became like hundreds of other "disappearances," where the mere fact that an individual had been "disappeared" convicted them in the public eye. After expressing regret and agreeing that by all accounts this unsavory police officer Mejía had done away with Ernesto, people I knew would pause and consider and then comment to me that they had privileged information about the Castillo family, that Ernesto was not really a student, that indeed it was just possible that to protect his dear parents he had left them in the dark about his plans to train at a secret camp where he had won a command in the People's Army, was dispatched to a mountain base, and killed in action. "Por algo será," they would say, it's for something.

In Peru, these types of stories are called *bolas*. They abound in politics and business. Their abundance of known facts and air of insider knowledge is seductive. In Ernesto's case, however, since I knew how far Zúñiga and the Castillos had advanced in their investigation, I perceived the degree to which this bola was fed by wishful thinking. Assuming the parents had been misled by a rebellious child, that they were acting out of love but were tragically misled, was a more comforting, reasonable narrative than boy is murdered and the crime is covered up by dozens of policemen, judges, and government ministers. Like the best bolas, this one hitched a logical assumption—that despite his parents' denials, Ernesto was involved with the Shining Path and had been grabbed that morning as he fled the police sweep—with a neat conclusion that absolved everyone of blame.

Perhaps something unique about Peru's conflict made this progression of event to bola so common, more so, say, than in Argentina during the dirty war or in Pinochet's Chile. But I suspect not. Wherever a government presides over atrocities, even on a grand scale, the majority can for a very long time convince themselves that the system is incapable of such extreme behavior. At the very least, victims must in some way deserve their fate or have a role in shaping it. Daily evidence is overlooked. Plentiful examples are explained away as isolated incidents or simply go unexplained, like the first ebb of Jews to the east under the Nazis. Bolas become self-fulfilling and circular. And, like an amulet, they appear to protect those who perpetuate them from a similar fate.

While the U.S. embassy officials I talked to acknowledged that human rights were a problem, they insisted that sanctions—a tougher stance, a cutoff of military aid—would be counterproductive. "Constructive engagement," a phrase used to describe U.S. policy on South Africa during apartheid and, more recently, on China, was the one they chose for Peru.

Zúñiga chose to attack on two fronts. He litigated on the habeas corpus, illegally ignored. But he was pessimistic about success, since few writs are ever honored in Peru. So he began a second case based on an event no one could dispute: the "abuse of authority" committed by high officials when police failed to provide Judge Minaya with the registry book. In press interviews, Zúñiga laid out his strategy in great detail. Given that it depended in equal measure on the legal code as written and the irrationality of political pressure, graft, fear, and pure venality at play in the courts, I found it difficult to follow. Zúñiga appeared to have meticulously weighed and measured each element and, like a roulette player with an unbeatable system, was walking directly to the big stakes table under the pit boss's alerted eye. It was his way, I supposed at the time, to show the government that they would have to go to great and perhaps damaging lengths to continue to protect Mejía and his superiors.

A superior court upheld the habeas corpus, forcing the government to appeal to the supreme court. The government's argument before these four justices was pure legalese: witnesses to Ernesto's arrest had not provided Judge Minaya with their addresses or identification card numbers. Zúñiga pointed out that this afforded them a certain protection from police retaliation. But the government countered that this procedural anomaly should invalidate the case, in effect freeing the police from having to account for Ernesto.

Before the justices on February 1, Zúñiga argued that police had made a laughable attempt to doctor the registry book. Furthermore, they had made no attempt to investigate that day's events. A report submitted by the Interior Ministry had not even managed to spell Ernesto's name correctly.

Zúñiga's knowledge of the law was formidable. The fact that he was impassioned must have rankled the justices, who probably knew even then that regardless of what he said they would vote in the government's favor. Where did this passion come from, they must have wondered, if the dead boy was just another terrorist? Was Zúñiga a terrorist? Was he Ernesto's terrorist godfather?

Before Zúñiga began his formal statement, all of this must have been visible to him, the play of impatience and lunch on their faces. Zúñiga recorded the remarks he addressed to the chief justice. First, he reviewed his work on Soccos, a man tortured in Cusco, and a "disappeared" journalist. Then he described the telephone death threats he had been receiving, "The first time," he said, "that I have received a direct threat against me and against my family."

This theme quickly exhausted the patience of the chief justice. Interrupting, he promised to order the interior minister to protect Zúñiga.

Weeks passed. Cromwell checked in frequently at the Palace of Justice to see if the court had ruled. Once, a clerk pulled him aside to remind him that the government prosecutor, known for his zeal in prosecuting terrorism cases, was handling this personally. "Don't expect too much," the man told Cromwell.

ON THE MORNING OF March 15, 1991, I was working at home, not far from Zúñiga's office. It was a balmy day, the end of southern hemisphere summer and already cool and misty in the late afternoons. My radio was tuned to the all-news station. I might have actually heard the explosion, since I remember listening to the news broadcast to find out which ministry or bank had been bombed. The breathless voice of the Radioprogramas Mobile Unit reporter broke into the quarter-hour news summary. A bomb had exploded at a neighborhood office. It was Zúñiga.

I ran across the Plaza Cáceres, where nannies with their charges had staked out the sun patches. When I turned onto the Campo de Marte, Lima's weedy Central Park, I could see cars and whirling lights. An hour earlier, a light-skinned woman with brown hair had gotten out of a black Toyota with smoked windows to deliver a legal-size envelope to the doorman. With deference, since she was clearly upper class, the doorman had received the package without requiring identification. He delivered it immediately to Zúñiga, just finishing a meeting and sipping coffee in his first-floor office.

Zúñiga was curious. He unfastened the staples and opened the paper mouth. One hand reached inside to tug at the contents. Too late to be called a premonition, he dropped the envelope. The bomb detonated.

That last bit of caution may have saved his life. Standing in the lobby, his assistant thought the explosion was outside and went to check. When he ran back, Zúñiga was still standing, in a room that had become the antithesis of everything legal and ordered he had ever defended. There was a black and smoking crater in the desk. Wall hangings were in ragged heaps on the floor. His books and papers were shredded. Somehow, Zúñiga managed to walk outside, leaving a trail of blood to the spot on the sidewalk where a coworker was hailing a taxi.

Until then, the letter-bomb had been unknown in Peru. But no one doubted the authorship of this missive. It was Mejía. When I reached the office, a lone policeman interviewed the receptionist. Cromwell was there, dazed. He had come to deliver documents. After speaking with the reporters who had begun to arrive, he wandered off, the documents still under his arm. When the coworker who had accompanied Zúñiga to the hospital returned, she brought the news that he was alive, but had lost his left arm. As she stepped into the building, I saw how the bright lights of the television cameras whirled to pin her in the doorway, her shirt brilliant white splattered with a red that could still be called damp, proof to someone watching that their day's labor had not been in vain.

AT THE TIME, news of the attack on Zúñiga was overshadowed by other tragedies. Cholera had broken out in Peru, product of the economic collapse. Whether it had arrived by ship, plane, or bus, no one knew. But within a month of the first outbreak in Chimbote, on the northern coast, thousands of people were infected. Although cholera is not a difficult disease to cure, many died, ignorant of how they had contracted it and too poor to get prompt treatment.

But the attack on Zúñiga did affect human rights workers. Kevin, a Christian Brother from Brooklyn who had lived in Peru for twenty years, began to lean to the left when he started his car, in anticipation of a car bomb. He directed a prominent human rights group, and though he rarely represented the group in public, one of his colleagues was usually making a stir over one case or another. So Kevin leaned.

"If I lean," he told me once, "with the door slightly open, chances are that the force of the blast will push me back and out of the car rather than against the seat. Otherwise, it will rip my balls off."

FIVE DAYS AFTER the attack on Zúñiga, the supreme court voided the writ of habeas corpus. When questioned about the protection the court had promised Zúñiga, the chief justice snapped that Zúñiga had never requested it in writing.

From his hospital bed, Zúñiga told Cromwell and Carmen Rosa he would remain on the case. But once recovered, he and his family flew to Sweden, where he was fitted for a prosthetic arm. The case was shifted to another lawyer who worked with a different human rights group. Yet the new lawyer seemed unwilling to pursue the case aggressively. Expenses were cutting into the Castillo's only source of income, the small paper-supply business that Cromwell had been forced to move into their home. When speaking of the case, Cromwell's tone became increasingly angry.

At about that time, the Castillos took part in a gathering of other families of the "disappeared" at La Recoleta, a stone church set on an oddly shaped plaza in downtown Lima. The plaza was home to a pack of winos, muggers and young pickpockets, who had glazed its granite base with their urine. As we gathered at the wooden doors, two of them began to fight with broken glass. The priest who had agreed to let the families use the nave for a ceremony to honor their lost family members had failed to notify the priest giving mass that morning, so we were shown instead to a side room, fragrant from the carnations and sprigs of rosemary left from a wedding.

Cromwell spoke, Carmen Rosa beside him. They looked physically diminished. For the first time in public, I saw Cromwell weep. These had been difficult months, for a parent difficult beyond imagining. The poor families gathered there also knew loss. Yet despite the gulf of privilege separating them from the Castillos, they listened with compassion. Grief was something they had no trouble understanding. Once, Cromwell had put great store in his *vinculaciones*, his connections. But they had served for naught. Once he had hoped to ease their way. Now, he had lost his own.

IN ONE INTERVIEW I did on human rights, an activist told me in hushed tones that thousands of bodies had been buried by the navy in the Huanta soccer stadium. A man who claimed to have escaped a torture center in Apurímac described prisoners drowned in vats of filth. Several times, I was promised evidence of crematoriums operating at Ayacucho's Los Cabitos army base, but it never arrived. Once, I was told that the smokestack of the burning chambers were visible from the airport's second-floor lounge. But there was no second-floor lounge at the airport.

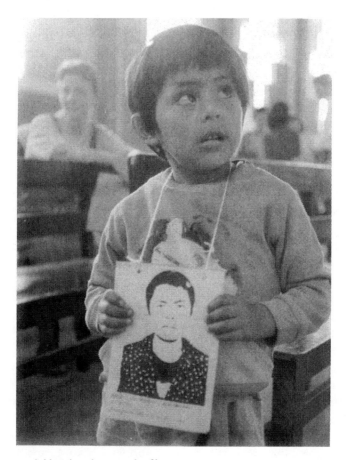

A Peruvian child with a photograph of his
"disappeared" father. © Robin Kirk

In Lima, the scandal sheets published reports of a *descuartizador*, a dismemberer, plaguing the shanty towns. Initially, I dismissed the story as fiction. But then I thought: and what of Mejía? How does a police colonel rid himself of the bodies left in his wake, taken apart by his explosives, perhaps, but there, in pieces, possible to find. What exactly does he do to tidy up? Later, however, I learned that the descuartizador had been identified as a doctor who bagged and dumped the bodies of women who had died from botched abortions.

Once, a student told me he had been tortured for a week in the Los

Cabitos barracks. I took notes. Then, he rolled up his sleeve and I saw the mauve scars left from the handcuffs, the iron ovals of chain as distinct as if they had been pressed in cold butter.

SEVERAL DAYS AFTER the gathering, Ernesto's case took a spectacular turn. During a rash of guerrilla attacks in Lima, police gave chase to a stolen car believed to have been used in a robbery. Police shot the driver in a middle-class neighborhood in Callao, Lima's port. Although police knew the man was probably a thief, not a guerrilla, they began a sweep for suspected subversives, much as they had done the morning Ernesto "disappeared." One of the men they stopped was Carlos Rodríguez Pighi, a medical student who had been walking to his girl-friend's house. Also stopped were two minors, Emilio and Rafael Gómez Puquillauri. Every day, the two boys walked to their mother's corner stand, where they picked up lunch for themselves and their younger siblings. A small suitcase broken open to reveal empty lunch containers was left at the spot where they had encountered the police.

By chance, a Channel 5 news crew had filmed the Gómez's arrest, capturing the face of Emilio just as he was shut into the trunk of the patrol car, its license clearly visible. Watching the video later, Cromwell found it almost unbearable. It was like getting a glimpse of Ernesto again, across a gulf of fear and foreboding that none of his efforts as a father had bridged. Another reporter was present during Rodríguez's arrest, though it was not filmed. When Rodríguez attempted to prove to police that he was just a passerby, the reporter said he was kicked unconscious. By afternoon, the three had been shot execution style and reported as terrorists killed in action.

This time, the eyewitnesses weren't local residents who had witnessed an arrest, but television newsmen who had film to back up their story. Two days later, the officers involved were arrested. One, the driver of the patrol car that had carried Rodríguez, later confessed. Officer José Infante Quiroz told the magazine Sí that an order in code came over the radio from Infante's superior, a major, as they left the arrest site.

"DX109 en DX24!" the major said. It meant "Kill them immediately."

The three police officers drove to the beach. There, Rodríguez was shot three times. Infante told the Sí reporters that Rodríguez didn't die immediately, but agonized in the car as they drove to the police station.

A march protesting the police murders
of Carlos Rodríguez and Emilio and Rafael
Gómez Puquillauri. © Orin Starn

In the garage, an officer pulled him out of the back seat and shot him a fourth time in the head as others watched. Rodríguez's body was loaded back into the patrol car and driven to a hospital.

For Cromwell, the incident became one more element to support the theory that Ernesto had been executed soon after his arrest. Clearly, this was police practice. They even had a code for it! And the officers had responded to the order immediately, with an assurance that seemed to speak of long practice. Their counterparts, with the two Gómez brothers in custody, had acted just as openly, ignoring the fact that the brothers' detention as well as their faces and the license plate of the patrol car had been filmed.

Cromwell and Rosa visited Rodríguez's father and the Gómez parents. They appeared with them at public events to demand justice. For a while, Ernesto's face appeared again in the newspapers. But Rodríguez's father was luckier, if it can be called luck, than the Castillos. His Callao neighbors, horrified, sponsored a protest march that attracted hundreds of people. Their lawyer successfully argued that the police should be tried in civil, not military court, up to then the rule for police officers implicated in abuses. Probably, the existence of the video played a role in fortifying the civilian courts in their bid to hear the case. Also important was the fact that none of the men charged held a rank higher than the equivalent of a U.S. beat cop. Eventually, five officers were convicted of manslaughter. The officers who gave the coded order were dismissed from the force, but never brought to trial.

BY THE YEAR anniversary of Ernesto's "disappearance," the case was at a virtual standstill. Meanwhile, the Castillos were increasingly worried about their daughter, Mónica, eighteen at the time of Ernesto's "disappearance." After going public with Ernesto's case, they had received telephone death threats. But they never talked of them publicly, for fear of scaring off witnesses. Yet Cromwell and Carmen Rosa knew that they were real. By grabbing Mónica, Mejía could shut them up for good.

Within a few weeks of Ernesto's "disappearance," the Castillos sent Mónica to Sweden, where she applied for political asylum. Yet even though her case might seem compelling, as far as the Swedes were concerned, she had received no direct threats and so was in no danger. As Cromwell told it, Mónica became desperate to bolster her claim. Other Peruvians she met at the offices of the Immigration Board counseled her to spice up her claim, give the Swedes something more tangible, yet something that, put in the scheme of things, wouldn't seem serious. Without first consulting her parents (such things were impossible to discuss over the telephone, which Cromwell believed was tapped), Mónica told her interviewer that she had distributed literature on campus for a group sympathetic to the Shining Path. Like her brother, Mónica studied at the Catholic University, and it was there that she set her deception, a kind of bola, really, something that, laced into a set of circumstances that were commonly held to be true about Peru, wouldn't awaken the least doubt.

At first, it seemed to work. Her case was accepted for review. When Cromwell visited several weeks later and learned what she had done, rather than feel angry or upset, he said he felt like he had failed his only child.

Mónica learned Swedish and resumed her engineering studies. Then the consequences of her bola began to unfold. A newly conservative parliament voted to restrict Sweden's asylum policy, one of the most liberal in the world. Instead of breezing through, Mónica's application stalled. Suddenly, there was talk of a denial and deportation to Peru. Through their Swedish lawyer, Cromwell and Carmen Rosa asked the Immigration Board to accept a revision of her statement. But the Swedes appeared intractable. In 1993 Mónica's application was denied. She went into hiding. Her lawyer mounted a media campaign to get the immigration service to reverse its decision on appeal.

The possibility that Mónica would be deported from Sweden to Peru kept Cromwell and Rosa in a state of near panic. If she had been deported in 1991 or even early 1992, they would have been able to bustle her from the Lufthansa flight onto a Quito-bound jet, anywhere, really, Santiago or Buenos Aires or Caracas. But in April 1992 President Fujimori had carried out what was later dubbed a "self-coup," suspending the constitution, seizing major media, and closing down the judiciary. Frustrated by a Congress that had attempted to block some of his more authoritarian initiatives to fight guerrillas, Fujimori responded by closing it down.

Fujimori's self-coup ended any hope of gaining justice for Ernesto in Peru. The Castillos' appeal of the supreme court decision, before a last-hope judicial body known as the Constitutional Guarantees Tribunal, was eliminated along with the tribunal itself. Fujimori replaced fired prosecutors and judges with his own appointees. They were given two new laws to prosecute those suspected of supporting guerrillas. The terrorism law made a crime out of "provoking anxiety," "affecting international relations," or seeming to favor or excuse the behavior of suspected guerrillas, called *apología del terrorismo*. For its part, the treason law took justice out of the hands of the courts entirely, diverting those accused of leading guerrilla groups, participating in armed attacks, or teaching guerrilla ideology in schools to military court martial and a life sentence.

Few in Peru, least of all Cromwell and Carmen Rosa, defended Peru's precoup courts. But the new courts provided little more than a rubber stamp for guilty verdicts. Mónica would be no different from any of the hundreds of Peruvians prosecuted on the basis of little more than bolas. Police were given the power to investigate and charge detainees, often holding them secretly until they could force a confession. Although the torture of suspects had long been routine in police stations, during these arrests, which lasted up to a month, people were whipped, near-drowned in filthy water, subjected to electrical shock, raped, told that their spouses or children had been arrested and tortured, deprived of food, water, and light and kept blindfolded.

Once charged, there was no hope of quick release. Suspects were imprisoned alongside convicts and made to mount a defense from prison, where they were subjected to rules harsher than those applied to convicted murderers.

Convictions poured out of the courts: a woman sentenced to twenty years because her sister was a guerrilla leader; twins given twenty years after police entered the house searching for an older brother; a sixteen-year-old sentenced to life for standing guard while others painted guerrilla graffiti. At some point, the Swedes illegally informed the Peruvian government of Mónica's initial claim to have distributed literature sympathetic to the Shining Path, ensuring at least a charge of terrorism and a possible twenty-year sentence. Peru's largest radio network and its most influential daily began circulating bulletins about the imminent deportation of "pro–Shining Path" Mónica Castillo.

IT WAS AS Cromwell and Carmen Rosa worked furiously to have the Swedish government suspend the order to deport Mónica that Fujimori ordered police to seize the Shining Path prisoners in Castro Castro prison, thus ending their dominion there. The police began with the 130 women in the Shining Trench, where Vera and I had taken our tour.

The women fought back with guns, crude lances, and pots of sulfuric acid. During the worst of the six-day battle, the prisoners hid in tunnels dug under the cell blocks and fortified with King Kong bricks. Via a cellular telephone, they sent progress reports to family members gathered outside.

On the TV screen, the prison looked like a city being shelled. Grenades tossed in holes blasted in the roof made the cell blocks chuff through their vents like mad machines. Police ran hunched and flak-jacket heavy on the roof. They blasted the Peruvian national anthem at earsplitting levels. The women answered with their own shouted anthems to Gonzalo.

More than fifty prisoners died. Three policemen were killed. According to reporters, when police finally forced their way in, they used lists to single out and execute Shining Path leaders, among them Janet Talavera, a former editor of El Diario.

A month later, I visited the women in their new prison, where they had been kept on twenty-four-hour lockdown since the siege. Under

Fujimori's new laws, it was there that Mónica would be taken if she returned to Peru, as a woman charged with supporting the Shining Path. The women had not been allowed to take any belongings, not even a change of clothes. Since so many items had been ripped and bloodstained, each two- and three-woman cell only had enough clothing for one person. The others, waiting their turns, covered their nakedness with a blanket.

Fiorella was there, but I did not see Gloria. I spoke to one prisoner through the cell bars. She spoke in a whisper about the maggoty food, the cold, the lack of water. At night, she said, male policemen would rampage through the halls, banging their night sticks on the bars and screaming insults. She wanted to take my hand, but the female guard, her expression scornful, prohibited any physical contact. This prisoner, I knew, had shot and killed a Peruvian admiral and perhaps others whose names I had never heard spoken aloud.

At their strongest, when I visited them in the Shining Trench, I refused their invitation to dance. If anything, their deeds since, especially the murder of María Elena Moyano, had made them contemptible to me. Yet I would have let her take my hand, for any good it might do. I had no illusions about the feeling that woman had for me—at best, I was a conduit through which her message might reach a sympathetic ear—or the murder she had committed, freely and sound of mind. I felt pity for her, pity beyond my ability to express in words. I was not like them; I was not so strong. And I could pity.

Worse awaited her. From that cell, she and her comrades were taken to Yanamayo Prison, at twelve thousand feet above sea level a frozen, air-deprived labyrinth meant to slowly kill. Much later, I had this thought: at least, Ernesto was spared. Not his parents, for their hell is beyond measure. But Ernesto rests.

Through the bars, our heads almost touched. I kept mine there, though the smell—of her sweat, her rotting teeth, her hot fury—made my eyes twitch and tear. Finally, fed up, the guard pulled me away.

SEVERAL TELEVISION INTERVIEWS seemed to turn the Swedish public in Mónica's favor. There was hope that an international letter-writing campaign would convince the authorities to rescind the deportation order. But the final appeal was denied. At an appointment at the Immigration Board, Mónica was arrested.

Cromwell made anxious plans in Lima. He called friends, journalists, and the human rights groups that had rallied to Ernesto's cause. The moment he learned which flight would return Mónica to Peru, he wanted to summon a crowd to receive her at the airport. With cameras rolling, he hoped to prevent the police from arresting her. Somehow, he would find a way to spirit her out of the country, driving her himself, he thought, or arranging some relay to get her to Chile or Ecuador in time to cross one morning as just another shopper taking advantage of the bargains on the other side of the border.

But the journalists were busy. Friends had left or were not available. None of the human rights groups would commit. Some would not even return his phone calls. Mónica's blunder had revived old suspicions about Ernesto and what exactly he had been doing that morning on the streets of Villa El Salvador. Her bola appeared to confirm the other bola about the family's complicity. And her bola could land her in one of those cells I had seen and that Cromwell and Carmen Rosa refused even to imagine. Their only daughter. Their only surviving child.

Throughout the war, Peru's human rights groups took information about "disappearances" and killings from families they believed had ties to the guerrillas and included it in statistics. But aggressive campaigns to win the freedom of those unjustly convicted were restricted to those they believed were innocent. It was perhaps an intellectually hollow position—after all, militancy in a guerrilla group does not presuppose a forfeiture of basic rights—but also a supremely practical one. With its deliberate use of violence, the Shining Path had aroused among the general population a deep revulsion. While some in the middle class, the class that supplies the employees who work in human rights organizations, acknowledged that profound injustice and inequality had given guerrillas a foothold, the Shining Path itself was viewed as a sect of fanatics, outside the accepted boundaries of revolutionary fervor and therefore shunned. Human rights groups believed—and they were probably right—that to defend equally the rights of all, including the Shining Path, was to effectively forfeit any persuasive power they had with the government or public. Therefore, only the innocents—completely, utterly, without doubt—were defended.

Mónica no longer qualified. The bomb-maker, far from finished with his work, continued to set off small explosions in the Castillos' lives.

The night Mónica was due to arrive, Cromwell alerted his contacts.

Only then did he realize he would be completely alone at the airport. He told me later that as he scanned the arriving passengers for Mónica's face, he felt a great rage. Where was justice that night, he thought. Or simple compassion? By chance, a member of one human rights group arrived on a different flight. The man had not been told of Mónica's arrival. At first he was cordial. But once Cromwell asked him to stay, just half an hour until the passengers on Mónica's flight cleared customs, the man explained that urgent business awaited him that foggy Sunday midnight, pressing commitments, he said. He walked away.

But luck was with Cromwell. The Swedish authorities had refused to tell the Castillos which flight would carry Mónica to Peru. So Carmen Rosa had installed herself and her single suitcase at a spot in the Stockholm airport where she could surveil all the ticket counter agents working South America–bound flights. During those two days, Carmen Rosa bought three full-fare tickets, each time convinced that Mónica was about to board. She even loaded her suitcase on one flight, but refused to board when she saw that Mónica had not come. The furious crew had to return the plane to the gate to unload her suspect luggage.

Finally, Mónica appeared, in the custody of two Swedish policemen. Carmen Rosa called Cromwell, then boarded the same VIASA flight, headed for Amsterdam. There, Mónica would be escorted to a Lima-bound connection. In her carry-on bag, Carmen Rosa kept a can of hair spray, and she planned to spray it in the eyes of the Swedish escorts in Amsterdam to give Mónica a chance to flee her seat and yell the magic words: asylum, asylum.

But such heroics weren't necessary. In Amsterdam, Amnesty International had made arrangements for Dutch police to take Mónica into custody. In the aisle, they granted her humanitarian asylum. For the first time, Carmen Rosa revealed herself as Mónica's mother. They left the airplane arm in arm. As they walked across the tarmac, Carmen Rosa told me later, she felt a great weight lifting from her shoulders. For all the rest of that day, everything—the air, the airport terminal, the skycaps, the taxis, even the office where they signed papers and were greeted with handshakes—seemed arrayed for them, for their enjoyment, special and new.

ALMOST FIVE YEARS after Ernesto's "disappearance," Peru's Congress passed a law granting amnesty to civilians and security force members who had committed human rights violations on the government's behalf from 1980 until the present day. The amnesty included not only the few men convicted of crimes and serving time, but also those who had merely been investigated or whose crimes have yet to come to light. Among them were the killers of Carlos Rodríguez and the Gómez brothers. The amnesty's supporters claimed it was time to forgive and forget, to wipe the slate clean. Critics—the predictable ones, and too few to raise much of a ruckus—said it is not possible to forgive what is not known, to forget what has never been acknowledged.

Ernesto's case was not mentioned in the commentary that followed the amnesty decision. From the front page, his case had faded for most Peruvians into a piece of news they might recall from a time most prefer to forget. The issue of justice for human rights crimes has faded with it. It is now an intensely private fight. No protestors mass at the Government Palace, no politicians champion cases. There are not even any victims' groups to circle tenaciously in Lima's central square, as the Argentine Mothers of the Plaza de Mayo still do. The Castillos press on in a silence that seems almost palpable and complicit in their son's disappearance, as if it were simply waiting for the proper time to pass to begin directing the show.

I would like to think the story of the monkey's paw might serve here as well, that I could say that this willed forgetting is sure to create the evil charm that, once invoked, will return Peru to those grim days of execution, disappearance, and torture. So long as the system that fostered abuse remains in place, the charm can work its dark magic. There is no more pressing issue for Peru's future, I want to say, than addressing the past.

Yet nothing ever seemed predictable to me in Peru. Perhaps the charm will linger. Yet it, like memory, may simply fade.

"One can never accept that only certain crimes merit the truth," Cromwell commented the last time I saw him in Lima. Beside him, Carmen Rosa fingered a cigarette. "This is illogical and immoral. And there is no justice without truth."

But what about divine justice, I wondered, since he had mentioned morality. Had the moral dimension of their loss and quest for justice ever turned them toward religious faith, since their faith in human nature had so betrayed them? It was not a question I felt comfortable asking in the pizzeria where we met most recently, bright and convivial and filled with other prosperous Limans, the Castillos graceful in their element.

I knew that certain questions could provoke a bitterness in Cromwell and in Carmen Rosa, who had only recently recovered a certain relish for talk unrelated to her son's death. Recently, Cromwell confided, a government emissary had offered them ten thousand dollars to drop their case at the Inter-American Court. "I wouldn't accept the entire national budget of Peru," he commented.

At least for the Castillos, there will probably be no completely satisfactory end, even at the court in San José. Although governments fight unfavorable verdicts, no criminal penalties apply. The only real sanction the court can impose is monetary: "just compensation," in court language. Human rights groups have contended that international treaties also include the concept of "reparation." Defined broadly, reparation includes criminal prosecution and public apology. But money and the occasional monument are about all the court has delivered to victims so far. In one 1995 case, the government of Venezuela agreed to pay $375,000 each to the families of fourteen men killed by the army, a bargain by the standards of U.S. litigation.

But the Castillos will take what they can get from the court, since I suspect that shame—in a moral sense, in the sense of the perpetrators recognizing their crime and feeling shame for it—is what money means to them, a way to force the men they believe killed their son, ordered it, and covered it up to own up to what they did and the world's contempt for it.

Just as they will never relinquish justice, so too do the men they seek in Peru appear unwilling to ever admit that what they did was not entirely right, indeed necessary, to protect whatever vision of the nation they share among themselves. When Zúñiga returned to Peru to visit, a reporter asked him if he could forgive the men who had harmed him. "I am willing to forgive," Zúñiga answered, "But I ask Mejía if he is ready to be forgiven. Forgiveness is only effective if the aggressor, not the victim, is willing to be forgiven."

The Castillos and I toasted to the success of their case in Costa Rica. We ate our fill. When it was time to leave, we navigated Lima's streets, sure of our way. No one followed us or took note of our passage or seemed to care about the hour we reached our destination. For all anyone knew, we had become ghosts, cold as fog and as visible.

7

HOME

Big stone, long stone
from the peaks
where I must leave you
you will not fall
you will not be lost
until I return
until I return
once again.

If I return
If I return once again
I promise that I will take you
in my right hand
I tell you that I will steal you
with my right hand.

Mother, I don't want you to cry.
Father, I don't want you to cry.

If I am still alive, I will return
to take with me the blood
that I love,
on the steep paths
of the heights
cradling you, hiding you
within my heart.

Ayacucho huayno

THAT NIGHT, THE night everyone remembers as if it were just yesterday, the men from Purus stiffened themselves with cane liquor before heading out on patrol. Between them, they had five Winchester rifles and a World War II–era Mauser, this last one bought with eight hundred dollars pooled by forty Purus families. The weapons were slim protection against guerrillas armed with AK-47s, which shot further and faster. But the Purus villagers had what they had. Each one had been a refugee, forced from the heights by war. But they had returned. They shared a resolve: no one would again drive them away.

Besides, months had gone by without a sign of guerrillas on the puna. Purus is at the cusp of the Andes, a clutch of mud and straw houses roofed in corrugated tin and straw. At thirteen thousand feet, it is barren and windswept, an unlikely place for human habitation. Even in the blazing sun, the cold penetrates. Hills seared brown surround the broad knob where the dwellings stand, overlooking the Huanta valley as it opens south. Gray-green eucalyptus in the crevasses below and the brilliant blue sky above provide the only variation in color.

Purus is neither the highest nor the last town on these moors. In 1994 refugees from five local communities—Purus, Uchuraccay, Cunya, Marccaraccay, and Ccarhaucc—returned to their homes, in ruins after a decade of fighting. At the end of a just-finished road, Purus has the most people. Every Friday, Purus expands with the vendors who drive up from the valley to trade city goods like salt and kerosene for the potatoes farmers have just begun to replant.

But on that night, the village looked empty. The men had to talk over the wind rattling the roofs. The women and children were in bed, the animals corralled. The only evidence of human habitation were wisps of smoke and the men, little more than wisps themselves against the great bulk of the peaks. Like over four thousand other mountain communities, Purus had a civil defense committee to resist guerrilla attack. The creation of these patrols was among the most controversial and misunderstood stories of the war, and people like me at first discounted them as merely army pawns, fooled into an unpaid, unprovisioned, and largely unarmed force that was little more than cannon fodder. In Guatemala and Colombia, army-linked civil defense wreaked havoc and amplified the state's ability to commit human rights abuses. In Peru, the thinking went, civil defense was the army's perversion of the good and pure patrols of the north, where peasants like those in Tunnel Six fashioned justice out of talk, not bullets.

But no soldiers were there that night in Purus to prod the men from the fire. Eventually, they began their climb above town to a mud-and-straw lookout. There, they planned to refortify themselves with liquor and huddle to await morning. Until the first wink of a flashlight appeared in the distance. No bigger than a dust mote, the light bobbed and swung with the motion of the person carrying it. Another light appeared, then another. By the time the men began to settle above the boulders marking the trail, twenty lights marked the length of la columna approaching Purus.

The guerrillas moved carelessly, perhaps believing the Purus villagers too weak or frightened to mount a challenge. The trail links the Huanta valley to the puna and the jungle beyond, known as Viscatán, where the guerrillas maintain their strongest redoubt. With the new moon, the villagers had no way to gauge how many they faced or the number or type of weapons they carried. Yet they would attack. The time of inaction, of allowing others to determine their fate, had passed. Silently, they took to the crags above the trail. Once the column was below, they struck. Stones came first, a sharp and sudden barrage. The flashlights swung wildly. Bullets ricocheted from the boulders, like a sudden lightning storm. Screams and the scramble of feet on rock drowned out individual voices.

When dawn broke over the moor, the people of Purus looked up in amazement. Not a single Purus man had been killed or even injured. Neither had the guerrillas left behind dead or wounded. But they had abandoned their backpacks and all that they carried: powdered milk, cheese, canned tuna, matches, tools, clothing, flashlights, wicks, oil, a radio, paper, rice, candles, carrots, books, onions, pens, batteries, meat, and even fresh lettuce. The patrol commander smiled broadly as he told me the story, a mischievous, pleased smile. Long black sideburns under the pediment of a tractor cap framed his face. "Comrade Feliciano likes to eat well," he commented, referring to the man who took command after the arrest of Abimael Guzmán in 1992. He patted the blue wool sweater that covered his stomach. "But, thanks to him, after so much suffering, the people of Purus ate like lords."

I WASN'T THERE. By then, Orin and I had returned to the United States. It would please me to say I left willingly, since months earlier I had come to understand that I was not made to live the life of an expatriate. I needed to go home. But the truth is we ran out of money.

The arrest of most Shining Path leaders and the migration of coca cultivation to Colombia meant that few newspapers and magazines were interested in stories. I wasn't willing to write for the business wires. In short, peace ended my Peruvian writing career. Orin was offered a teaching job at a U.S. university and we left. I wept on the flight back. I thought nothing truly interesting would ever happen to me again.

Instead of looking forward, I looked back. I took every opportunity to return. There were stories I wanted to finish, places I had never been. One of them was Purus.

When I left Peru, Purus was still outside the membrane of the Peru considered possible for a foreigner to visit. Barring a special arrangement—like the time Ruth searched out the Shining Path column and met Lydia—meetings between journalists and guerrillas tended to end badly. For them, the idea that journalists were without political bias was absurd. I tended to agree. But they took this conclusion to an extreme, threatening and killing journalists who strayed into their sights after accusing them of being lackeys of a reactionary state.

My writing had drawn special ire from the Shining Path. In one issue of the *Red Flag,* a pro–Shining Path magazine, I had been singled out for vintage Guzmán insults, called a "reactionary feminist," a "rat," a "pseudo-scholar," "an old trafficker of Third World struggles," "filthy," a "villain trafficker," a "pseudo-journalist and human rights trafficker . . . totally reactionary, bourgeois, imperialist, old and rotten."

But the danger wasn't just personal. People I talked to or walked with risked execution later, infected by imperialist cooties. Often, I was mistaken for a nun or missionary. It was no comfort. While most Latin revolutionaries exempt religious workers from attack, the Shining Path seemed to take special relish in killing people they considered emissaries of "the cooperativist fascist" pope and CIA agents working through "nefarious" sects, like the Presbyterians.

So when I first went north out of the city of Huanta on the road to Purus in 1995 and pierced that membrane, I experienced intense anticipation edged in fear. Huanta is both the city and the province surrounding it, which forms the northern extreme of Ayacucho State. The route was a primer on the history of the war: here a wealthy farmer had barricaded himself in his house until guerrillas shot him out; there a police station was blown up and remained abandoned; here a vacant central square marked an infamous massacre. This had been Betty's region and Augusta's, Guzmán's wife. On either side of the road stood abandoned houses, their adobe walls blackened from fire. Some walls had fresh coats of paint. But through it, I could still make out the red graffiti that had once lined the road like billboards hawking revolution.

The road looped up the valley, frequently turning on itself and exposed to any eyes that cared to see. Once, at mobile checkpoints set up along certain stretches, guerrillas had screened travelers against carefully copied-out lists, seizing those marked there for swift execution. Months had passed, I had been told, since the last checkpoint had appeared. Yet I sensed it was not so much that the danger had ceased to exist, but that an absence has been created, a void. As we churned over the ruts and potholes, Robert, the driver, would crane his neck out of the window of his king-cab Toyota pickup to try to glimpse beyond a blind curve. They had been here. Something had happened. His memory marked these spots with more precision than any milestone.

Beside Robert was a humanitarian aid worker, also on his first trip to the heights. Pepe, our guide and an anthropologist who works with returning refugees, was at the passenger window. In the backseat, I was wedged between two of Pepe's students. Adrián, born and raised in Purus and a member of the civil defense patrol, rode in the bed.

As we drove, I noticed that Pepe seemed to know everyone. Pepe is dark, *moreno* in local parlance and with a moreno's cap of black, kinky hair. People always ask him if he is from the coast. When he starts to speak Quechua in front of peasant women who don't know him, their mouths drop open and they look at each other and laugh uproariously. But he is a Huanta boy through and through. He had recently run a spirited, though unsuccessful, campaign for congressional office. Added to his work with refugees, the campaign meant that he had often traveled this route and had helped many of the people to rebuild their homes and farms. From the pickup, he called out names, thumping the door and waving his long arm and giving high fives.

That he knew people in town isn't unusual for a man born and raised in one place. But even beyond the peopled stretch of road, when an hour would pass between that boy leading a donkey and the old woman crouched in the thin shadow of a pole, Pepe would still be calling out names, by then in exuberant Quechua, transforming the seemingly sullen, blank faces I was used to seeing out of car windows throughout Peru into animated ones that reminded me of people I knew.

Internal refugees returning to the Huanta
heights in 1995. © Orin Starn

The humanitarian aid worker and I had come to learn about the return of refugees to the heights. The aid worker kept his questions
pointed and pressed for dollars-and-cents answers: aid received, families
counted, government programs launched. These numbers went into a
spiral notebook that bounced and slithered on his knee. Peru, the aid
worker had already commented, appeared to be pretty mainstream,
refugee-wise. The people forced to flee were never concentrated at one
time or in one place, and as a group went largely unnoticed. Few
Peruvians left the country, so never qualified for international protection or aid as refugees. Instead, they fit into a category called internally
displaced persons, IDPs. Although there are more IDPs in the world
than refugees, he noted, no international treaties protect them, so they
go largely uncounted and unprotected.

What the aid worker found unusual about Peru was the Shining
Path. "I mean," he said to Pepe, "if they are fighting for the peasants,
why did they kill them? Why did they drive them away?"

Pepe thumped on the door, releasing a whoop loud enough to make
a man plowing a field with an ox look up and wave excitedly. Although

I had heard Pepe asked and answer the same question before, he seemed to mull it over, placing his finger perpendicular to his lips. For those with a romantic view of revolution, the Shining Path is a hard pill to swallow. Despite ample evidence that revolutions can devastate the very people supposed to benefit most—China, Russia, Ethiopia, Cambodia—among both Peruvians and Americans on the left, there remained a stubborn assumption, nurtured by the relatively gentle revolutionaries of El Salvador and Nicaragua, that guerrillas by definition protect and help the poor, and are the good guys. It is as if the words themselves—guerrilla, revolution, the people—were coins with constant, intrinsic value.

Pepe began where he always did, with chutos.

"Peasants," Pepe began, "are called *chutos, sallqas,* which mean dirty, savage, pagan, from the puna. This is a great divide we must still cross. Huanta society is deeply divided by race and social class. For instance, although I am a moreno, my family is considered misti, white above the brown."

Although he spoke to a small audience in the confines of the truck, his tone was rounded and deep, built to project to the furthest wall in a drafty classroom. "For instance, the Quechua I learned as a boy is different from the Quechua a chuto speaks. When I slip into chuto Quechua around my mother, she calls me to task and corrects me. Why must I spend so much time with these chutos, she wants to know. After Adrián visits, she cleans the house. My mother has many fine qualities. But some things will not change."

For Pepe, who came of age in the midst of war, the story of violence was as much personal as it was cultural or historical, a product of particular idiosyncrasies, and friendships he witnessed, and people he probably would still recognize if he saw them on the street. In fact, as he told me later, he had seen a cousin of his recently who went underground in the 1970s and just reemerged, thinner now and nervous as a cat. When he threw his arm around her shoulders, as Pepe does, he felt the bones beneath her sweater and smelled sickness and fright on her breath.

At the National University San Cristóbal of Huamanga, where Pepe studied and later taught, colleagues and some students were Shining Path. He read their dissertations and attended their lectures and went to the debates where they faced off against other Marxists, against

Pepe, and hurled the insults that would one day reverberate with the crunch of homemade grenades. When the navy occupied Huanta in 1983, he knew them too, pale Limans who saw little difference between his moreno face and the copper-skinned highlanders. Peru's navy is the most anti-Communist and race-conscious of the armed forces, and draws its officers from the middle- and upper-class descendants of the European families who immigrated to Peru but did not mix with the natives. To the navy, Huanta was Communist, Huanta was brown, and so brown equaled Communist and vice versa. From the stadium, where the navy is said to have buried the "disappeared," hair, no longer straight or moreno, but in tufts, used to tumble down the streets, collecting dust and twigs and banking against the adobe bricks of the locked and shuttered houses.

Pepe also knew the peasants the Shining Path planned to recruit, peasants who had once served his family and the families of his childhood friends, delivering sacks of corn and potatoes and the suckling pigs to the entrance of the house and no further. As a youth, he had taken an interest in them. He learned their names and where they came from, a pursuit his mother viewed with indulgent horror. I would bet she thought he'd grow out of it. He didn't.

Pepe used our route to underscore his answer. To reach Purus, Robert had to take the right-hand fork that begins the final ascent through a narrowing canyon where the town of Chaca and its former estate are located. Chaca overlooks the Chocay-Paqchanqa River, which cuts a surprisingly gentle path through the canyon as it tilts toward the valley below. Protected from the moor wind, Chaca felt almost tropical as we got out to tour the ruins of the estate house.

From the conquest until Velasco's land reform, chutos worked the huge estates that used to dominate rural Peru. The ruins of the Chaca estate house still overlook the town, a panorama that takes in the river and fields and the blue shimmer of the deeper valley beyond. The house was built of fieldstone and roofed in red tile. Arranged in a square around a central patio, the house was distinguished by a graceful arched colonnade that provided an inner ribbon of shade. Each of the rooms had a door connecting it to the next room, creating a breeze that swept through in a continuous, currentlike stream. Owned by the Lama family, the Chaca estate used to include much of the valley as well as the puna around Purus.

"It was here that the whipping would take place," the mayor offered as he swept his arm across the patio. A compact man with a brown, leathered face, he had come from the fields where he was planting potatoes. Although reforms of the estates were periodic, and some of the worst abuses were outlawed before the first conquistadors began to die of old age (a small number, since so many died violently), Chacans remember the Lamas with anger and resentment. "Here they had the stocks, where they would leave you in the full sun without a hat. Women and children, too. They wouldn't even give water."

The Lamas had been forced out by Velasco's land reform. Since then, the estate house has been used as a stable, military garrison, and shelter for itinerant travelers. The last inhabitants had been a Protestant group, the mayor said. Outside the estate house walls, a work crew building a new school was systematically cannibalizing the site for stone. Next to the entrance sat a blackened and rusted tractor, burned by guerrillas early in the war.

It was at Chaca, Pepe said, that Osmán Morote, a Shining Path leader Pepe knew, did research for a master's degree in anthropology in the late 1960s. Morote, Pepe said, was painfully thin, a chain-smoker among peasants who couldn't afford the vice. His father was a professor, and he had been well if strictly educated. Although the Morotes lived in Ayacucho, Osmán spoke no Quechua, relying on interpreters to interview the peasants at Chaca. His hostility toward the Lamas was apparently reciprocated in full by Consuelo, the Lama who met him on the steps of the estate house when he first arrived. Later, Morote recounted his version of their exchange in his thesis: "I already see you coming, you good for nothings, you'll get nowhere with us, guerrillas, we're not dead yet, we own this estate, we work for ourselves, you good-for-nothing communist murderers."

The thesis was unusual even for the heated political standard of the day. On the first page, Morote introduces himself by predicting that other university academics, whom he calls "the preachers of feudal traditionalism, of pro-imperialist servility . . . gorilla intellectuals," will be made to tremble by the class struggle.

"They sharpen their knives," Morote wrote. "So we must also have our knives ready."

Following Guzmán, Morote believed the Huanta heights were semi-feudal and semicolonial. Only a "scientific" Marxist analysis was appropriate to understand the culture. Morote railed against the "bourgeois" professors and students who paid attention instead to outside influences as a source of change, like the construction of a road or the radio. Instead, he argued, the only valid objects of inquiry were the "internal contradictions" created by Chaca's progress on the inevitable march toward Communism. For Morote, the estate system was a mere wheel in a global domination machine. To confront it, Morote wrote, intellectuals were obligated to prepare a "payback" in revolutionary violence.

"But he ignores a crucial fact," Pepe commented as we stood in the ruined patio, the mayor at his side. "A year before his master's thesis was submitted, the government implemented the land reform. The estates were broken up and each family received title to the land. No longer did peasants owe labor or crops. For the first time any of them could remember, they had a legal stake in the land, something that was theirs."

The Shining Path dismissed the reform as a sop, a rearrangement of the old order. True reform, Guzmán insisted, lay in toppling the system and extirpating its remains. His absolutism echoed something of the priest Francisco de Avila, who, as Guamán Poma was writing his letter to King Philip III, combed the mountains around Lima for pre-Conquest idols and mummies to cart to the giant bonfires lit at the steps of Pizarro's palace. Only cleansed by fire, De Avila believed, would Peru be safe for God. Like him, Guzmán and Morote were not chutos but outsiders. And like him, Pepe suggested to me, their radicalism and belief in total destruction rested upon a deep and unacknowledged prejudice about chutos.

For Guzmán, chutos were not equals, but masses that would "overflow," "flood," and "inundate" the enemy on demand, less a human force than a natural phenomenon that could be pooled and directed and worked once the dam of revolution had been erected. In 1983, when Guzmán wanted to demonstrate precisely how far the Shining Path was willing to go to seize power, he used chutos to do it. On April 3, "the masses," as Guzmán called them, fell on the town of Lucanamarca, which had spurned his recruiters. They killed eighty men, women, and children with machetes, clubs, and rocks. "There was an excess," Guzmán allowed years later in the self-proclaimed Interview of the Century with the pro-guerrilla newspaper *El Diario.* "What we needed was for the waters to overflow, for the landslide to appear, sure that when it appears, it devastates, but then returns to the riverbed."

A destroyed farm near Purus.
© Orin Starn

Perhaps, Pepe said, Guzmán didn't want to see that the estates themselves were the frame that made the chutos into such a convenient crowd. In Morote's thesis, not once is an individual other than a Lama named, described, or quoted. For Morote, their identities seemed beside the point. With the reform, though, they put their thumbprints on land deeds, scrawled their names or just a scraggly X on the line that meant owner. "The chutos were no longer just chutos, but the Huamanis, the Silvas, the Mendozas. Their identities were no longer meaningless."

Or perhaps it would seem so now, standing in Pepe's shadow, as he greets and chats and embraces the men and women who contrive to pass by, chutos all. Despite having lived in Peru so many years, these highlands were as foreign to me as Oz. Language was just one barrier. I understood bits of Quechua, but not enough to speak to the women, uniformly monolingual. In a way, I may have seen them as Morote did—exotic, thrilling, even brutal.

A man began tinkering with the charred tractor, trying to pull off a

175

metal plate to cannibalize parts. The mayor shook Pepe's hand vigorously, extracting a promise to return later in the week. The humanitarian worker was wondering about lunch. We rejoined the driver and started on the last climb to Purus.

FOR AS LONG AS anyone has written its history, rebellion and forced flight have been part of Huanta's story. Newly arrived in Cuzco and contemplating expansion, the Incas' first challenge was to overcome the Chankas to the north and west, in what are now the departments of Ayacucho, Apurímac, and Huancavelica. Descendants of the Wari, whose empire had disintegrated around A.D. 1000, the Chankas were a federation known for their own dreams of empire. To the Incas, they may already have been chutos, "savage and brutish" according to one chronicler of the Conquest.

Inca history-telling is famously slippery, reflecting a lack of interest, wrote historian María Rostworowski, in "the supposed *truth* or exact *chronology* of events." It is not clear exactly when the Chankas attacked the Inca capital or who led them. In the version written by Garcilaso de la Vega, son of a conquistador and an Inca noblewoman, the Chankas took advantage of dissension within the royal family to attack the Inca capital at Cuzco in the mid-1400s. Garcilaso was an accomplished storyteller, but a biased one, seeking as he did to highlight Inca nobility by emphasizing the brutishness of their rivals. As he tells it, the Chanka reputation for ferocity convinced the reigning Inca to capitulate without a fight, and he fled with his court.

But one son refused to surrender. Later to take the name Pachacútec, this Inca warrior defeated the Chankas at the city's edge in a battle so bloody that the gorge called Ayahuaicco, Gorge of the Cadavers, bears that name today. Garcilaso claims Pachacútec was hated by his father, who considered him a warmonger, "harsh, unbending, cruel." But in Garcilaso's telling, the son is portrayed as visionary, brave, and regal. To the Spaniards who were Garcilaso's public, themselves just recently victorious over the Moors, such a king was indeed admirable. Pachacútec chased the Chankas north, launching the Incas into an expansion that ended only with Pizarro's arrival in 1531. He made the Chankas he could catch into *mitimaqs*, forced to move north to settle the empire's new holdings. In turn, other mitimaqs, from Cuzco, Lake Titicaca, and the coast, occupied their farms.

The Chankas who managed to remain in present-day Ayacucho sent tribute to Cuzco while awaiting their moment to rebel. It came with the Spanish. Pachacútec's descendants, the brothers Huáscar and Atahualpa, fought over the Inca throne, a civil war that ended with Huáscar's murder and Pizarro's arrival. Atahualpa considered the Chanka his brother's allies and systematically burned their houses, sacked their grain stores, and stole their animals. When news came that Pizarro had captured Atahualpa, then had him garroted, the Chankas greeted the Spanish as liberators. After Manco Inca, another brother, escaped from the Spaniards and led a rebellion, the Huanta highlanders rebuffed his call to arms and harassed his men as they crossed the heights.

Little was written about the Huanta heights again until the Independence War. Peru was among the last of Spain's colonies to embrace Bolívar and his army, which trapped the royalists near Huanta in 1824, defeating them. Ironically—and painfully for latter-day nationalists searching for a Peruvian hero of the Independence—the royalist army was exclusively Peruvian, while the liberators were mostly Colombian and Argentine. Two years later, the chutos rebelled—this time, for the royalists and against the leaders of the new Republic. Although they came from across the heights, they were identified as Iquichans, a village near Purus on the puna's eastern edge.

A Republican soldier described one battle in a letter: "Huge crowds of people organized in parallel lines covered the Arco clearing. The simultaneous, thundering shouts of more than 4,000 Iquichan Cossacks made the land they desired to seize tremble beneath their feet. Reinforcements did not come and the spirits of many of the militia members forced to remain behind the walls began to waver."

After resisting the Inca and helping the Spanish topple their king, why did chutos fight for a monarchy that had shown them only cruelty, want, and disease? For local historians, the answer lay in their chutoness. "[This uprising] is simply a demonstration of their rebellious nature and barbarity," wrote one. "They repeat names and words whose meaning they do not know, and they kill and force others to kill obstinately, which could be called heroic were it not just blind and savage instinct."

But there were other answers. Under the Bourbons, Peru's economy had stalled, and city-based families saw their fortunes diminish, spurring talk of independence from Spain. But highlander villages were "relatively prosperous, relatively stable," according to historian Patrick Husson. Amid the great reshuffling described by Guamán, the chutos gained a certain independence and self-sufficiency missing since their defeat at the hands of Pachacútec.

After independence, however, the Peruvian government levied new taxes, payable in coca leaf, and tried to run community affairs. Peru, wrote historian Pablo Macera, was "a colony without a king, more feudal and like a colony than before." Led by Antonio Huachaca, a chuto who had served the Spanish army, the chutos seized Huanta in 1827. To la indiada, the Indian horde, gathered victoriously at Huanta's central square, Huachaca proclaimed his intention to retake Peru for Spain.

For reasons that remain mysterious, however, Huachaca abandoned his plan, and his army melted back into the puna. Peru's army retaliated by burning puna villages, beheading captured Indians, and staking their heads around the same square where Huachaca had made his proclamation.

Fifty years later, the highlanders rebelled again, this time against taxes levied to finance the army of Andrés Avelino Cáceres against the Chilean invaders. During a battle on the streets of Huanta, the Huamanga bishop was killed, earning the city residents the epithet of "bishop killers." At the time, one scandalized official sputtered: "[these] half-savages . . . only obey authority when it is convenient. . . . Without the force of bayonets, my authority is illusory, and it will always be so if a new conquest is not waged against them so as to replace this indomitable race with a more docile, rational one."

In 1896 the chutos returned to Huanta, this time to protest the new tax on salt, an essential addition to a diet based on potatoes. When their petition to suspend the tax was rebuffed, they massed on the hilltops surrounding the city and fell on it, seizing control. "The Indian rabble has taken possession of Huanta, where they took their revenge with pillage and barbarity," wrote the prefect to the president in Lima. The vice-prefect and mayor were killed.

Almost a century later, the chutos led protests against the government plan to charge a school fee. Protestors again marched on Huanta's central square in 1969. Afterward, a Huanta schoolteacher wrote a song that became an anthem of protest in Peru: "La Flor de

Retama," the Broom Flower. A huayno, "The Broom Flower" describes how the protestors were fired on by police. Stanzas describing the protest are interspersed with praise for the yellow broom flower, said to flourish on bloodstained earth. The song ends with an implicit threat:

> La sangre del pueblo tiene rico perfume
> Huele a jasmines, violetas, geranios y margaritas
> A pólvora y dinamita
> ¡Carajo!
> A pólvora y dinamita.
> [The blood of the people has a rich perfume
> It smells of jasmine, violets, geraniums and daisies
> Of gunpowder and dynamite
> God damn it!
> Of gunpowder and dynamite.]

A decade later, the Shining Path adopted "La Flor de Retama" as a kind of unofficial anthem (the official one being "The International"). Even though the song predated the Shining Path, performers who included it in their repertoire risked arrest.

The first time I heard the song was live, during a concert to celebrate Peasant Day in the Campo de Marte in 1991. As the lyrics reverberated unexpectedly from the bandshell, the crowd fell silent. The singer stood alone at the microphone, her band in the shadow at the back of the stage. When she got to the defiant last verse, I could see that others in the crowd—people holding their babies and with baskets of lunch—were riveted. The singer was no guerrilla; but by singing the song, as the policemen sent to monitor the event looked on and listened, she performed a singular act in full public view, whether brave or foolish it was too early to tell.

Since, I have heard the song many times, by artists aware of its history and others, less effective, who sing it to spice up their repertoire. Hearing it, I remember that moment as her voice faded and the crowd, rapt, had yet to respond. It was as if someone had declared their love or made a threat or announced a vocation to join the priesthood in our collective midst. It was an act of such pure and complex passion that no precise response was possible, and only after several breaths did the applause begin and a low murmur of astonishment ripple through the crowd.

WHEN WE ARRIVED at Purus, the market was at its peak. The hillside the Purus villagers had used to ambush the Shining Path was dotted with donkey caravans. In the packed-dirt plaza, the vendors piled plastic sheets with tools, canned tuna, matches, rolls, evaporated milk, sugar, salt, and clothing. The pickups that make the Friday trek, yellow, green, blue, orange, and white, seemed decorative elements in the generally festive air. Children stroked them and sniffed at their grease and mud-splattered chassis.

Pepe acted as host, pulling over people he knew and locating chairs. One man complied with a grin and a shy blink. "This is Fortunato," Pepe told me, "Fortunato speaks Spanish."

Thusly qualified, Fortunato sat. It was strange to me to talk only to men, since in the past I had found that my best interviews had always been with women. But without Quechua, I was cut off from them. Pepe was pulled away by an old woman in a ballooning skirt, who patted his hand and pointed to a dim shack where soup had been ladled into a tin bowl.

Fortunato wore a polyester sweater patterned in brown, green, and white leaves and a brown fedora. He looked at me just as the guerrilla Gloria had, with all the enthusiasm of someone awaiting a tooth extraction. I explained that I was interested in refugees who had recently returned to the highlands. Fortunato brightened. He had never left, he said. He was the president of Huaychao, about a three-hour walk away. Throughout the 1980s he and his neighbors had lived in caves on Razuhuillca, the peak that dominates the heights.

Huaychao holds a unique place in the history of the war. On January 21, 1983, the Huaychao villagers ambushed and killed seven Shining Path guerrillas. Although it was not known widely at the time, these killings were part of a larger pattern of attacks by local farmers on the Shining Path. At least seventeen other guerrillas had been killed that month, beaten to death and buried in unmarked graves.

Unlike the ambush a decade later above Purus, the one in Huaychao had depended entirely on subterfuge. As Fortunato told it, he and his neighbors had become increasingly unhappy with the guerrillas' behavior. By the end of 1982 the Shining Path had closed the nearest market, and farmers from the valleys on up were ordered not to plant for sale or trade and to grow only enough for themselves, the first step in the Shining Path plan to starve the cities. Guerrillas carried out "popular trials" in nearby villages, killing men and women accused of crimes against the revolution. They used the puna and Huaychao as a transit point, dipping into the more populated valleys to attack the police, bomb state offices, and kill local authorities. Afterward, they would retreat to the heights, where the chutos were expected to provide food and shelter. In December, President Belaunde placed six highland provinces, including Huanta, in a state of emergency, ceding control to the military.

The Huaychao villagers knew the guerrillas by name, high school boys who had spent the past months crisscrossing the heights. That January day, they met them with red flags and chanting Party slogans. But the guerrillas were nervous and kept their weapons close at hand. In the community center, the boys began to lead the slogans in praise of the people's war. Imperceptibly, the people closed in. Under their wool ponchos, they held clubs and knives. They fell on the boys, and beat them until they were dead.

Until Huaychao, news about the war had been bad. Police stations had been abandoned, local officials had been murdered or had fled. So on January 23, when Gen. Clemente Noel announced in a press conference that peasants in Huaychao had killed Shining Path guerrillas, there was a sense of victory and relief. The news seemed to show not only that the guerrillas were more vulnerable than previously supposed, but also that their support in the countryside was crumbling. General Noel confidently declared that the tide was turning against the delincuentes subversivos. For his part, President Belaunde described the killings as a "gallant action," high praise from the misti architect to the Huaychao chutos.

Journalists, especially the ones working for leftist newspapers, were skeptical, even derisive. Why would peasants kill Communists, their defenders? What was the general hiding? It was well known that the navy and anti-terrorist police were on the heights. There were rumors that the military was organizing its first civil defense committees. Perhaps the seven dead were really innocent peasants, killed by out-of-control soldiers. Or a cabal of armed chutos led by the police was loose. Stories about Huachaca and the bishop killers reappeared in the press.

Eight reporters decided to see for themselves. They set off at dawn on January 26, hoping to reach Huaychao by nightfall. Their driver let them out at Toccto (TOCK-toe) Lake, on the highest pass accessible to vehicles, an area then considered "liberated" by guerrillas. Although shielded by the peaks surrounding it, the pass is a barren, inhospitable place, used mostly for pasturing sheep and llamas. On their way, the reporters were joined by Juan Argumedo, the half-brother of Octavio Infante, editor of Ayacucho's daily newspaper. Argumedo knew the area and agreed to guide them to a spot near a village called Uchuraccay. Along with Argumedo, Infante and Félix Gavilán, who wrote for the leftist *El Diario de la Marka,* spoke Quechua. From Uchuraccay, they could start the final leg to Huaychao.

The men took longer than expected, wheezing as the air thinned and the path grew steep and rocky. Suspecting that they might encounter danger, Gavilán had packed a white sheet. But even he could not guess how agitated the families on the heights were in the wake of the attacks on the Shining Path. Although many mistis still believed the Shining Path was chuto, the chutos knew otherwise. So far, almost all the guerrillas had come from the valleys and few even spoke the chuto language. Many of the chuto women had recently converted to Protestant sects and were convinced the violence heralded the Judgment Day. Catholics and Protestants alike expected and feared the Shining Path's revenge.

Armed with farming tools and the slingshots they used to hunt, their only hope was vigilance and surprise attack. Several villages had discussed the matter and agreed to fight the guerrillas. In Uchuraccay, more than two hundred people had gathered on January 25 to discuss strategy. It was this meeting that was just ending when a sentinel spotted the journalists approaching.

What happened next remains in some doubt. Apparently, the peasants took to the heights, then fell on the men by surprise. One of the last photographs taken by Willy Retto, who worked for *El Observador,* shows a journalist kneeling. His hands are up as a man in a wool poncho approaches, his face set in a grim mask. Another demonstrates how the shoulders of the reporters are hunched, as if to duck a hail of stones. A woman seems to shout. The reporters' satchels and Gavilán's white sheet lie in a heap. Then the camera angles to the ground. Talk had served for nothing. The penultimate photo appears to be one of

the reporters on the ground, his temple opened into a gaping black-
ness. The last photo, never published, is said to show the face of the
person who killed Retto.

All eight men were beaten and stabbed. The guide was caught later.
When he didn't return home, his mother and sister went to Uchuraccay to look for him. There, they were captured and accused of being
terrorists. Imprisoned in the community building, they discovered that
thirteen other people were there, all accused of supporting the Shining
Path. The Iquicha lieutenant governor had a Shining Path flag knotted
around his neck. The thirteen were tried in a community assembly that
numbered in the hundreds. Four were taken away and probably killed.

Argumedo's mother and sister swore on the cross that they were not
terrorists and that they would say nothing of what they had seen. But
when they got home, they found the police there looking for the
missing journalists. When the authorities helicoptered to Uchuraccay
and exhumed the journalists's bodies, they discovered that each one
had been ritually mutilated: eyes and tongues removed, ankles broken,
buried face down outside the community boundaries as befits humans
who make pacts with the Devil. The clubs and knives used to kill the
men had not even been cleaned and were crusted with blood and hair.
Blood stained the dense puna grass. Although the Uchuraccay villagers
told the police the journalists had unfurled the red hammer-and-sickle
flag, the only flags found in Uchuraccay were the red one seized in
Iquicha, the white one brought by Gavilán, and the national flag, the
red-and-white bars that drew them together in a perverse pact.

A government commission that later investigated the massacre concluded with "absolute conviction" that "all of" Uchuraccay committed
murder. At the same time, the commission defended the highlanders
by saying they had been subjected to tremendous pressure by the
guerrillas and the authorities, yet had been given no real protection by
anyone. Critics answered that the army and Sinchis had either been
directly involved (the district attorney who handled the case pinned
blame on an "extraterrestrial" wearing shoes and polyester pants partially captured by Retto's camera) or had incited the people of Uchuraccay to kill guerrillas. Among the commissioners was novelist Mario
Vargas Llosa, who later wrote about Uchuraccay and its meaning for
Peru. Already fighting the political battle that would lead to his presidential candidacy, for him, Uchuraccay demonstrated "how vulnerable

democracy is in Latin America and how easily it dies under dictator-ships of the right and left."

But that's not the lesson Fortunato seems to have drawn from Uchu-raccay. After the massacre, every Huaychao family packed its belong-ings and moved to the caves, where they spent most of the next decade. From their icy perch, they watched the countryside around them empty. Their lesson was vanish.

The military perceived the Shining Path as imported evil, intro-duced like a virus into the body politic. Although their attitude was certainly nurtured by U.S. Cold warriors, it also reflected persistent fears about chutos, who they believed had embraced Communism much as they had monarchism two centuries earlier—out of igno-rance, without understanding. For the military, the chutos were not a military threat, but a biological one, to be quarantined and extermi-nated before infecting the entire country.

And for the Shining Path, they were the sea, the flood, the tempest itself. Like these natural forces, they had to be dealt with decisively. Thus began what Pepe calls el éxodo, the exodus. Although he is not a religious man, Pepe saw the first refugees as figures in a biblical trag-edy, expelled against their will, often penniless, without a clear destina-tion or plan. Typically, families would move from village to town to city, stopping for weeks or even months along the way as they looked for work and sold off animals. By the time they reached the city slum where a relative or former neighbor lived, they would be exhausted and starving.

Mistis suffered, and lost family, farms, and businesses. But they were already city people and had city skills. The chutos did not. Only the men spoke Spanish, often haltingly. They knew primitive farming, enough trading skills to supplement their potatoes and corn with store-bought noodles, some sugar. Although the young men were used to spending part of the year in the jungle or on the coast, usually working as day laborers, they always returned. Becoming refugees meant not only losing a home and livelihood, but also language, iden-tity, and self-respect.

By 1985 thousands of refugees lived in the slums of Ayacucho and Lima. Others went to the jungle, where there was work in the coca fields. Few noticed. To Limans still untouched by war, they were indis-tinguishable from the economic migrants who had come in the 1940s and 1950s looking for work (and ruining the city, according to my landlady María). Only there was no work. Economic collapse had sucked the life from Peru's fragile industries: the textile and paint factories, the fish meal plants, construction, the mines that used to power a small, but striving working class. Refugee men worked as day laborers, brick-makers, ice cream vendors. Refugee women washed clothes, sold the rotted food others discarded. Their children—unschooled, poorly fed and dressed, often scarred by the skin sores that breed in filth—worked with them.

As for Uchuraccay, things went badly. The political left saw them as filthy chutos for killing reporters. They were filthy chutos to the right as well, which mistrusted their resolve. The courts issued seventeen arrest warrants for the village's leaders, meant to symbolize its collective guilt. Since they were chutos, the reasoning seemed to go, it didn't matter whether those tried had actually taken part in the killing. One chuto was the same as any other. And they were all, in a way, guilty.

THE FIRST REFUGEE settlement I visited in Lima was called Chincho, after the Huancavelica village they had abandoned in 1984. Stuck up one of the dry and rocky canyons that connect Lima to the Andes, it was a desperate spot. The only water was far away on the canyon floor, collected from irrigation ditches used to grow vegetables. People shit into it and washed their cars in it. Concentrated there were all the pesticides that had drained out of the surrounding fields, keeping the water free of algae and smelling of paint. The refugees had no choice. The Central Highway and its buses and markets and water pumps was a good hour away on foot. Nearby settlements refused to let the Chincheños in to draw water. For the Chincheños, water was only one problem, anyway. They had no food to put in the water or fuel to cook it or a roof to keep the fire they didn't have from damping out in the fog that clung to the canyon rock like their own misfortune. Chincho overlooked a police training facility where the president and his ministers would occasionally congregate to watch the officers pour kerosene on bales of seized cocaine and burn it. The Chincheños were perplexed by the acrid smoke that bit their eyes and made their children weep. But they never moved. To them, the very undesirability of the spot, its impracticality and noxiousness, made it the perfect place to hide.

A local parishioner found the Chincheños huddled on their hill,

An internal refugee from Chincho.
© Robin Kirk

awaiting the new calamity that was sure to befall them. Instead, they met the engine of their salvation. "Ay," Sabina would say to me when I asked about the Chincheños. "You are not going to believe the story I am going to tell you."

A broad-hipped, cushiony woman, Sabina had come to Lima from the mountains two decades earlier to marry a factory worker. He had built her a house to raise her children. By the time I knew her, her children were grown and her heart was lonely. So she crowded it with Chincho. Sabina brought clothes, some stoves, blankets, and food donated by the Catholic church. She was devout, nosy, kind, distracted, full of charity and loved to chat.

From my point of view, she had only one failing: she was a terrible interpreter. She would relate perhaps the first three sentences of a story before falling silent, take someone's hand and pat it. Minutes would tumble by, and I would discretely prod her to summarize. "Ay!" she would say. "I have never heard anything so sad!" And she would listen, murmuring "Mamita!" or "Papito!" until the story finished.

To me, her heart never revealed any hardness or ran out of room. During our chats, she would put her hand over it and tell me a story of near death or grief that she had just heard from a new refugee, drawn to Sabina like a plant to water. They were all incredible, horrible, beyond empathy: barefoot women who carried babies over fifteen-thousand-foot passes at midnight, hid from rampaging soldiers in thorn bushes, saw their houses and all their possessions burn, saw relatives and friends cut down in cold blood, saw bodies carved like backyard pigs. By 1990 Sabina was finding people who had lived for a year or more as *masas*, communities controlled by the Shining Path. After escaping, they felt as hunted by their former guerrilla patrons as the army. They saw and saw and saw, and arrived in Lima knowing no one, speaking no Spanish, and willfully blind and lame, sick to their bones. And Sabina would find them, and murmuring "Mamita!" and "Papito!" gently dab open their eyes.

The Shining Path threatened her in a kind of off-hand, intimate way. For them, her work was "a curb to the explosiveness of the masses." They would pass the word along secondhand, through people they knew she knew and knew would rush to her house where she would sit heavily in a chair, place her hand over her heart, and say "Ay!" But they never got around to actually killing her. I suppose the cadre who worked the area also ate off Sabina's charity, from the sacks of U.S. wheat and French cooking oil and Canadian powdered milk Sabina would extract from the church's huge Lima warehouse and finagle truck drivers into delivering to the soup kitchens wedged up the canyons. Sabina never announced her visits to the refugee settlements, to minimize the risk of an attack. Occasionally, when I traveled with her, I would be made to overhear someone who seemed to casually ap-

Bishop Richter in the Huamanga cathedral.
© Robin Kirk

proach and remark about imperialism and the masses and a time coming when all this would be ashes. "Ay!" Sabina would whisper under her breath. And they would smile and drift away.

The church was not the same everywhere, though. Ayacucho bishop Federico Richter barred church social workers from his diocese, describing them as terrorists in disguise. For a while, a U.S. Jesuit named Carlos Schmidt fought him. "Say mass and lock the door, that's his style of religion," Schmidt once said to me of Richter. A burly, profane priest,

I think Schmidt would have liked to arm wrestle the bishop for the prize of the city itself, which during the 1980s almost doubled in size as its slums filled with chutos. But Bishop Richter preferred political duels. He managed to get Schmidt recalled all the way to the United States.

Locals told me about sheep airlifted in army helicopters to the cathedral and bishop's residence, where Bishop Richter would have his servants roast them over pits dug into the rose garden. I'm not sure how I got this impression, but I imagined the bleating beasts slung beneath the helicopters coming directly to the cathedral, where the bishop would winch them down as maids tended glowing coals and primped the laden tables where the banquet would be served to generals. When I interviewed Bishop Richter in his residence, I saw no evidence of feasting or barbecue pits. But he did have a throne, which he posed in for a photograph. It was a wooden chair with broad, dark arms. The wood was elaborately carved with leaves and curling vines and lions' feet and upholstered in cherry-red leather and velvet. Bishop Richter's only concession to the war raging around him was to set up three small orphanages, only, he told me, for the children of parents killed by the terrorists. The terrorists, he said, could take care of their own.

He was especially proud of the use he had made of the gift Pope John Paul had given him during a 1985 visit. The pope's airplane had paused at the Ayacucho airport just long enough for the pope to wave from the airplane's opened door and hand Bishop Richter a check for fifty thousand dollars.

"Some people said I should spend it," Bishop Richter told me, the glint in his eyes like that of canny money men the world over. "But I invested half, so that it will rise with the dollar." As a parting gift, he handed me a 45-rpm record that featured songs by Lima society matrons. It was called "A Song for Sleeping Love."

BY 1990 MORE than six hundred thousand people had become internal refugees. Their settlements had a particular character that contrasted sharply with neighborhoods built by economic migrants. In settlements like Huáscar, the archaeology of construction pointed to slow but consistent progress: straw huts to adobe and tin shacks to houses made of iron rebar and concrete. But among refugees, the straw matting bought on arrival remained a year or two later, gray and rotted and patched with bits of cardboard, burlap, and plastic. Cooking was done on evaporated milk cans beaten flat, over a twig and garbage flame. The men learned only the Spanish they needed to work. Women remained monolingual. Men and women alike suffered from "nerves" and "anguish," which translated into physical symptoms like headaches, a lack of will, and pain in the arms, legs, and belly.

One social worker termed it *sicoseado*—psychotized, traumatized, but worse. The Fujishock had drawn a sharp line between early refugees, from the 1980s, and the ones arriving after August 1990. Sabina no longer made any pretense of finding them jobs or getting free medical treatment. It was enough to find a roof for them and keep them from dying of cholera. It was enough to endure.

For its part, the government ignored the refugees. If at all, they were considered carriers of the guerrilla virus, an annoyance in the mountains but a real threat to the cities. In Lima's Chincho, the security forces would patrol at night in the small tanks Limans called *tanquetas*. Sabina was constantly going to the prefecture, where she would sit with her battered vinyl handbag on her lap until some young police officer would take pity and tell her what had happened to Florencia or Porfirio or Andrés, picked up overnight for not carrying their identification cards, cards that had already been seized or burned before they fled their homes.

Sabina always got them out. For a mother, she wasn't big on lectures to be careful, to watch out, to avoid trouble. How could they? They were a people carrying trouble in their handbags, in their pockets, like bus change. Sabina would help them solve their problems, what she considered God's work.

Sabina would accompany them on the bus back to the parish, where they would get off and start the walk to Chincho. Sometimes, Sabina would pause to rest in the chapel she and her husband had helped build, a stocky little building with a single pane of stained glass. In the dark, when it was quiet, with the dust gently spiraling, she would sometimes doze off. But then her companion would touch her shoulder. "Mamita!" they would whisper. Sabina would pat her handbag. "Ay!" she would say. They would continue on their way.

AT THE TIME, it was easy to divide the conflict into describable chunks, good guys and bad guys and the victims in between. Some journalists and human rights groups put the civil defense committees squarely in the bad guys camp, together with their allies, the army. The refugees were the good guys, farmers who hadn't wanted to take sides so were forced to flee. It was widely believed that peasants were forced to join the civil defense committees and used as cannon fodder.

There was some truth to it. By 1990 civil defense committees were taking the brunt of the casualties, fifteen hundred dead compared to three hundred policemen and soldiers. Typically, the committees would walk ahead of the soldiers, absorbing the force of guerrilla attack. Once the soldiers were back in their barracks, the committees faced the guerrillas alone. Many civil defense committees were based in *núcleos,* valley camps set up by the army to house families moved from villages still considered to be in guerrilla zones. Although residence was obligatory, the army provided no shelter or food or water.

Of course, the núcleos became prime targets. The guerrillas would wait until the men left, to the fields or an army patrol, then raze them, killing everyone left behind. Or they would attack just at dusk or dawn, when the darkness heightened the effect of their guns and the firestorm they rained on the straw-roofed huts.

In 1990 I made a special trip to meet the man who formed the núcleos. At the Ayacucho airport, César, the driver, met me, and we made the hour drive to Huanta to interview him. I never learned his real name, since army officers in the emergency zones always used "war names," to prevent guerrillas from tracking them down later (and, according to human rights groups, to elude responsibility for atrocities). Local reporters called him El Platanazo, the Big Banana.

He commanded the Huanta army base and was said to have launched a campaign of terror with the help of an aide known by the nom de guerre "Centurión." Besides Pepe, Centurión was supposed to be the only other moreno in Huanta. The Big Banana gave peasants a choice: join the civil defense patrols or leave. Many joined, even former Shining Path militants. Within weeks, there were reports that the guerrillas had been forced to retreat from the valley and were trapped on the heights.

But even the chuto villages, beyond the Big Banana's reach, started to form civil defense committees. They refused the guerrillas food and water, cut off the passes, and began hunting down and killing known leaders. Although some were forced into núcleos, others formed them willingly and sent delegations to Huanta to ask the Big Banana for guns and bullets. I was prepared to hear of chutos being forced into combat; instead, I learned that the army itself had changed, and no longer considered the chutos the enemy.

My first night in Ayacucho, a veteran journalist told me, "As a strategy, it leaves much to be desired, but at least the soldiers see the advantages of getting the peasants on their side and have devoted time and energy to the committees. The Shining Path's trained soldiers are still out there, but their ability to move in the countryside and find support has eroded dramatically." Among other things, the journalist pointed out, the éxodos of the past had tapered off. There was a sense, fragile but persistent, that the worst of the war was past.

On the way to Huanta, César and I stopped at one of the Big Banana's núcleos, called Flor de Canela, Cinnamon Flower. Made up of seventy families from the surrounding heights, Cinnamon Flower was a perfect square of shoulder-high huts roofed in dried broom and grass. At night, the families gathered to sleep in a single long hut, bunkered and roofed partly in tin. Cinnamon Flower had been attacked repeatedly, and guard posts had been set at each of its corners.

On the day we visited, most of the residents had gone to Huanta to raise the national flag and sing the national anthem, a common Sunday ritual in Peru. In Huanta, though, attendance was obligatory. Anyone who failed to appear risked arrest by the Big Banana's men. The man who had remained to guard the straw huts came out to meet us. Although he would never have survived an attack—Cinnamon Flower was precisely between the two cities, and he had no radio—he was in a relaxed and talkative mood. When I gingerly asked what he would do if he saw the guerrillas, he showed me the evaporated milk can he carried with him. Inside was gunpowder mixed with nails. A lamp wick was stuck in the top. The homemade grenade was not to attack the guerrillas, though. Before they burned Cinnamon Flower, he said, he would start the flames himself.

As we drove on, I remember observing the land's harsh beauty, rounded mountaintops washed brown, white, and faded green. In my journal, I wrote: "It reminded me of New Mexico, but without the strong reds and blues of the plateaus. There are no people—no one in the houses along the road, no one walking the paths, no one glimpsed against the horizon."

Yet even as I smelled the broom flower that crowded the shoulder

Internal refugee with homemade grenade
near Huanta. © Robin Kirk

and felt the grit on my skin and in my eyes, I felt distant from it, too casual a visitor to ever fully understand the weight of the choices presented and the decisions made and the particular history that inhabited each curve and sweeping vista. After spending some months in Peru in the 1930s, U.S. journalist Carleton Beals described the Andes as "too brutal, too vast, too remote. They have lifted me to frightful agony of body and soul, to grand awe, but I always want to escape quickly."

193

I thought of the man with the homemade grenade and his willingness to set his last home afire simply to deny guerrillas the satisfaction. I found nothing brutish in him, only the set of choices he had been given, destroyed to destroy. It made me afraid and ready to leave.

César stopped once, sure he had heard a whistle that could have meant a surprise attack by the Shining Path. When he shut off the car, the breeze was surprisingly gentle for such a desolate place. We saw no one and continued on to Huanta.

As we pulled up to the central square, the flag-raising parade had just begun. There were sharpshooters in the church's twin bell towers. The local authorities stood shoulder to shoulder on the curb, which they used as a reviewing stand. Among the military men, I tried to guess which one was the Big Banana. But none of them seemed particularly evil or despotic. There were no morenos, either. The soldiers led the parade, followed by the police. By far the most dramatic marchers were the civil defensemen. They wore an approximate uniform, black or dark-blue shirts and pants and the black balaclavas that had earned them the Shining Path insult of *yanaumas* (yah-nah-OO-mah), blackheads.

Along with the weapon war, an insult war raged between the defensemen and the Shining Path. Yanauma was among the tamer insults. The Shining Path considered the committees military pawns, traitors, dupes. In the field, the guerrillas called defensemen pus heads, said they slept with their mothers and ate their own shit, they fucked sheep, they gave venereal diseases to their sisters who passed it along to the soldiers who passed it along to each other. The defensemen would respond by calling the guerrillas traitors and blood-drinkers, suggesting that President Gonzalo was a homosexual, that the guerrillas had lice, that they gave venereal diseases to their sisters who passed it along to their leaders who passed along to each other.

As they paraded, the defensemen carried their weapons at an angle in front of their chests: Winchester rifles, old hunting guns, knives, clubs, more homemade grenades. Some had long poles with the blades of kitchen knives lashed to the tips. Others carried *tirachas*, homemade guns of wood and pipe as dangerous to the shooter as the target.

"We need guns," one defensemen with a tiracha commented as I passed, my journalist notebook conspicuous. "These aren't good for shit."

In the parade, the defensemen were followed by the teachers, nurses, and schoolchildren. Several of the girls were dressed in nurse costumes and carried a stretcher loaded with a bundle of rags made to look like a body. There were no spectators for the parade, unless you counted the sharpshooters, just marchers.

After the flag was raised, I milled among the defensemen. A week earlier, other journalists had filmed them, and they were excited and flattered by the attention. The man who had commented about his tiracha agreed to talk only, he emphasized, because he thought publicity would bring guns, munitions, binoculars, night-vision equipment, radios—all the things they needed to fight. For the past four months, he said, the entire lower valley had been grouped into núcleos. "We are an army," he said.

Suddenly, he froze. His eyes fixed over my shoulder. The spectators who had been listening drew away. Behind me, an army jeep had managed to pull up without a sound. It was driven by the Big Banana, clad in camouflage and wearing mirror shades.

"I'll see you at the base," he said. The jeep pulled away.

An aide met me at the entrance and left me in the Big Banana's office, chosen, I guessed, for its windows facing away from the heights and therefore less vulnerable to attack. On his hat rack hung a noose. All his desk objects—pen holder, paper clip holder, clipboard, lamp—featured a design of real bullets. On his desk was a copy of a newspaper featuring an exposé on him, the civil defense committees, and Centurión. Several peasants had anonymously declared that they had seen Centurión kill suspected guerrillas on the base. Secret cells were supposed to be dug under the buildings and the very office where I sat, waiting for the Big Banana.

For a tall man, he walked fast, and I dropped my notebook as he entered. He was furious. The newspaper was full of lies, he said. "Journalists!" he spit.

His cheeks were burned a cherry red. He was as handsome as a movie star. As he spoke in a kind of controlled shout, he clasped his own torso and rocked, rocked, rocked. Despite his taste in office decor, he saw himself as a kind of evangelist of decency, of admirable, healthy virtues, like working together and planning for the future and getting up off your lazy butt and controlling your sexual urges and not living like chuto animals in pigsties, fucking, fucking, fucking. Bullets glinted in his hands as he talked, as he rubbed them and tapped them on the metal desk and bit them, tenderly, then stopped talking long enough to look and see if his teeth had made a dent.

"We make them understand," he said, looking sharply at me. I noted down each word. "They can do things one way or the other, one way or the other. They waste their time squabbling over small things, rivalry, living so far apart they can do nothing against the Shining Path. So I teach them to work together. Well, things used to be pretty slack around here, the *terrucos* could just come in and kill. So we went village by village, village by village. And we made them understand."

To illustrate, he swept his long arms up, suddenly huge in the confines of the office. "Look here! This base was built in twenty-five days, there were four thousand people who did it. Each village built four feet of wall. Imagine! If you can make an army base together, what else can stop you?"

He was proud of the fact that he had set up núcleos in the hill overlooking the base, to secure the area. Seen from another perspective, he had shielded himself with civilians, with chutos, which the Shining Path had no qualms about cutting through. But it worked. Months had passed since the last potshots had been taken at the base. Dozens of *arrepentidos*—repented ones, former guerrillas or their supporters who surrendered to the authorities—had been converted by the Big Banana into civil defensemen. One of his main problems now, he said, was his own soldiers getting bored and drunk and sometimes going a little too far with the townspeople.

He was full of aphorisms: "The people are mine!" "I make the necessity"; "Union creates strength." Near the end of the interview, his voice dropped conspiratorially. Evil forces were at work, he said. He hunched again over his bullets. "What I have achieved, what I have achieved," he said, "is with precisely no help from anyone. When I asked for help, I got a deaf ear." He seemed to mean the government and his own commanders. To them, he had a specific message. "If they don't help me, I'm going to blow this all up."

Later, a Huanta journalist told me the Big Banana would herd guerrilla suspects into a trench and have Centurión shoot them one by one until the survivors confessed. He also said the Big Banana had recently been airlifted from the base in a straitjacket, "just like," he noted, "the American soldiers in Vietnam." It was one of those stories, like the one about the bishop airlifting in sheep, that was tempting, but impossible to confirm.

After thanking the Big Banana for his time, I found César sucking a Popsicle at the entrance to the base. We started down the hill. Before reaching the plaza, we were stopped by an army patrol. A soldier—in a black T-shirt emblazoned with a skull, the emblem of the base—stuck his head in the window.

"Are you from the United States?" he asked. His face was deeply tanned, and he had a thick, black moustache.

I nodded. The soldier fumbled in his pocket.

"My sister lives in Los Angeles," he said. "I don't get the time to call her and besides. . . ." He shrugged, meaning that Huanta was far from anywhere. He had her name and telephone number on a slip of lined paper. He had also left his name—Johny. "I would greatly appreciate it if you could call her and tell her Johny is alive."

The message didn't strike me until later, when César let out a long, relieved sigh.

"That," César said, "was Centurión."

REFUGEES WOULD OFTEN tell me they had been caught between *la espada y la pared* (the sword and the stone). On one side was the Shining Path, on the other the security forces. I heard the phrase so often I finally put it down to something unconsciously taught, probably by the kind of young and eager social workers who worked with Sabina and helped tend to the refugees' most catastrophic needs, finding doctors to remove life-threatening tumors for free, Quechua-speaking teachers to tutor severely depressed and violent children, parishes to donate plots of land over the energetic objections of parishioners convinced their families would be contaminated by the terrorist virus. The social workers, a bright and whirring presence against Lima's wasted countenance, had a stake in the innocence the phrase implied, in seeing these refugees as victims of implacable, cruel forces.

Otherwise, what was the point? If they were simply ministering to failed terrorists, the chutos who killed, pillaged, and raped, then they might as well be joining public relations firms or leaving for Miami, where they would be guaranteed a steady salary and could forget the hellish three-hour commutes to the nook-and-cranny settlements where the refugees holed up.

Of course there were innocents. I met a few, mainly children. But after a while, the simple stories seemed only the ones I didn't know much about. Once I began to explore and compare them with the few knowable facts at hand, or simply moved on to the next village or house where relationships within the same story would often be described as radically reversed, so that I was always, miraculously, in the immediate presence of perfect innocence, a doubt would arise, ultimately without solution but persistent, nagging.

It was easy, I ended up thinking, to choose among the varied qualities ascribed to chuto-ness when it came time to lay blame. If the chutos were the victims, then it was their apolitical urges that came into play, their position outside civilization, history, time. And if the chutos were guilty, then their unfettered brutality could be mined for context, converting them into engines of destruction. For the Big Banana, all it took was a little muscle, a little etiquette training, and he had a chuto army. An Ayacucho sociologist warned against arming chutos, for fear of losing control of these unpredictable highlanders, conjuring fears of Huachaca's sieges. To some degree, I also embraced the idea of the chutos. They had become a sort of prize, the authentic article that symbolized truth and pure, unmuddled experience. I often didn't even take their full names and just scribbled down some best approximation of where they were from, assuming some desperate, generalized need for anonymity. They were in my dreams, the focus of my memories, when I felt like I closed in on eternity itself with my notebook and pocket camera. When I succeeded in snapping a chuto's photograph or scribbling down captured words or the hint of a provable fact, I felt like I had finally reached the true center of things, the soul of the hard mountain.

I don't mean to make excuses. But eventually, I got tired of all that nameless suffering. Weren't there other stories among the chutos? In a way, it was my American-ness erupting, my need to take names and assign responsibilities. It was also part of my realization that it was time to go home. I understood enough to suspect I was being lied to, and I thought, What's the point? Everything I put up with—the risk, the pollution, the thieves, the señoras—entitled me, I thought, to at least a little honesty.

In interviews, I was grumpy and impatient, and the thought occurred to me that this was all some sort of grand conspiracy whose

Sabina with internal refugee woman.
© Robin Kirk

motives I couldn't guess. Why was every story so slippery? Why were there no dates, no places, no names? Complicity came to seem more admirable, for god's sake, taking a stand.

In an interview with two refugee women who said they had recently escaped a battle, after a point I didn't even press Sabina to interpret. First they said the battle had taken place in spring, then fall. They claimed the attackers had been Shining Path, but transported in helicopters, impossible.

"Sabina," I said wearily, "let's wrap it up." The interview was useless. I had seen the same expression of fear dozens of times. I had three hours of Lima traffic to slog through before getting home. I closed my notebook.

Sabina squeezed my hand.

"They will tell you nothing," she murmured. "You see, they think you are Shining Path. Your eyes, your skin, the color of your hair. The Shining Path women look just like you. They even dress like you. Even though I have assured them otherwise, they are afraid and are being purposefully vague."

I can feel it still, that icy grip of dismay. As if blinded, I blinked my eyes rapidly. With an almost physical reaction, I understood the full meaning of the still palpable fear I recognized on their faces. It was fear of me.

To me, they were female chutos, a subgroup of a species worthy of study but whose interior particularities held no interest. They had also seen me as a type, the type who had come fully armed into their midst with her mind made up. I tried some response before remembering that they spoke no Spanish. Sabina embraced them and pressed some medicines in their hands.

To Sabina, I apologized. I felt like jumping out of my old skin, leaving it for some refugee to patch their rotted roof.

"Never underestimate fear," was Sabina's reply as she patted my arm.

ONLY THREE MEN were prosecuted for murdering the eight journalists at Uchuraccay and Juan Argumedo, the guide. They were the three who had voluntarily presented themselves at court after being summoned. None spoke Spanish. No interpreter was provided. The men were convicted.

In prison, Simeón Aucatoma, seventy, succumbed to tuberculosis. Dionisio Morales, who maintained that he had been in Iquicha the day of the massacre, served his time, then dropped from view.

When I met Mariano Ccasani years later, he said he did not want to speak about the reporters. Of the three, Mariano had never claimed to have been anywhere but Uchuraccay at the time. He had been released after serving seven years and was living with his wife and daughter in a refugee camp run by the Protestant church. They lived in a barracks-like row of rooms. There was no one else from Uchuraccay. They owned a stool. They slept in their clothes and cooked over coals on the floor.

My notebook made Mariano nervous, so I put it away. By then, Uchuraccay had been completely razed by the Shining Path. The survivors were scattered between Huanta and Lima. Even to other refugees, they refused to identify themselves. Now, they were not only "bishop killers" but "journalist killers."

What Mariano wanted to talk about was home—when he could go, how he would go, what he would do. Since his arrest, when his picture had been frequently in the newspaper, he had lost weight and looked as young as a teenager.

"Here," he said, "everything has its price."

His wife listened to the few words he spoke, clearly nervous about what he would say and how I would react. I didn't ask for the lesson of the massacre and Mariano didn't offer it. I'm not sure I would have believed him if he had.

It surprised me to hear that Mariano felt in more danger in the city than in the place where he had perhaps seen those men killed and had had a hand in the killing. For him, his city persecutors—hunger, damp, disease—were more relentless. He wanted to go home. At this point, he preferred to take his chances with whomever he might find in the rubble of Uchuraccay. That was all he had to say.

That is what Sabina might say about Uchuraccay: never underestimate fear. Or, mistakes are made. Even the best-laid plans go awry. Some people in Uchuraccay, like people everywhere, made a mistake. Hounded by fear, they acted rashly. In light of their recent experience, they struck first. But she wouldn't say the defense of democracy was uppermost in their minds (though I know that's not what Vargas Llosa meant) or they acted out of ancient custom. They acted humanly, fallibly, and according to their experience, out of incomplete information and assumptions that proved tragically wrong. And for it, they paid. And paid again, in all that they had or had hoped to have, and in the pounds of flesh that had been taken out of Mariano Ccasani, like fat sucked by a nakaq.

I could say Peru took something out of me as well. It took my faith in the innate goodness of humankind; it made me afraid to travel at night. It taught me to do body counts and describe torture in precise, technical terms. It taught me there is much, so much, I will never know or be sure of. There is no limit to cruelty or savage prejudice. Privilege marks me like a flame that burns through the night. There are limits to my ability to love. And endure. I wanted to go home. But I could not be sure even home would satisfy me any more.

WHEN I MADE MY trip to the Huanta heights, thousands of refugees were heading home. Not all or even most, by any means, but enough to reanimate villages abandoned since 1980 or build entirely new ones. The civil defense patrols were the key. Though it pained and disturbed me to admit it, the Big Banana's strategy had proved effective. No group returned without some weapons and an agreement with the

Civil patrol members near Iquicha.
© Robin Kirk

army to patrol and take part in counterinsurgency operations. Aid
groups scraped together some seeds and tools, tin roofing and blankets, and enough food for a couple of weeks. With their belongings on
their backs, the chutos headed home.

Even Uchuraccay was populated again, with sixty families. Because
of its past, it was the most famous returnee village, and the government poured in aid. They paid an engineering firm by the meter to
build a road to it, which now coils tiresomely up a broad and dry valley
past no other place of note and avoiding several of the larger villages
that remained intact and fought the Shining Path during the long years
of war. Even Fujimori visited, and awarded Uchuraccay two trucks,
four computers, and an electric generator big enough for a settlement
of five hundred. However, no one knew how to drive, so they had to
hire a city man to keep the truck in the nearest town and make regular
trips. But since the president had given the trucks to "the community
of Uchuraccay," no one felt obligated to pay a fare to ride it. And there
was no money anyway, for that or for the driver's salary or gasoline,
including the gallons and gallons needed to run the huge generator

and thus power up the computers, which were useless anyway since not a single soul in Uchuraccay knew how to read or write much less use Microsoft Word on the Japanese-language keyboards tucked into their factory-sealed bags. The president's gift came with an agreement not to sell or give any of it away, so the trucks were motionless in a city three hours away, and the generator was packed with the computers in their boxes under a plastic tarp made brittle by the nightly *heladas,* frosts that crisped the grass the color of uncarded wool.

Ironically, things seemed better in areas where little government aid was sent. Rather than taking whatever the government doled out, peasants brought what they had to the heights. One such place was Ayahuanco, a district that forms Huanta's northern edge and is Ayacucho's border with the neighboring state of Huancavelica.

In all indicators, Ayahuanco is dead last—no roads, no doctor, no telephone, no potable water. To get there, I had started in an entirely different state, in Junín. From Huancayo, Junín's capital, a dirt road crosses Huancavelica and ends at the state-owned Cobriza mine, where ore is pulled from the rock above the Mantaro river and rinsed in its waters, turning them from blue-green to black. Across the river, there is a single foot bridge. On the other side is Ayahuanco.

Even its name is unlucky. In Quechua, it translates as "Enshrouded Cadaver" district in "Corner of the Dead" state. But an unusual alliance of city-based refugees and farmers desperate to get back had made Ayahuanco a model for the return. I went to Ayahuanco with Edilberto Oré, president of the Ayahuanco Reconstruction Committee and an organizer of the return.

In some ways, he was like Pepe—more comfortable in the country than the city, a man who relished particularities and had a gregarious nature. Slim and gray-haired, Oré was also from a misti family that had once owned land. A generation earlier, his family had lost its fortune and slipped down the economic ladder. But Oré had insisted on remaining in the country. While Pepe was still a misti, Oré had embraced the role of chuto, farming his plot with a mattock and crowbar, using chuto Quechua, living in a chuto house.

He was no romantic, and like Pepe had run for political office on the promise to bring roads, clean water, and a medical clinic to the district. He kept a house in the city, where his wife worked for a state agency and his children went to school. But his sensibility, his position, was not one of an outsider, however well-connected and intentioned, but a chuto looking out.

"For instance," Oré pointed out as we climbed from the footbridge up the steep and rocky trail that would lead us to Ccochacc, a new village built by returning refugees three hours' distant, "one day a truck arrived at the mine to off-load some sheep for a village further north, a donation, they explained, from the government to the refugees. No one had asked for it, no one knew about it, because of course, anyone familiar with that area would know that it is too hot and dry there for sheep; it is goat country, and besides the people there know nothing about them. But the sheep were delivered and in a couple of weeks they were gone, slaughtered and eaten before they died of thirst. Such useless gifts only teach failure, passivity. And these are not passive people."

Ayahuanco had been one of the first areas to fall under Shining Path control in the 1980s. During that time, Oré had come and gone secretly, never announcing his destination and careful to leave before word spread of his presence. Still, he can only go by daylight to the puna, where the trail that passes above Purus crosses, then dips to Viscatán. But week after week, he walks with his knapsack to the villages that have been rebuilt on the lower hills, calling meetings, distributing tools and seeds, taking requests back to the city where he raises more help.

I was curious about the genesis of the name Ayahuanco, and Oré explained its history. "This is Chanka land, and the place where many families fleeing the Inca settled. After the Conquest, they harassed the defeated Inca army without mercy. Once, they ambushed the army of Manco Inca, retreating through Ayahuanco pursued by the Spaniards. Thus the name, for the dead collected along the river."

The climb was exhausting. Although Ccochacc was visible from the mine, the trail started at the riverbank and climbed what seemed a goat path over a huge shoulder. On a small plain at the foot of the mountain where most of the families used to have their houses, Ccochacc was a fortress. It is edged on two sides by a gorge that drops straight to the Mantaro hundreds of feet below. The rest is protected by a wall and guard towers, which took one month to build. Outside the wall, the returnees planted fields of prickly pear cactus. The cactus had a double function. While protecting what Oré called "the perimeter," the cactus also nourishes cochinilla, an insect that produces a red dye much valued by the textile industry. Since the cochinilla began producing, Ccochacc has converted the proceeds into guns and munitions.

Inside the fortress, we were met by Julio, the president of Ccochacc's civil defense committee, who invited us inside his home to eat. His wife handed me a tin plate heaped with rice and potatoes yellow with the oil they had been fried in hours ago. The sun had just gone behind the mine, and a cold wind pushed dust through the gaps in the adobe wall and it swirled above the layer already crusted on the food. While Julio's wife squatted beside the fire, I sat next to Oré on the single bed, my head ducked between the clothes hanging from the roof beam. The guinea pigs underneath nibbled at my boots. I found myself almost giddily grateful that none had ended up a grinning carcass on my plate.

Julio himself did not eat, anxious to be a good host. He was probably no more than thirty, and had a goofy, chip-tooth smile. Like his neighbors, Julio had fled Huanta in 1983. The stories of why they left were mythic in their brutality—children swung against rocks, bodies abandoned at trail side. But I had no reason to doubt them. On the walk up, Oré had pointed to the spot where concrete gravestones had been placed to mark where people fell or were killed as they fled.

For years, Julio lived in a slum beside the mine called Expansión. Every day, he could look across the Mantaro and see his ruined house and his untilled fields. To survive, he sold vegetables to the miners. Finally, he said, he had had enough. Along with the other Ayahuanco refugees, he voted to go home in 1989.

By then, he was a pastor in a Protestant church known as the Witnesses of God. While the Shining Path preached a doctrine of utopia on earth, Julio came to believe in the life of purity—no drinking or adultery, thrift and hard work—that would lead to his reward in God's kingdom. He saw himself as a soldier in a holy war, battling the Satan that was the Shining Path so that his flock could aspire to grace.

For that and because Julio led the civil defense committee, the Shining Path despised him. Having a pastor as military leader was far from unique to Ccochacc. Throughout the heights and in the valleys that cut to Peru's eastern jungles, the battle between guerrillas and the peasants who chose to return had taken on the quality of a holy war. Many civil defense committees and particularly their leaders were inspired by a militaristic, evangelical fervor. Few priests or nuns had remained in the battle zones, and in Ayacucho, at least, clerics the likes of Bishop Richter had kept their Catholicism firmly irrelevant. So the Protestants took over. In tiny Ccochacc, for instance, there are three Protestant congregations and not a single Catholic Church.

Two hundred families crossed the Mantaro River together. But instead of returning to their houses, they built Ccochacc. The Shining Path attacked repeatedly. The first time, they shot flaming coals onto the roof of the community center, made of straw. Ccochacc switched to tin. In 1991, while Julio was at a prayer meeting, guerrillas sneaked over the wall and headed for his house. His wife, eight months pregnant, had stayed behind to rest. They killed her and left her naked on the floor. It was their message to "Hawk," the name he uses as head of the civil defense committee.

Since then, Julio had chased the Shining Path as far as Viscatán. Huachaca hid there when the first "pacification" swept through the highlands. Now "Feliciano," said to command the Shining Path army, used it as his base. The trail, Julio told me, was booby-trapped—"holes with stakes dipped in shit, trip wires, ambushes." The military forced him and the men of Ccochacc to walk in front of the troops, but was still too scared, Julio said, to go all the way in.

"If they would just give us their guns and bullets," Julio said, "we could finish off the terrucos in a week."

Talk turned to Ccochacc's future. By then, three thousand people, one-third of the Ayahuancans who originally fled, had returned to the district. Oré could look through any kitchen and tick off the implements he had personally carried in and distributed—bowls, hoes, blankets, pots, sweaters, notebooks, shoes. But it wasn't enough.

"Maybe we should have killed ourselves some journalists," muttered one of the civil defensemen who was squatting in a corner in Julio's house.

So far, Oré hadn't come up with what Julio said people really wanted—a road to connect them to the international markets they now saw as essential to survival. Although Julio chose to return to the farm and in essence remain a chuto, he harbored little nostalgia for the way things were before the war. Along with his neighbors in Viracochán, an hour's walk away, Julio wanted a city plan for Ccochacc complete with layout for streets, house lots, electric lights, and sewage. Already, Oré had arranged for university students to come and mark out streets with stakes and chalk. Then the chutos themselves were going to get their mattocks and hack some modernity into the hard earth. To me, Ccochacc wouldn't look much different from any village seen from the bus: steep and rocky lanes, mud slides when it rains and dusty chutes in the mid-day sun. To them, though, it would be a dream city, a piece of progress won from a land of little mercy.

Paradoxically, the decade-long quest of the Shining Path for peasant utopia had instead inspired in Ccochacc a hunger for the city—for its schools and lights and clinics and television and doctors—that had never been so acute. Although Julio himself planned eventually to rebuild his farm house high in the hills, he had no intention of living there. The daughter just then learning to crawl and fiddling with the frayed laces on Julio's cast-off army boots would live in the adobe structure where we bent over our plates, what he called his "town house." There, she would keep her school uniform and books, her keepsakes when she eventually left for high school in Huanta and university in Ayacucho or maybe Lima.

Someday, Julio mused, she might even arrive home in a bus, and he would greet her like the proud father he already was, with open arms. By then, the lamps had grown dim and the light from the fire had faded to a dim, red glow. Julio was due on patrol. The men who would accompany him were already gathered at his door, their guns a dull glint of blue and black in the starlight.

"Hawk," murmured one, "it's time to go."

ONCE, WHILE DRIVING through a shantytown, I saw a wall that stopped me cold. Painted on the massive concrete canvas was a six-foot high PCP, Partido Comunista Peruano, the Shining Path's official name. Afterward, however, someone had carefully matched the paint and, risking their lives, had added to the design. PCP now read BOB.

Ridicule was the surest sign that something had changed. A week later, on a public bus, the driver shouted out the stops: "Arequipa, Cuba, Perestroika, Estalinismo, Maoismo, Pensamiento Gonzalo (Gonzalo Thought)." After a brief silence, and no protest, the passengers smiled.

ADRIÁN WAS ESPECIALLY proud of the new school at Purus, and led me away from the market to see it. Like the Chaca school, it was being built partially from the ruins of the estate house. It was the most elaborate school I had ever seen in a village the size of Purus: four fully fin-ished classrooms, with concrete floors and blackboards, and a detached house for the teachers. Although simple adobe was good enough for the Purus houses, it did not fit the high purposes of the school. New brick had been hauled in all the way from Huanta.

As I viewed the school from the ruined walls of the estate house, a copse of eucalyptus rustled around me. Their gray-green leaves flick-ered, as if each contained its own miniature light. Pepe joined us. For several minutes, the three of us sat in silence, watching the men lay the bricks that defined the school patio.

Adrián's most distinctive feature were the aviator sunglasses he had worn ever since his left eye was gored by a bull. Although he is among the best Spanish speakers in Purus, he finds the language unwieldy, like an ill-fitting jacket. He has been the president of Purus and its civil defense committee. But he drinks a bit and was currently at loose ends. Pepe admired his eloquence and ability to inspire his neighbors to great acts of courage. For his part, Adrián seemed to consider Pepe a kind of wise older brother, someone he could depend on in a pinch.

I asked Adrián to tell me about the estate.

"Ay!" said Pepe, "how many days do you have?"

Adrián grinned. Doña Guillermina, he told me, was the last of the Leandros to live at Purus.

"When I worked at Doña Guillermina's house in Huanta, I remem-ber seeing the peasants arrive from the estate at Purus carrying huge sacks of grain or potatoes. They would not step inside, but would nod, to show that they had come as ordered. It was a day's walk down, more going up. But they weren't allowed to step inside the house to rest."

Although Adrián spoke freely about the abuses, he made a distinc-tion between systems and individuals. Unlike the Lamas, who are still battling the peasants of Chaca to reclaim their estate, Doña Guiller-mina signed hers away days before the land reform took effect in 1969. The last time she rode down the mountain, the peasants of Purus followed her singing and wearing flowers.

As a young man, when Adrián went to Huanta to sell his corn, townspeople would call him a "swinish chuto." Perhaps some of that hatred still existed, he allowed. But on this brilliant day, Adrián seemed to hold no grudges. Purus is once again his home. He asked to be photographed with Pepe, in front of the school. In the photograph,

Pepe with Adrián at the Purus school.
© Robin Kirk

Pepe smiles a broad, moreno smile, looking as if he has just told a new and excellent joke. Beside him, Adrián seems more reserved. But it is Adrián whose right arm is draped around Pepe's broad shoulders.

Not all the men and women who fled will return to the heights. One census prepared by the church estimated that only 20 percent of the six hundred thousand people displaced since 1980 will go home. Of those, the majority are older, people who were already farming and heads of household when they fled. Their children are less willing to return, whether because of school, jobs, or an unwillingness to become chutos again. Many still fear the guerrillas, who will probably continue to harass villages into the next century. But the ones who are back say they won't leave again.

Adrián has his city plan, too, like Julio. He pointed to the place where they will install the *parabólica*, the dish that will connect them like an invisible bridge to the cities that are now as much a part of their imaginative life as Lima: Buenos Aires, Mexico (through the tearjerker soap operas they love, when the Doñas, like Doña Guillermina as they think of her now when she last left Purus, weep with huge, mascara-stained tears, black and rich), New York, Los Angeles (where people, someone notes, seem to have a lot of the kinds of guns that would prove especially useful in Purus the next time the Shining Path makes the mistake of using the trail above town).

Once the school is finished and the streets are dug and the generator is in place, what's next, I asked. Shops, telephones, a video cinema?

Adrián smiled, a brief, furtive smile. He looked away from the school. Before him was the unpeopled mountain, as wild as it had ever been, and as beautiful. So much had happened there. As desolate as the peaks looked, they were shrouded in stories. For Adrián, there could be no knowable limits to what humankind was capable of.

So why not a video cinema?

BENEATH THE AIRPLANE wing, Peru lay in its glory. The sere coast was crumpled with shadow. Beyond it were the Andes, blue as my eyes. Clouds billowed behind them, over the jungle. I tracked the wing as it revealed each settlement: Chincha, Chimbote, Trujillo, Piura. For a moment, I saw below me the undulation that was the Quiroz Valley, its gentleness belying the hot grit of its earthly skin.

From above, Peru was a geography lesson. Every climate and terrain known on earth was visible to the naked eye and in its proper relation to the sea and sky. Much of it I had experienced, on foot or by truck, train, and bus. When I closed my eyes, I could still feel the thrill of what I now think of as a rebirth in Ayacucho, when the physical space—land and sky and the knife-sharp air—dazzled me with its brilliance.

Closer in, I had learned, the view was never as clear. I had seen so much only to end my stay by following people as they returned to less than what they had called their own when I first arrived in Peru. They rebuilt not from scratch, but ashes. Hope drew them, perhaps, but also despair. Their misfortune was their citizenship, their grief a passport home.

These had been brutal times, and splendid. I had paid a price for my seeing. I had also been paid. The airplane climbed into the nationless space above the clouds, and the land was lost to me. Perhaps that is the natural home of people like me, who shed houses and cities as easily as clothes. But I felt only emptiness there and an impatience to find a home. There, I knew, the dreams would find me and the memories of other places, other people, I had been. For they were part of me as surely as my blood and bone. That was the ultimate risk I bore—that Peru would change me and not in any way I planned.

I began this book by posing a moral question. Can I bridge the gap between Peru and me, between privilege and want, between fear and security? Through this book, I tried to measure out just how wide that gap is, and deep. At times, I felt as if I were slipping in. But usually, I kept it at a distance, with my notebook and my paragraphs and my instinct for not going too far, too quickly.

There were moments, though, when I crossed. Holding Marco in his burial cloth, for instance, or when I sat with Betty. When Sabina said to me, "Never underestimate fear." I was not brave in these moments or particularly admirable. But I was, completely, there.

SELECTED BIBLIOGRAPHY

Andreas, Carol. "Women at War." In *Fatal Attraction: Peru's Shining Path*. NACLA: Report on the Americas, vol. 24, no. 4, December–January, 1990–91.

Arendt, Hannah. *The Human Condition*. Garden City, N.Y.: Doubleday, Anchor Books, 1959.

Arguedas, José María. *Yawar Fiesta*. Trans. Frances Horning Barraclough. Austin: University of Texas Press, 1985.

Beals, Carleton. *Fire on the Andes*. Philadelphia: J. B. Lippincott, 1934.

Becker, Jillian. *Hitler's Children: The Story of the Baader-Meinhof Terrorist Gang*. London: Pickwick, 1989.

Blondet, Cecilia. *Las Mujeres y el Poder*. Lima: Instituto de Estudios Peruanos, 1990.

Bourque, Susan C., and Kay Warren. *Women of the Andes: Patriarchy and Social Change in Two Peruvian Towns*. Ann Arbor: University of Michigan Press, 1981.

Bryce Echenique, Alfredo. *Dos señoras conversan: Novelas breves*. Barcelona: Plaza y Janes Editores, 1990.

Burgler, R. A. *The Eyes of the Pineapple: Revolutionary Intellectuals and Terror in Democratic Kampuchea*. Saarbrücken, Germany: Verlag Breitenbach, 1990.

Chatwin, Bruce. *What Am I Doing Here?* New York: Viking, 1989.

Chávez de Paz, Dennis. *Juventud y Terrorismo*. Lima: Instituto de Estudious Peruanos, 1989.

Colegio de Periodistas del Peru. *Sendero de Violencia: Testimonios Periodisticos*. Lima: Colegio de Periodistas del Peru y CONCYTEC, 1990.

Comisión investigadora sobre la masacre de Uchuraccay. "Informe sobre Uchuraccay." Lima: Government of Peru, 1983.

Cook, David Noble. *Demographic Collapse: Indian Peru, 1520–1620*. Cambridge: Cambridge University Press, 1981.

Cooper, H. A. "Woman as Terrorist." In *The Criminology of Deviant Women*, ed. Freda Adler and Rita James Simon. New York: Holt, Rinehart and Winston, 1976.

Cravero Tirado, Juan M. *Terror, Sangre, Muerte en los Andes: Uchuraccay Mudo Testigo*. Ayacucho: Self-published, 1992.

Degregori, Carlos Iván. *El Surgimiento de Sendero Luminoso: Ayacucho, 1969–1979.* Lima: Instituto de Estudios Peruanos, 1990.

——. *Que Difícil es Ser Diós: Ideología y violencia política en Sendero Luminoso.* Lima: El zorro de abajo ediciones, 1989.

Elshtain, Jean Bethke. *Women and War.* New York: Basic Books, 1987.

Golte, Jürgen, and Norma Adams. *Los caballos de troya de los invasores: estratégias campesinas en la conquista de la gran Lima.* Lima: Instituto de Estudios Peruanos, 1990.

González Carré, Enrique. *Los Señoríos Chankas.* Lima: Universidad Nacional de San Cristóbal de Huamanga / INDEA, 1992.

Gorriti, Gustavo. *Sendero: Historia de la guerra milenaria en el Peru.* Lima: Apoyo, S.A. 1990.

Guzmán, Abimael. Attributed. "Interview with Chairman Gonzalo." Lima: Red Banner Editorial House, 1989.

Hemming, John. *Conquest of the Incas.* New York: Harcourt Brace Jovanovich, 1970.

Husson, Patrick. *De la guerra a la Rebelión: Huanta, Siglo XIX.* Lima: Centro de Estudios Regionales Andinos "Bartolomé de las Casas" and Instituto Francés de Estudios Andinos, 1992.

Lázaro, Juan. "Women and Political Violence in Contemporary Peru." *Dialectical Anthropology* 15 (1990): 233–47.

Macera, Pablo. "Sendero y Mama Huaco," in *Cambio,* 1988.

Malpartida, Daniel. "Madonnas Dentadas," in *Cambio,* 1988.

Morote, Osmán. "Lucha de clases, en las zonas altas de Huantas (distrito de Santillana)." Master's thesis. Facultad de Anthropología, Universidad Nacional San Cristóbal de Huamanga, 1970.

Niles, Blair. *A Journey in Time: Peruvian Pageant.* Indianapolis: Bobbs-Merrill, 1937.

Núñez Rebaza, Lucy. *Los Dansaq.* Lima: Museo Nacional de la Cultura Peruana, 1990.

Ono, Kazuko. *Chinese Women in a Century of Revolution.* Stanford: Stanford University Press, 1989.

Oré Cárdenas, Edilberto. "El Problema de los desplazados: una historia que se repite después de cien años." 1995.

Policía Nacional del Peru. "Participación de la Mujer en la Subversión y en las Fuerzas Antisubversivas," VI Curso Superior de Guerra Política y Seguridad del Estado. Surquillo, November 1990.

Pratt, Mary Louise. *Imperial Eyes: Travel Writing and Transculturation.* New York: Routledge, 1992.

Rostworowski de Diez Canseco, Maria. *Doña Francisca Pizarro: Una ilustre mestiza, 1534–1598.* Lima: Instituto de Estudios Peruanos, 1989.

——. *Historia de Tahuantinsuyu.* Lima: Instituto de Estudios Peruanos, 1988.

SEPAR. *Cifras y cronología de la violencia política en la región central del Peru: 1980–1991.* Huancayo: SEPAR, 1992.

Saywell, Shelley. *Women in War.* Markham, Ont.: Viking Books, 1985.

Silverblatt, Irene. *Moon, Sun, and Witches: Gender Ideologies and Class in Inca and Colonial Peru*. Princeton: Princeton University Press, 1987.

Starn, Orin. *Con los llanques todo barro: Reflexiones sobre campesinas, protesta rural y nuevos movimientos sociales*. Lima: Instituto de Estudios Peruanos, 1991.

——. "Uchuraccay y el retorno a los Andes." In *Quehacer*, 1995.

Starn, Orin, Carlos Iván Degregori, and Robin Kirk, eds. *The Peru Reader: History, Culture, Politics*. Durham, N.C.: Duke University Press, 1995.

Stern, Steve, ed. *Resistance, Rebellion, and Consciousness in the Andean Peasant World*. Madison: University of Wisconsin Press, 1987.

Stern, Susan. *With the Weathermen: The Personal Journey of a Revolutionary Woman*. Garden City, N.Y.: Doubleday, 1975.

Terrill, Ross. *Madame Mao: The White-Boned Demon*. New York: Bantam, 1984.

Tristán, Flora. *Peregrinaciones de una paria*. Lima: Editorial Cultura Antártica, 1946.

Vargas Llosa, Alvaro. *The Madness of Things Peruvian: Democracy under Siege*. New Brunswick, N.J.: Transaction Publishers, 1994.

Vargas Llosa, Mario. *Contra viento y marea*. Lima: Promoción Editorial Inca, S.A., 1990.

——. *El pez en el agua*. Barcelona: Editorial Seix Barral, 1993.

Wickham-Crowley, Timothy P. *Guerrillas and Revolution in Latin America: A Comparative Study of Insurgents and Regimes since 1956*. Princeton: Princeton University Press, 1992.

Wilentz, Amy. *The Rainy Season: Haiti after Duvalier*. New York: Simon and Schuster, Touchstone, 1989.

Witke, Roxane. *Comrade Chiang Ch'ing*. Boston: Little, Brown, 1977.